PROTEST AND PUNISHMENT

PROTEST
AND
PUNISHMENT

The Story of the
Social and Political Protesters
transported to Australia
1788–1868

BY

GEORGE RUDÉ

OXFORD
AT THE CLARENDON PRESS
1978

Oxford University Press, Walton Street, Oxford OX2 6DP

OXFORD LONDON GLASGOW
NEW YORK TORONTO MELBOURNE WELLINGTON
KUALA LUMPUR SINGAPORE JAKARTA HONG KONG TOKYO
DELHI BOMBAY CALCUTTA MADRAS KARACHI
IBADAN NAIROBI DAR ES SALAAM CAPE TOWN

© *Oxford University Press 1978*

British Library Cataloguing in Publication Data

Rudé, George
   Protest and punishment.
   1. Penal colonies, British   2. Social reformers
   – Great Britain   3. Social reformers – Canada
   4. Australia – Exiles
   I. Title
   365′.3   HV8950.A8   77–30539
   ISBN 0–19–822430–3

F1"

*Printed in Great Britain
at the University Press, Oxford
by Vivian Ridler
Printer to the University*

TO

THE MEMORY OF

PETER ELDERSHAW

PREFACE

THIS book is the product of research, spread over more than fifteen years, in archives and libraries in Australia, Ireland, Canada, and the United Kingdom. My thanks are therefore due, in the first place, to archivists and librarians in a dozen cities: at Canberra, Sydney, Perth, and Hobart in Australia, at London, Preston, and Edinburgh in the United Kingdom, at Ottawa in Canada, and Dublin and Belfast in Ireland; and, most of all, to the officers of the State Archives of Tasmania, of whom I must pick out for special mention Geoffrey Stilwell, now Keeper of the Special Records at Hobart, and the late Peter Eldershaw, to whom I owe a particular debt.

My thanks are due also, among Australian historians, to Manning Clark, Alan Shaw, and Lloyd Robson, who helped me over the first hurdles and whose work has provided important pointers for my own. I must also thank the University of Adelaide, the Australian Research Grants Committee, and the Canada Council for generous support at various stages of my travels and research.

And, as ever, words cannot adequately express my gratitude to my wife, Doreen Rudé, whose patience and sympathy have, in this case, had to be extended over so many years and who has so long endured talk of the activities of Ribbonmen, Whiteboys and Fenians, Canadian *habitants*, and Luddites, Chartists, and 'Captain Swing', both in their homelands and in their Australian exile.

G. R.

Beckley, Sussex
July 1977

CONTENTS

ABBREVIATIONS

ADB	*Australian Dictionary of Biography*
Ann. Reg.	*Annual Register*
ANU	Australian National University
Arch. NSW	Archives of New South Wales
Arch. WA	Archives of Western Australia
CON	Convict Department Records, Hobart
CSO	Colonial Secretary's Office
Eng. Hist. Docs.	*English Historical Documents*
DNB	*Dictionary of National Biography*
GO	Government Correspondence, Hobart
Hist. Stud.	*Historical Studies* (Melbourne)
HO	Home Office Records, Public Record Office, London
HRA	*Historical Records of Australia*
JRAHS	*Journal of the Royal Australian Historical Society*
LRO	Lancashire Record Office
ML	Mitchell Library, Sydney
NSW	New South Wales
Petitions (Farrell)	Prisoners' Petitions 1836–40 in Patrick Farrell's Inventory, SPO, Dublin
PP	Parliamentary Papers
PRO	Public Record Office (London, unless otherwise stated)
RO	Record Office
SPO	State Paper Office, Dublin
SRO	Scottish Record Office, Edinburgh
Tas. Arch.	Tasmanian State Archives
Tas. Hist. Assoc.	*Tasmanian Historical Research Association. Papers and Proceedings*
VDL	Van Diemen's Land (Tasmania)
WA	Western Australia

Introduction

BETWEEN 1787 and 1868 nearly 162,000 men and women were transported as convicts to Britain's Australian colonies, New South Wales, Victoria, Western Australia, and Van Diemen's Land (the present Tasmania). About three-quarters of these came from Britain —England, Scotland, and Wales—a little less than a quarter from Ireland, and a few hundred more from Canada, India, and a handful of other British possessions overseas. Their story has been told, and the problems relating to the convict system have been discussed, in the work of earlier historians and most recently and most thoroughly by Dr. Lloyd Robson and Professor Alan Shaw of Melbourne.[1] From their work we now know fairly exactly what sort of men and women the convicts were, their occupations and ages and the background from which they came, and what happened to them after they came to Australia. Thus the transportation of convicts has been placed in a proper historical setting and many old myths relating to the convicts, their judges, and their gaolers have been laid to rest.

The purpose of this book is not to go over all this ground again. It will focus not on the 'convict settlers' as a whole but on those among them whose crime was to have rebelled or protested against the social conditions or institutions of the country from which they came. This is not to suggest that the problem of the 'protesting' convict, as opposed to the ordinary common-law offender, has been entirely neglected by previous historians: Shaw and Robson both agree that while the great majority of convicts were transported for larceny and other common-law offences, a minority—considerably larger among the Irish than among the British[2]—had been found guilty of 'political' or 'social' crimes.[3]

So to make such a distinction is not original in itself; but to explore the matter in depth by identifying individual protesters and

[1] L. L. Robson, *The Convict Settlers of Australia* (Melbourne, 1965); A. G. L. Shaw, *Convicts and the Colonies* (London, 1966).

[2] For convenience the term is here used to include Englishmen, Welshmen, and Scotsmen, but not Irishmen whether from North or South.

[3] Shaw, pp. 152-3, 182-3; Robson, pp. 9, 56-7, 180. Specifically, Shaw argues that three in four of the Canadians belong to this group, one in eight ('nearly 5,000') of the Irish, and considerably less than one in 100 of the British. As will appear later, the only figure seriously in dispute is that relating to the Irish.

counting heads, and by focusing not on samples but on the case-histories of the protesters as a whole, may claim to be so. Moreover, it is proposed to give the problem a new dimension by studying it from both ends: both in the Australian context and in that of the countries and counties in which the protests were made. Treated in this way, transportation ceases to be merely a reflection of crime and the prison system of the countries that gave them birth: it also becomes a projection of the popular and protest movements of nineteenth-century Britain and Ireland—and, to a lesser degree, of Canada, which became involved in a dual rebellion in 1837 and 1838.

But, practically, how do we make such a distinction? How do we separate one type of convict—the protesting convict—from the rest? This proves to be no easy matter. First, there is the problem of definition and selection. How do we distinguish between 'protest' crime and crime in general? The law knows no such distinction, and it never has: a breach of the law by a protester is at law a crime like any other. So criminologists and others, with some notable exceptions, have not surprisingly tended to ignore the distinction or, at best, to blanket it behind such omnibus labels as crimes against property and crimes against persons;[4] and in the numerous volumes of the Parliamentary Papers devoted to crime and punishment protest as a category of crime has no part to play at all. Such a view is broadly shared by those conservative historians and other stern upholders of law and order to whom protest appears as a crime against established society. But there are others who, more liberally, see it the other way round. To them it is not so much that all protest is a form of crime as that all crime is a form of protest. For, they have argued, if protest is a social phenomenon so is crime, and how can one sensibly distinguish between the conscious rebel against society and the man whom society drives, or appears to drive, to crime? So it has been claimed that all convicts, whether sentenced to prison or transportation, were the victims of the society that left them out

---

[4] Among these exceptions is a paper by V. A. C. Gatrell and T. B. Hadden, 'Criminal Statistics and their Interpretation', in ed. E. A. Wrigley, *Nineteenth-Century Society* (Cambridge, 1972), pp. 336–96. The authors draw particular attention to records (such as the Criminal Registers in the HO Papers and depositions and indictments in certain County Record Offices in England) which help to identify 'social' and 'political' offenders at times of unrest (pp. 348–9). Similarly, in France, P. Petrovitch, in a recent study of crime and criminals in eighteenth-century Paris, attributes to the corn-rioters of May 1775 qualities that are not shared by the criminal population at large. P. Petrovitch, 'Recherches sur la criminalité à Paris dans la seconde moitié du XVIIIe siècle', in *Crimes et criminalité en France sous l'Ancien Régime 17e-18e siècles*, Cahiers des Annales 33 (Paris, 1971), pp. 187–261, at pp. 259–61.

in the cold. The Hammonds, the British social historians, saw it somewhat in this light when, in viewing the imperfections of society in the early stages of the industrial revolution, they concluded that there was a common bond of culpability between the arsonist and urban thief and the county justice or High Court judge who sent them to the convict-prisons of Van Diemen's Land and Botany Bay.[5] Engels, perhaps more realistically, distinguished between crimes against property and others when, in his *Condition of the Working Class in England*, he attributed the sevenfold increase in crimes against property in the past thirty-seven years (he was writing in 1844) to 'want in some form'; for 'what a man has, he does not steal'.[6]

I would not quarrel with this judgement as far as it goes: it was made at a time when the close connection between poverty and crime—and, more certainly, crimes against property—was evident for all to see. But I believe it is necessary, in attempting to identify protest, to be more discriminating still and to distinguish between the common-law offender who, however acute the provocation, simply helps himself or settles a purely private score and the one who either acts with others or appears to do so in pursuit of common political or social goals. Such distinctions or lines of demarcation are never, of course, likely to be very precise. Mr. Edward Thompson, for example, in a recent book, distinguishes between 'social' crimes involving 'common rights', such as deer-hunting, poaching, and smuggling, and the activities of the robber, the gangster, or the urban thief.[7] The distinction is, I believe, a reasonable one to make, though we need to go further. It is fair enough to argue that the man who steals bread, shoots game, or traps rabbits in order to feed his family when in need is performing an act of natural justice which has little in common with the activities of the professional thug or what Henry Fielding described as the 'gangs of robbers' in eighteenth-century London. But though a social act, it is still a private act that has little to do with protest. Protest, in the sense in which I am here using the term, is also a *collective* act though it may not always be carried out in the company of others. Such acts are fairly easy to recognize in the case of trade-union militants, machine-breakers, food-rioters, demolishers of turn-pikes, fences, or workhouses,

---

[5] See J. L. and B. Hammond, *The Village Labourer 1760–1832* (London, 1913), p. 239: 'The village Hampdens of that generation sleep by the shores of Botany Bay.'
[6] Frederick Engels, *The Condition of the Working Class in England in 1844* (London, 1952), pp. 130–2.
[7] E. P. Thompson, *Whigs and Hunters* (London, 1975) esp. pp. 142–6, 172–5, 196.

administers or receivers of unlawful oaths, treasonable or seditious persons, armed rebels, and city rioters—all those, in fact, who generally protest within the context of a 'popular movement'— (and all of these appear on the lists of transported convicts). But there are others: those whose activities belong to that shadowy realm between crime and protest where it is often no easy matter to tell the two apart. I refer to such types of law-breaking as rural incendiarism, poaching and smuggling, cattle-maiming, assaults on peace officers, and the sending of anonymous letters. These types of *marginal* protest (and there are of course others) have to be judged, as it were, on their merits and treated with care and discrimination. Here there are no easy blanket-definitions to fall back on and they can neither be dismissed out of hand as unworthy of further consideration (as some would have it) nor can they be counted *en bloc* as forms of protest (as favoured by others). It all depends on the precise nature of the act and where and how and against whom it was committed; it may even depend on the traditions or *mores* of the community to which the victim and his assailant belonged. For instance, in both England and Ireland an assault or the threat of an assault against a person in authority like a policeman, a landlord, a magistrate, a wealthy farmer, or an employer, or (in Ireland) against a rival claimant to a piece of land, may reasonably be taken as a form of protest even when made by individuals rather than organized groups; whereas a scuffle in a pub, the murder of a relative in a family quarrel, or a simple act of highway robbery may not. Again, the burning of a hayrick or a barn may be done for kicks in the course of a night on the town or it may be done (as arson so often is in cities) to claim the insurance or to settle a personal score; but it may also be an act of reprisal against a landlord, employer, or parson, or it may be set in the context of a wider movement of protest—as, for example, was often the case during the long years of the land-and-tithe war in Ireland and with the numerous conflagrations left by the rick-burning labourers in the English southern counties in 1830 and 1831.

But a word of caution here. Even such wider movements have to be viewed with discrimination, for in the course of the Irish land war (as in the Rebellion of 1798) there were plenty of unlawful activities going on that had little to do with protest. Rural arson, which was common on both sides of St. George's Channel in the 1840s and early 1850s, is a further case in point. In the records relating to Ireland, one is struck by the large number of young women (their average age is 23) who were transported to Tasmania as arsonists during these years: I have counted no fewer than 234 compared with a mere fifty men. Here, then, one is naturally inclined to believe, is a form of social protest in which women played an altogether outstanding role.[8] There is some truth in this as the number of protesters among Irish women transported for arson in the 1840s was considerably greater than among men. Yet the difference is not so great as appears at first sight; for, on closer examination, the Tasmanian records reveal that nearly one in seven of these women, according to their own 'confessions' on arrival, had committed the offence in order to be sent to Australia either to 'better their condition' or to join a parent, a son or a daughter, a brother, sister, or lover who had gone out before them. Others, the records tell us, had past records that seem to accord ill with social protest (though this is, admittedly, a difficult point to decide); while many others proved to be totally ignorant of the names of their accusers.[9] So, clearly, a fair proportion of these women must be excluded from the numbers of protesters; and the same applies, though the reasons are different, to the men. Unfortunately the records, however we read them, do not permit of a precise enumeration; but if we add to these 'defaulters' the very considerable number of *urban* incendiaries from both England and Ireland,[10] protesters (as I have defined the term) are likely to account for no more than a third of the thousand arsonists transported to the three main convict settlements of Australia between 1820 and 1868.[11]

Some types of marginal protest were more characteristic of one country than they were of others, or they might have a significance in one country that they did not have elsewhere. In England, sheep-maiming or killing, like sheep-stealing, was a common rural crime; but it appears most frequently to have had the object of selling the carcass for profit or feeding the labourer's family; and the killing or maiming of cattle from revenge—which alone can be seen as a form of social protest—was comparatively rare.[12] In Ireland, however, the maiming or 'houghing' of cattle was a traditional and

[8] See, for example, Shaw, p. 183.

[9] For further evidence in support of this view, see John Williams, 'Irish Convicts and Van Diemen's Land', *Tas. Hist. Assoc.* xix (Sept. 1972), 117.

[10] In the case of Ireland, the point is well illustrated by the Returns of Outrages reported to the Constabulary Office for 1844. These show that only 121 out of 525 incendiary fires for that year occurred in country districts. PP 1845, xxi, 118–19.

[11] See also Part Three, chap. 6 below.

[12] Dr. A. J. Peacock, however, argues that, in East Anglia at this time, cattle-maiming was a frequent and recognized form of agrarian protest: 'Village Radicalism in East Anglia 1800–50', in ed. J. P. D. Dunbabin, *Rural Discontent in Nineteenth-Century Britain* (London, 1974), pp. 40–5.

recognized form of reprisal which, in the context of the Rebellion of 1798, assumed such dimensions in certain counties of the west that special punitive measures were applied to repress it;[13] and, judging by the transportation records, the same pattern continued, though generally pitched in a lower key, into the 1830s and 1840s.

Poaching, on the other hand, was a peculiarly English crime (no poachers were transported from Ireland and less than a handful from Scotland and Wales), which might on occasion be considered as a form of social protest. It might be so in the sense that a poacher might be asserting his right as a free-born Englishman to fish in the river and hunt in the forest and to hell with the landlords' property rights and the gamekeepers who got in his way;[14] but, equally, poaching might, like stealing bread or the carcass of a sheep, be undertaken to meet a pressing personal need; or, again, it might, when professionalized, be a substitute for any other form of private enterprise or self-help. The following case, taken from the Gloucester prison records of 1845, may serve as an example:

> Edwin Padbury, 33, earthenwareman of South Cerney, charged with having at Ampney Crucis (being armed with a gun) assaulted William Ginks. Has two brothers; *all three live by poaching* [my italics].

There are plenty of similar cases among poachers sent out to Australia. Among other seeming professionals there was Henry Pegg, a 34-year-old Staffordshire labourer, who had already been in prison five times for poaching before being transported for life in 1841.[15] Again, while most poachers were servants or labourers, there were others whose occupations lead one to suspect that they were in the business not so much to assert their rights as free-born Englishmen or to keep hunger from their door as to make out of it what they could: such, one may reasonably suspect, was the case with the half-dozen pork-butchers and gamekeepers who were among the transported poachers that came out from the English counties to Tasmania between 1830 and 1850. With such considera-

[13] See an instruction from Dublin Castle, dated 20 Feb. 1799, placing the counties of Mayo and Galway under Martial Law as 'the pernicious practice of houghing the cattle has spread to so alarming a height as to threaten their total destruction'. PRO, Northern Ireland, D 272/16.

[14] This, however, is pure surmise as there is no way of telling the *intentions* of transported poachers from the Home Office or Australian records; even the Tasmanian 'conduct' registers (see p. 7 n. 18), so invaluable for revealing the intentions of other protesters of the 1840s, cannot help us here. But the phenomenon is likely to have become a dwindling one by the time the first great wave of transported poachers began to arrive in the 1830s; and it is perhaps significant that poaching plays a comparatively minor part in A. J. Peacock's study of East Anglian 'village radicalism' of the period. [15] Tas. Arch., CON 33/16.

tions in mind, it would be quite unrealistic to put the number of protesting poachers at more than one-third of the whole.[16]

But, having decided what offences to look for, we are still faced with the problem of identifying those who committed them. (Admittedly, we have jumped the gun by mentioning some of these cases already; but that, as I hope the reader will appreciate, could hardly be helped.) The problem is not so great in the case of prisoners arriving after 1826, when the 'indent', which generally accompanied them to the port of arrival,[17] and other descriptive records[18] gave the crime for which they had been transported; and the task of identification becomes all the easier when, as in the Tasmanian 'conduct' registers of the 1840s (and sometimes before), the prisoner supplements the charge on which he has been convicted with an explanatory (or justificatory) statement of his own.[19] But before 1826 the crime rarely appears on the accompanying record at all. So it has to be sought elsewhere: for example, in the case of London, in the printed *Proceedings* of the Old Bailey, or, in the case of English and Welsh counties, in the Criminal Registers among the Home Office Papers.[20]

As most of the English—and Scottish and Welsh—protesters came out after 1825, in their case the problem is not such a formidable one. The Irish present a far more intractable problem, as the bulk of the political Irish, and a large part of the social protesters

[16] This, of course, does not exhaust the types of 'marginal' protest for which convicts were sent to Australia. Protest may even lurk behind such crimes as 'robbery' and 'burglary'. Once more, it depends on the context and the occasion. For examples of the first, see the term 'robbery' often applied to rioters levying money on unwilling farmers and landowners, particularly in Hampshire and Berkshire, during the labourers' revolt in 1830; and for the second see the charge made against several of the United Irishmen engaged in political activities in County Armagh in 1797 (*Commons Journals of Ireland*, vol. xxvii (1798), Part 2, Appendices). Such charges also appear frequently in the Criminal Registers for England and Wales against the names of Chartist rioters convicted by Special Commission in Staffordshire, Lancashire, and Cheshire in 1842.

[17] Convict indents for New South Wales are in the Mitchell Library in Sydney: Arch. NSW, 4/3998–4019 (1788–1835), with printed copies for 1830–42; and for Tasmania in Tas. Arch., CON 14/1–47 (1827–53).

[18] The most useful of these are the 'conduct' registers in the Tasmanian archives (CON 31, 33).

[19] Some historians (e.g. Robson) have called these statements 'confessions'. But they are quite often denials of guilt ('I wasn't there' or 'I was drunk at the time') and, at their most useful, they give a more precise, and often extremely revealing, description of the offence committed.

[20] PRO, HO 26 (London), 27 (English and Welsh counties): from 1805 on. Unfortunately, they do not include the Scots, who are not so well served in the meagre information provided in the proceedings of the Courts of Judiciary in the Scottish Record Office in Edinburgh.

as well, were transported between 1798 and 1824; and, for this period, records that allow for reliable identification are far harder to come by than they are for the British. In fact, some early transports from Dublin and Cork carried shipping lists that not only failed to convey the nature of a man's crime but also the term of his sentence; and we find Governor Hunter complaining to the Home Secretary after the *Marquis Cornwallis* arrived in Sydney in March 1796, that 'every ship . . . [has] omitted to bring out any account of the conviction or term of transportation of those they bring out'.[21] Moreover, the extensive criminal and convict records that were once held in the Four Courts in Dublin[22] were almost totally destroyed by fire, during the Civil War, in 1922. All this, of course, adds to the researcher's frustration and confusion. But, fortunately, there are other records in both Sydney and Dublin that provide some degree of compensation: such as the muster-rolls (giving crimes) relating to a score of Irish convict-ships arriving between 1816 and 1825, the Rebellion Papers and prisoners' petitions of 1778–1836 in Dublin Castle, the lists of prisoners convicted at assizes in the Journals of the Irish House of Commons for 1798–1800, and the long lists of persons arrested and sentenced under the Insurrection Acts in the British Parliamentary Papers for 1823 and 1824.[23]

From these records, with all their gaps and imperfections, we can construct a plausible—if not fully accurate—picture of the number of political and social protesters (in the sense in which I have attempted to define the term) that arrived in Australia as convicts between 1788 and 1868. According to my calculations, they included 2,250 Irish, 1,200 Britons (English, Scots, and Welsh), and 154 Canadians.[24] (I have omitted all military deserters from India,

[21] HRA, 1st series, i, 555–6. One ship—*Friendship II*—which brought a large batch of rebels of 1798 to Sydney in 1800 arrived without a shipping list of any kind. In some cases (though not in this one) the list followed later.

[22] They are listed in Wood's *Guide to the Irish Records* (Dublin, 1920), pp. 207–8.

[23] In addition, there are (quite exceptionally) detailed lists of prisoners—also giving crimes—for two ships bringing large numbers of rebels of 1798: the *Minerva* (Jan. 1800) and the *Anne I* (Feb. 1801). For details of these 'compensatory' records, see Bibliography.

[24] Shaw's estimate of one protester in every eight of the Irish prisoners (see p. 1 n. 3 above) will be seen to be more than twice as high as mine (2,250 out of 39,000). But as I am concerned not so much with global figures as with counting individual heads, it is perhaps natural that I should have been more selective and that my calculations should have been more conservative than his. However, as records relating to the early Irish prisoners often make positive identification an uncertain business, it may well be that, in the case of this earlier period, I have erred on the side of caution. On the other hand, Shaw's lower estimate of the number of British protesters is due to his omission of poachers, arsonists, and the like.

Bermuda, and Canada, though there were certainly protesters—
mutineers and others—among them.) These national groups are
composed as follows:

Irish

Defenders of Ireland and rural protesters before 1798	160[25]	
Rebels of 1798, 1803	329	
Transported under the Insurrection Acts of 1814–25,		
to New South Wales: 571		
to Van Diemen's Land: 18	589	
Armed rebels, Whiteboys, Ribbonmen etc., engaged in the tithe		
and land war,		
arriving in NSW, 1827–40: 604		
arriving in VDL, 1840–53: 339	943	
Young Ireland movement of 1848 (arriving VDL, 1849–51)	12	
Fenians (to Western Australia), 1868	62	
Marginal protesters:		
Arsonists: to NSW 58 men, 9 women;		
to VDL 50 men, 234 women;		
to WA 1 man	352	(117)*
'Houghers' and maimers of cattle:		
to NSW 25 (4 women);		
to VDL 13;		
to WA 8	46	(35)*
Destroyers of trees	2	
	2,495	(2,249)*

* Estimated number of protesters in brackets. These are liberal rather than conservative estimates.

British

Scots Jacobins, 1793, 1798	6
Naval mutineers, 1797	15
Luddites, 1812–13, 1817	42
Agricultural labourers (Isle of Ely), 1816	7
Pentrich Rebellion, 1817	14
Scots radical weavers of Glasgow and Bonnymuir, 1820	19
Cato Street Conspiracy, 1820	5
Yorkshire radical weavers, 1821	12
'Swing' rioters, machine-breakers and arsonists (inc. 2 women)	483
Bristol Riots, 1831	26
Welsh industrial riots, 1831, 1835	7
Tolpuddle Martyrs, 1834	6
Battle of Bossenden Wood, 1838	3
Welsh Rebecca Riots, 1842–3	5
Chartists: 1839: 11 (4 to NSW, 7 to VDL)	
1842: 75 (to VDL)	
1848: 16 (to VDL)	102

[25] Here I have accepted Shaw's estimate (p. 171), as, owing to the paucity of records
for the period, I have been unable to identify more than a handful of Defenders and
have no alternative figure of my own to put forward.

British (continued):

Marginal protesters:

Arsonists:	to NSW	32 men, 8 women;		
	to VDL	199 men, 46 women;		
	to WA	360 men;		
	to Victoria, 7 'exiles'		652	(218)*
Poachers:	to NSW 146;			
	to VDL 66;			
	to WA 12;			
	to Victoria, 2 'exiles'		226	(75)*
Cattle-maimers:			31	(20)*
Destroyers of fences, trees, etc.			10	
Other categories:				
Machine-breakers			22	
Riots			52	
Wages movements			15	
Assaulting peace officers, 1841–52			18	
Miscellaneous protest			15	
			1,793	(1,197)*

* Estimated number of protesters (after 'correction') in brackets.

Canadians

Anglo-Canadians, Americans, 1838: to VDL	96	
French Canadians, 1838: to NSW	58	154

So we arrive at a total of 3,600, or about one in forty-five of all transported convicts; 120 of them were women. This, then, is the size of the problem. Behind these figures are the faces of the men and women (women, as our calculations show, were mainly in evidence as arsonists) who are the subject of this study. Their case-histories, based on their records in both Australia and their British, Irish, and Canadian homelands, provide the main ingredients from which this book has been constructed. It is divided into five parts. The first gives, for each country in turn, a picture of the protest that led to their conviction. The second deals with the repression of protest and, in particular, with transportation as a means of punishment. The third presents, in miniature, the case-histories of a representative number of protesters up to the time of transportation. The fourth describes the Australian convict system and relates the experiences of the protesters in Australia; and the fifth discusses in what ways the protesters differed from the common run of convicts. Such a comparison may show that they at least—or a large part of them—deserve the title of 'village Hampden' which the Hammonds, with perhaps excessive generosity, bestowed on the convict settlers as a whole.

PART ONE

PROTEST

1. In Britain

THE years when Britons were transported as criminals to Australia (1788 to 1868) were also years when the country was being transformed from a predominantly rural to an industrial society. They were years of dislocation and uprooting, of large-scale Irish immigration and rapid city growth. By 1841, 400,000 Irishmen had arrived in the United Kingdom over the past twenty-five years and a further 2,700,000 followed in the course of the next ten. Like thousands of others—demobilized soldiers and displaced villagers—they were drawn to cities that were already expanding and even bursting at the seams. London's population trebled in the first half of the nineteenth century, Leeds' and Sheffield's doubled, and Birmingham, Manchester, and Glasgow saw theirs multiplied by more than three.

It is evident that this disruption of old communities and creation of new ties had a great deal to do with the growth and patterns of crime and protest in the course of these decades. This relationship has been the subject of frequent comment[1] but it will not be restated here. Having noted, but not explored, the causes, all I propose to do is to record the volume and follow the respective patterns of crime and protest with the aid of the criminal returns and the studies of protest movements. As has been said often enough,[2] there are obvious dangers in placing too great a reliance on the annual criminal statistics, but they have some limited use and should not be dismissed out of hand. Even if exact numbers should be treated with the greatest reserve,[3] they are at least useful in establishing

---

[1] Among a medley of social commentators, criminologists, novelists, and historians we may note B. Disraeli, *Sybil, or the Two Nations* (1845); F. Engels, *The Condition of the English Working Class in 1844* (1845); H. Mayhew, *London Labour and the London Poor* (1864, repr. 1961–2); J. L. and B. Hammond, *The Skilled Labourer* (1919) and other works; L. Radzinowicz, *A History of English Criminal Law and its Administration from 1750* (1948–68); J. J. Tobias, *Crime and Industrial Society in the 19th Century* (1967).

[2] Already a century ago by William Hoyle, *Crime in England & Wales in the Nineteenth Century* (London and Manchester, 1876), pp. 53–5; and, most recently and most explicitly, by V. A. C. Gatrell and T. B. Hadden, 'Criminal Statistics and their Interpretation', in ed. E. A. Wrigley, *Nineteenth-Century Society* (Cambridge, 1972), esp. pp. 336–40, 361–2.

[3] One problem is the transference of certain types of offence from certain courts to others at various times in their history. Specifically, we may note that from 1847

trends and all the more so when the mere record of annual national figures of committals or indictments (from 1805) become supplemented with a breakdown into types of crime (in the early 1820s) and into counties (in 1835). Even the global figures, published from 1805 on, enable us to trace the steady, almost unbroken, rise in the incidence of crime over a period of fifty years. Broadly, the picture is as follows: a steady advance from 4,605 recorded committals for indictable crimes in 1805 to 13,698 in 1824 and further advances to 22,451 in 1834 and 30,349 in 1848 (with a peak of 31,309 in 1842), followed by a levelling-out between 1849 and 1855 and a steady decline (though only in *indictable* offences) in the fifteen subsequent years.[4] So these *global* figures, whatever else they do not and cannot tell us, have the virtue at least of establishing that indictable crime (as measured by commitals before assizes and quarter sessions) rose six and a half times in forty-five years (1805–1848) at a time when the national population, rising from roughly $10\frac{1}{2}$ million to 16 million in England and Wales, expanded by a factor of a little over one and a half.

With the breakdown into counties after 1834 we learn something about the geographical distribution of crime as well. The following are the total of committals for indictable offences in fifteen representative English counties over a twenty-year period between 1834 and 1853. (As will be seen, they are presented in a descending order of magnitude.)

Middlesex (including London)	70,514	Warwickshire	16,188
Lancashire	57,623	Cheshire	15,147
Yorkshire	32,019	Devon	12,886
Surrey	18,491	Norfolk	12,654
Gloucester (including Bristol		Essex	11,347
from 1837)	17,334	Suffolk	9,829
Staffordshire	17,180	Sussex	8,520
Kent	16,959	Bedfordshire	3,137[5]

onwards, and more particularly with the Criminal Justice Act of 1855, a large part of larcenies, assaults (including some assaults on peace officers) and juvenile crimes were transferred to magistrates' courts and so, ceasing to be indictable offences, disappear from the returns of indictments with which we shall be mainly concerned in this chapter and the next. Another, larger, problem is, of course, that such records, even at their most sophisticated, are only able to measure *detected* crime.

[4] These figures appear in various volumes of the Parliamentary Papers; but, for convenience, I have taken them from Hoyle, pp. 14, 25, 29, 37.

[5] Numbers of persons committed for trial or bailed in England and Wales, 1834–53, P(arliamentary) P(apers) 1835, xlv, 156–7; 1836, xli, 126–7, 1837, xlvi, 124–5; 1838, xliii, 118–19; 1839, xxxviii, 358–9; 1840, xxxviii, 448–9; 1841, xviii, 320–1; 1842, xxxii, 318–19; 1843, xlii, 64–5; 1844, xxxix, 66–7; 1845, xxxvii, 68–9; 1846,

If allowance were made for the size of population (difficult to assess over a twenty-year span), it is evident that the order would be different and the great gap shown between the larger 'urban' counties—such as London, Lancaster, and York—would be somewhat narrowed in relation to some of the smaller 'rural' counties, such as Bedford, Suffolk, and Sussex. But the fact that leaps to the eye is the evident relationship between urbanization and the volume of crime. The counties with the largest urban population—not only Middlesex, Lancashire, and Yorkshire, but also Warwickshire, Surrey, and Gloucester—are also those with the largest volume of crime. Crime is shown to be an essentially *urban* phenomenon which grows with the growth of cities and towns. The same is true of Scotland (though, as Scottish annual returns only began in 1839, a direct comparison is not possible), where the urban areas of Edinburgh and Lanark and Renfrew (between which Glasgow is divided) have, over a similar time-span, between them an aggregate of crime almost equal to that of the twenty-nine other Scottish counties combined.[6]

The record of protest—in terms of indictments for what I have termed 'protest'-crimes[7]—follows a different pattern. Sometimes, it is true, the peaks of the two coincide—as in the crisis years of 1831 and 1838 and, most strikingly, in 1842 when, in England and Wales, the figures for 'protest' and over-all crime are higher than for any other single year.[8] But these are exceptions and, generally speaking, there is little concordance between the two. It is true that the volume of protest tends, like that of crime, to rise in some decades, as in the 1830s and 1840s, and to fall in others (notably, once more, in the

xxxiv, 68–9; 1847–8, lii, 242–3; 1849, xliv, 118–19; 1850, xlv, 518–19; 1851, xlvi, 86–7; 1852, xli, 64–5; 1852–3, lxxxi, 644–5; 1854, liv, 62–3. Of the thirteen Welsh counties (including Monmouth for historical-political rather than administrative reasons), only two—Monmouth and Montgomery, with 4,965 and 3,908—had totals higher than Bedford's 3,137. Radnor, a fairly typical small Welsh county, had only 411; and even Montgomery, the scene of considerable Chartist activity in 1839, had only 1,260.

[6] Numbers of persons committed . . . in Scotland, 1839–58, PP 1841, xviii, 436; 1842, xxxii, 434; 1843, xlii, 180; 1844, xxxix, 182; 1845, xxxvii, 107; 1846, xxxiv, 185; 1847–8, lii, 359; 1849, xliv, 335; 1850, xlv, 733; 1851, xlvi, 307; 1852, xli, 187; 1853, lxxi, 69; 1854, liv, 181; 1854–5, xliii, 287; 1856, xlix, 293; 1857, xlii, 115; 1857–8, xlvii, 625; 1859, xix, 555.

[7] These appear under the following thirteen heads in the annual returns after 1834: arson; cattle-maiming; game laws (poaching); smuggling; riot and destruction of buildings and machinery; destruction of cloth in the process of manufacture; destruction of threshing machines (up to 1837 only); threatening letters; unlawful oaths; conspiracy to raise wages; assaulting peace officers; seditious riot; high treason.

[8] In Scotland, these peaks come later: for crime in 1848 and for protest in 1849.

1850s). But the over-riding pattern—certainly up to 1852—is one of fluctuation rather than of any steady rise or fall.[9] Some of these fluctuations are, not surprisingly, far more dramatic than others: sharp increases are, for example, observable in the crisis, or near-crisis, years of 1831, 1834, 1839, 1842, and 1847-8 (in 1842, Sir Leon Radzinowicz reminds us, there were over a thousand commitments in connection with the North-Country disturbances in August alone[10]).

Once more, as with crime, these global figures, though instructive, cannot take us very far. It is a different matter, however, when they become supplemented first by the returns of committals for individual acts of protest (starting with 1820) and later when these (after 1834) become broken-down into counties. These two innovations combined enable us to follow the course of different crimes of protest, occurring in England and Wales, over a thirty-four year period, between 1820 and 1853.[11] To begin with the most constant protest-crime of all: arson. It appears from the indictments that acts of arson tried at assizes and quarter sessions almost doubled between 1821 and 1822, fell gradually during the next six years, sharply increased, in the context of general rural unrest, between 1829 and 1832 (reaching a peak of 107 cases in 1832), levelled out between 1833 and 1836, fell sharply again between 1837 and 1841, and rose to new heights in the 1840s with peaks of 225 in 1844 and 206 in 1851. What is noticeable here is, on the one hand, the fluctuating pattern of arson as a form of crime (whether as a form of social protest or not); and, on the other, that it sometimes coincided with a wider protest-movement, as with the 'Swing riots' of 1830 and 1831, but sometimes most evidently not, as in the years of relatively muted protest of 1844 and 1851. Other rural protest-crimes, like poaching and cattle-maiming, followed a pattern all their own and can at no time be related to wider movements of protest. The peak-years of poaching, as shown in the limited record of the indictments, were 1823 (223 cases), 1827 (284), 1828 (366), 1832 (213), 1843 (236), and 1849 (201), none of

---

[9] The annual returns of wheat-prices suggest that, throughout this period, protest was more responsive than crime to their short-term fluctuations. This seems particularly evident in 1831, 1838, 1841, and 1847-8. Yet it is likely that, as in the case of crimes of violence, the fall and gradual levelling-out of wheat-prices after the mid-1850s contributed to the muting of protest in the next quarter of a century. See G. Rudé, 'Protest and Punishment in Nineteenth-Century Britain', *Albion*, v (i), spring 1973, pp. 16-17.

[10] Radzinowicz, iv, 232.

[11] Records of persons committed, convicted, sentenced to death, and executed for crimes of protest in England and Wales in 1820-40 are in PP 1839, xxxviii, 245-8; 1840, xxxviii, 325-8; 1841, xviii, 259-63.

which—with the possible exception of 1832—were years particularly noted for protest as a whole. Cattle-maiming was a late starter never attaining more than a dozen cases in any one year until 1831, a 'Swing' year when it rose to nineteen. It rose again to 33 cases in 1833, to 41 in 1834, to 42 in 1837, and 43 (the highest point reached) in 1844. Assaults on peace officers (another 'marginal' type of protest) only appear among the indictments after 1833. Here the peak year is 1835 (844 cases), followed by 700 cases in 1836, 626 in 1834, 590 in 1837, and 549 in 1841 and, perhaps surprisingly, never attaining any figure higher than 467 in any of the three years of greatest Chartist activity: 1839, 1842, and 1848.[12] So, by and large, these 'marginal' protest-crimes were not central to other, wider forms of protest and more generally followed a pattern all their own.

Other forms of protest that appeared in isolation, though for quite different reasons, were the administration of unlawful oaths and conspiracy to raise wages. (The first of these, as we shall see in our next chapter, formed an integral part of the wider rural movement in Ireland.) After playing a considerable role at the time of the Luddites, they only appear as a major indictable offence in the return for 1834—with minor offshoots in 1835 and 1836—having in that year been used as the major charge against the Dorchester labourers who were sentenced for forming a trade union. Other forms of collective protests—acts of violence and sedition of the more 'conventional' kind—appear strictly within the context of wider movements. Thus high treason (again after 1834) virtually only appeared within the context of Chartism, fourteen such cases being tried in 1840 and twelve in 1848. Acts of seditious riot (and other variations of the term) were almost exclusively confined to the two major Chartist years of 1842 and 1848, as machine-breaking, 'felonious' riot, and the sending of threatening letters were conspicuously associated with, and formed an integral part of, the 'Swing' movement of the early 1830s. And, surprisingly perhaps in view of the great numbers of arrests and committals in the northern districts in 1842, it was not Chartism but the 'Swing' movement that provided the bumper year for protest activities of every kind: with 1,350 indictments in 1831 for protest-crimes (excluding assaults on police officers, which were not yet separately recorded, and the numerous cases of 'robbery', which were disguised forms of extortion of money by riotous

---

[12] Admittedly, by 1847, some cases of assault (including, presumably, some cases of assault on peace officers) had been transferred to magistrates' courts (see p. 13 n. 3 above). But 1848 was not nearly so turbulent a Chartist year as 1842.

labourers), compared with 1,242 cases (502 in Lancashire alone) in 1842.

Once more, the county breakdown after 1834 adds a further significant dimension, as it makes it possible to distinguish the more 'riotous' or 'protesting' counties from the rest. This may be measured in one of two ways: by placing protest in its regional context or by comparing the over-all volume of protest in one county with that in the next. In adopting the first method, one is struck by the tendency of some types of protest to cluster in some counties and in some years rather than in others. Arson is a case in point. Between 1834 and 1853 there were 139 indictments for arson in Norfolk, 133 in Devon, 130 in Suffolk, 120 in Essex, 99 in Yorkshire, and 85 in Cambridgeshire. So, apart from Yorkshire and Devon, it was overwhelmingly an East Anglian affair: strikingly so in the second, and greatest, round of rural conflagrations in 1844, when the East Anglian counties alone (including both Cambridge and Essex) accounted for no fewer than 113 out of a total of 254 indictments throughout the kingdom as a whole. It will also be observed that of the half-dozen leading incendiary counties only one, Yorkshire, may reasonably be called conspicuously urban. In fact, in the great centres of urbanization—Middlesex, Lancashire, Warwickshire in England and Edinburgh, Lanark, and Renfrew in Scotland—arson appears to have been comparatively rare, at any rate as an indictable (or capital) offence: there were over this period only 72 indictments for arson in Lancashire, 62 in Middlesex, 48 in Gloucester, 38 in Warwickshire, 17 in Edinburgh, and 52 in Lanark and Renfrew combined. Arson, like poaching and cattle-maiming, proves to have been essentially—though, of course, not exclusively—a rural phenomenon; and it is probably only in its rural context (though not always then, as we have seen) that we should treat arson as a form of social protest rather than as an ordinary common-law crime.

Among other rural protest-crimes, the killing or maiming of cattle appeared most frequently in Norfolk (39 indictments), Yorkshire (32), Essex and Staffordshire (25), Suffolk (24), and Devon and Somerset (22). So, like arson, it features high on the list of rural offences in the East Anglian counties. But, as we have already observed, it was also a fairly common phenomenon in the early 1830s and it is with the 1830s that Dr. Peacock is mainly concerned in his essay on village 'radicalism' in East Anglia in the earlier part of the century.[13] Offences against the game laws, like arson, were more widely spread; yet they were quite evidently a more frequent

[13] Peacock, pp. 43–5.

occurrence in some counties than in others. Here the indictments serve as a very imperfect measure, as it seems that only about one in seven of all poaching offences (at least in the late 1820s) was tried at assizes or quarter sessions. We get some indication of this disparity from the publication in 1831 of a return of all poaching offences committed and tried by junior courts between 1827 and 1830. Yorkshire heads the list with a total of 766 convictions, followed by Lancashire with 694, Sussex with 598, Nottingham with 476, Suffolk with 442, and Stafford with 374.[14] The order changes somewhat—and there are a few surprises—when we turn once more to the indictments of 1834–53. Yorkshire (with 29 indictments in 1834 and 26 in 1843) again appears high on the list, as do Stafford, Suffolk, and Lancashire—but not Sussex or Nottingham which are replaced by Gloucester and Chester and, most conspicuously of all, by Norfolk which now tops the poll with a total of 179 indictments. So, in terms of rural protest-crimes, East Anglia occupies once more a commanding position.

Among other similar offences appearing in the indictments, smuggling was, by its very nature, an affair largely of the ports; so it is hardly surprising that it was mainly to be found in coastal counties, headed by Cornwall with nineteen indictments over the twenty-year period, which was followed by Dorset and Kent with twelve and Devon with nine. (Sussex, rather unexpectedly, recorded a mere three.) Assaults on peace officers, alone among these 'marginal' crimes of protest, was an urban rather than a rural phenomenon; and here Lancashire heads the list with 1,002 indictments, followed by Middlesex with 531, while Stafford, Devon, Surrey, Warwick, Essex, and Chester record between 200 and 300 apiece. (Devon, an essentially rural county, is in this case the odd man out.)

Other, more 'conventional', forms of protest included the destruction of property (buildings, machinery, 'hop-binds', or cloth in manufacture) and 'seditious' and other types of riot. In the late- and post-war years and the 1820s such activities generally took place in the countryside: we may instance, for example, the destruction of 1,300 or 1,400 stocking-frames by the Luddites between 1811 and 1816,[15] the revival of machine-breaking in East Anglia and Yorkshire in 1816 and 1822, not to mention the massive destruction of threshing machines (921 committals in a single year) in the southern and Midlands counties in 1830–1. But, in England, rural machine-breaking

---

[14] Returns of convictions under game laws for 1827–30 in PP 1830–1, xii, 575–89.
[15] F. O. Darvall, *Popular Disturbances and Public Order in Regency England* (London, 1969), p. 209.

was virtually finished by the mid-1830s and the last destruction of
a threshing machine is recorded in the Leicestershire indictments
of 1837. Riots involving the large-scale destruction of property
moved into the towns in the early 1830s: at first into old-established
towns and cities in the course of the Reform Bill agitation (Carmarthen, Derby, Nottingham, and Bristol, above all, are notorious
examples) and later, with Chartism, into the manufacturing centres
of northern England and South Wales. We can measure its extent
and distribution from the 'Chartist' indictments tabulated in
separate reports in the Parliamentary Papers of 1840, 1841, 1843,
and 1849:

Lancashire	742;
Stafford	305;
Chester	170;
Monmouth	67;
Montgomery	51; and
London (Middlesex and Surrey)	43.[16]

We come to the second way of measuring the scale of protest: by
comparing its incidence in one county with that in another. This we
can do, most simply and most crudely, by presenting protest-crimes
as a percentage of all criminal indictments in selected counties. The
results in the fifteen English counties that we listed above are as
follows (and we must stress that we are not measuring here the scale
of protest in itself but of protest as an element in detected crime):

Bedfordshire	6%	Lancashire	3·2% (13% in 1842)
Suffolk	5% (10·8% in 1844)	Yorkshire	3% (9% in 1842)
Stafford	4·5% (8·6% in 1842)	Kent	2·9%
Norfolk	4% (9% in 1834)	Warwick	2·5% (7·4% in 1834)
Devon	3·8%	Surrey	2·1%
Essex	3·8% (8% in 1844)	Gloucester	2% (3·7% in 1834)
Chester	3·6% (6·4% in 1842)	Middlesex	0·9% (1·6% in 1848)
Sussex	3·4%		

Thus, over all, we see that rural counties, partly because they are
among the least 'criminal' (see the order in which they appear on
p. 14), tend to come high on the list (only Staffordshire spoils an
interrupted sequence of half a dozen leading rural counties); that
manufacturing centres, until the 1840s at least, come somewhere
in the middle; and that Middlesex (with London as its nucleus) falls
far behind the rest.[17] But the figures in brackets suggest that with

[16] PP 1840, xxxviii, 335–6; 1841, xxviii, 260; 1843, xlii, 6; 1849, xliv, 56–8.
[17] The position of Scotland is similar, the lead being taken by rural counties, while
the main centres of population trail far behind. A sample of seven Scottish counties
goes as follows: Haddington 9·28%; Dumfries 7·25; Perth 3·2; Inverness 2·7; Edin-

the early 1840s there is a certain rescrambling with some of the manufacturing counties moving higher up the list. How and why this
happened will become more evident from the paragraphs that follow.

So far we have dealt with protest in terms of individual committals
and indictments. This is not the whole story for three very good
reasons. First, because the indictments barely extend beyond a third
of the whole period under review; secondly, because even for the
period they cover they are an inadequate record (particularly, as we
have seen, in the case of 'marginal' protest-crimes, like arson and
poaching, which more often than not were tried at petty sessions
or by other junior courts); and, thirdly, because by focusing on those
cases that came before the courts we lose sight of the popular movements of which the protests were a part. Admittedly, these movements, unlike the court-cases, are not susceptible to any precision
of measurement; but, apart from the inadequacies of the earlier
method of inquiry, to fail to take account of them would seem to be
another case of playing *Hamlet* without the Prince of Denmark.

So we turn briefly to the movements themselves. Those relating
to the transportation of British protesters extend over a seventy-
year period, roughly from the early 1780s to the mid 1860s; so they
are essentially an early-nineteenth-century phenomenon though including a couple of decades from the Revolutionary and Napoleonic
years. They fall into eight or nine phases of collective protest which
may, for convenience, be chronologically grouped as follows:
1793–1800, 1811–22, 1826–7, 1829–32, 1837–9, 1841–3, 1847–9, the
1850s (largely in Scotland), and the 1860s (largely in England). In
addition to these there were two minor phases—in 1833–4 and
1843–5—which fall somewhat outside the mainstream of our
chronological pattern.

The first phase belongs to the Revolutionary wars and related to
the government's fears that the contagion of Jacobinism might
radiate outwards from Paris; it found expression in such 'conspiratorial' episodes as the activities of the Scottish Jacobins in
1793 and of the English and Irish naval mutineers of Spithead and
the Nore in 1797; there were also food riots in south-eastern England
and food and enclosure riots in Wales between 1793 and 1801.[18]

burgh 1·17; Lanark 0·86; Renfrew 0·7. (It will be noted that it is only in certain
manufacturing regions in England, like Lancashire and Staffordshire, there is a
certain uneasy balance between the two.)

[18] See (for England), J. Stevenson, 'Food Riots in England, 1792–1818', in eds.
J. Stevenson and P. Quinault, *Popular Protest and Public Order. Six Studies in British
History* (London, 1974), pp. 33–74; and (for Wales) David Jones, *Before Rebecca.
Popular Protests in Wales 1793–1835* (London, 1973), pp. 13–66.

This earlier phase was followed by the far more widespread movement of social protest of 1811 to 1822, also beginning before the end of the wars with France. It saw the eruption of Luddism, or machine-breaking, in the hosiery and textile counties of the Midlands and North which, in some districts, continued intermittently until 1817.[19] There was also a resumption of food-rioting at Falmouth, Bristol, Sheffield, Nottingham, and Carlisle in 1812 and there were demonstrations against the new Corn Law in London in 1815. In 1816 there were the Spa Fields riots in London, the march of the unemployed 'Blanketeers' from Manchester, a great strike of iron workers in South Wales, and extensive agrarian riots against food prices and the use of machinery in East Anglia, followed by further outbreaks in 1822.[20] Meanwhile, the movement for political reform had found a working-class base in the Pentrich rebellion in Derbyshire, when Jeremiah Brandreth and his companions attempted to seize Nottingham Castle in June 1817; and in the great weavers' rally in St. Peter's Fields, in Manchester, in 1819; and, in 1820, the Cato Street conspirators in London plotted to blow up the Cabinet.[21] And, in Scotland that same year, there was the first large-scale wave of rioting over the repeated attempts to 'clear' the Highlands, in which women played a characteristic front-line role;[22] and in the Scottish Lowlands there was a radical rebellion of miners and weavers centred on Bonnymuir, near Glasgow.[23]

The third phase was the shortest of them all. It came in the wake of the financial crisis of 1825 and took the form of riots in Sunderland, Glasgow, and other cities of the North and a recurrence of machine-breaking in Yorkshire.

The fourth phase, though also a short one, was one of the most explosive in modern British history. Disturbances were, broadly, of three kinds. There were the agrarian riots (associated with the mythical 'Captain Swing') in the wheat-growing regions of the

[19] The best recent accounts are by F. O. Darvall (see p. 19 n. 15 above); E. P. Thompson, *The Making of the English Working Class* (London, 1963), pp. 494–602; and Malcolm Thomis, *The Luddites, Machine-Breaking in Regency England* (Newton Abbot, 1970).

[20] See A. J. Peacock, *Bread or Blood. The Agrarian Riots in East Anglia in 1816* (London, 1965); and (for Wales) Jones, *Before Rebecca*, pp. 69–85.

[21] For these events, see John Neal, *The Pentrich Revolution* (reprint Derby, 1966); R. J. White, *Waterloo to Peterloo* (London, 1957); and Thompson, *passim*.

[22] For these and later episodes in the anti-Clearance rioting in the Highlands, see Eric Richards, 'Patterns of Highland Discontent 1790–1860', in *Popular Protest and Public Order*, pp. 75–114.

[23] Peter B. Ellis and Seumas Mac A'Ghobbainn, *The Scottish Insurrection of 1820* (London, 1970).

South and East; they took the form of rick-burning, wages rioting, the sending of threatening letters (often signed 'Swing'), and the massive destruction of threshing machines in a score of counties.[24] There were strikes and industrial riots, including machine-breaking, in the manufacturing districts around Manchester and in the coal-fields of Durham and South Wales, and in the Midlands hosiery counties and the industrial North: violence was most prolonged in Wales where the movement extended from industrial riots in Merthyr in 1831 to the nightly visits and depredations of the 'Scotch Cattle' in 1832 and 1833. And there was also the great agitation over the Reform Bill of 1832, centred on London and Birmingham but break-ing out in violent riots in Derby, Nottingham, and Bristol in the autumn of 1831.[25] (The first of the two minor phases—that of 1833-4—was really a continuation by other means of the strikes and wages movements in the northern manufacturing districts: it was the period of Robert Owen's Grand National Consolidated Trades Union, with its offshoot in an agricultural workers' branch in Dorset, six of whose members—the Tolpuddle Martyrs—were transported to Australia in 1834.)

The next three phases—those of 1837-9, 1841-2, and 1847-9—were dominated by Chartism, the first and only *national* workers' movement of the time. Chartism began with attacks on workhouses in the North, was given unity and coherence by the great petitions for a People's Charter presented to Parliament in 1839, 1842, and 1848; and assumed a variety of guises, as in the armed rebellion at Newport in 1839, in the union-led strikes and 'sacred months' of 1839 and 1842, the destructive rioting in the Staffordshire towns (the 'Potteries') that year, and the great political public rallies to promote the Charter in London, Birmingham, Leicester, Glasgow, and many other towns.[26] The most dramatic and protracted episode of all, and that which sent a far larger contingent of workers into exile in Australia than any other, was known as the Plug-Plot Riots which

---

[24] J. L. and B. Hammond, *The Village Labourer* (London, 1911; and several later editions); E. J. Hobsbawm and G. Rudé, *Captain Swing* (London, 1969).

[25] See G. Rudé, 'English Rural and Urban Disturbances on the Eve of the First Reform Bill', *Past and Present*, no. 37, July 1967, pp. 87-102; and (for Wales) Jones, *Before Rebecca*, pp. 86-158.

[26] For good recent accounts of Chartism and Chartists, see ed. A. Briggs, *Chartist Studies* (London, 1959); F. C. Mather, *Public Order in the Age of the Chartists* (Manchester, 1959); and ed. Dorothy Thompson, *The Early Chartists* (London, 1971). For the Plug-Plot Riots, see G. Kitson Clark, 'Hunger and Politics in 1842', *Journal of Modern History*, xxv (1953), 355-74; and F. B. Smith, 'The Plug Plot Prisoners and the Chartists', *ANU Historical Journal* (Canberra), no. 7, Nov. 1970, pp. 3-15.

took place in the industrial villages and towns of Lancashire, Stafford, and Cheshire in the summer of 1842. After one of the many incidents attending these riots, Christopher Holmes, a 'fire-beater' at John Hargreaves's steel-mill at Accrington, described 'how a large body of people came to [my] master's mill and said they wanted to stop it'. 'They asked me', he continued, 'where the plugs were. I told them to wait ten minutes whilst I drew the fire or it would blow up the boiler. One of the men said, "Damn the boiler, you must buy fresh ones." Another of the party then struck me across the back with a bludgeon and told me to find the plugs or he would stick me in the fire.'[27]

Chartism was accompanied, during its first and second phases, by the 'Rebecca' riots in North and West Wales, when farmers and labourers, wearing women's skirts, rode together down country roads, pulling down turnpikes and tollgates;[28] and by a further round of resistance to the Clearances in Sutherland and Inverness; while the fiasco of April 1848 in London was preceded by food riots —among the last of their kind—in the north-west of Scotland. (The second of my minor protest-phases forms an interlude between the last two phases of Chartism: it marks the second great upswing of rural incendiarism, in 1843–5, which was centred mainly on East Anglia and Devon, and which continued with interruptions into the 1850s.)[29]

As has often been observed, after the collapse of Chartism public protest in Britain became less frequent and more muted; and compared with the riots and rebellions of the Regency and the 1830s and 1840s those of the 1850s and 1860s—the last two of our phases— seem, except in the Highlands, to have been less of a bang than a whimper. Yet there were violent clashes between Protestant English and Catholic Irish workers in Stockport in 1852; there were riots in Hyde Park in London over Sunday trading in 1855; and there were further outbreaks of rural resistance to enclosure in the Scottish Highlands in 1852, 1853, and 1859. This last year also saw the beginning of a two-year builders' strike in London. In the 1850s and 1860s, there was a further crop of attacks on the 'new' police, after earlier waves in the 1830s and 1840s, mainly in the northern manu-

---

[27] County of Lancaster RO, QJD 1/89 (13 Aug. 1842).

[28] David Williams, *The Rebecca Riots. A Study in Agrarian Discontent* (Cardiff, 1955).

[29] It will be observed that I have omitted poaching and other offences against the game laws from this record. Poaching was a fairly constant activity, occurring regularly and not merely in fits and starts; moreover, it did not, like arson in the early 1830s, ever appear in association with a wider movement of protest.

facturing towns;[30] there was a minor Reform Bill riot in London in
1860; and, at Sheffield in the same year, there were the 'outrages'
that recalled the 'direct-action' methods used in Wales and the
Potteries a quarter of a century before.

If we now look back on these seventy years, we shall see that the
geographical pattern of protest had undergone a series of changes
and that there had been significant shifts in its location and distribution as it moved from one part of the country to another. The picture
is roughly as follows. In the first phase—that of the early war-years
of the 1790s—it is hard to pinpoint protest exactly, as it had, to a
large extent, been driven underground; but of the protest that
emerged in the daylight—the tip of the iceberg, as it were—we may
note the 'conspiratorial' Jacobin movements in cities such as
London and Edinburgh (with 'Church and King' counter-responses
in Manchester and Birmingham), and the food-rioting in south-
eastern England and parts of Wales. In the second phase—that of
the late-war and post-war period of 1811–22—protest resurfaced
and became widely diffused all over the country, including both
rural and industrial Wales. If, in addition to our protest time-chart,
we plotted a protest *map*, we should pin on it a number of large cities
like London and Manchester; old centres of declining industry like
East Anglia; established and ongoing industrial centres like the iron
districts of South Wales and the hosiery counties of the Midlands
and the West Riding of Yorkshire; new textile areas like Lancashire
and Cheshire; parts of the Highlands of Scotland; and such widely
scattered food-rioting market towns as Falmouth, Nottingham,
Bolton, and Carlisle. So there is a certain neatness of balance and
evenness of distribution between city, market town, and country
and between North, Midlands, and South. In the third phase
(1829–32) there is a new and decisive shift to the new manufacturing
districts of the Midlands, South Wales, and the North (including the
coalfields and the Clydeside in Scotland); a temporary shift from
London to Birmingham and certain of the old chartered towns
(Nottingham, York, Derby, and Bristol); and a final and dramatic
upsurge of the rural counties in the south of England; from now on
such rural protest as lingers on in the South, as in East Anglia or
Devon, is of the more muted 'marginal' kind until agrarian trade
unionism takes over in the 1870s.

In the three Chartist phases of the 1830s and 1840s, the more

[30] For this later phase, see J. D. Storch, 'The Plague of the Blue Locusts. Police
Reform and Popular Resistance in Northern England 1840–57', *Internat. Review of
Social History*, xx (1975), 61–90.

overt agrarian protest is limited to the 'Celtic fringe' of West Wales
and the Scottish Highlands (though there is an exception in the
strange, millenarial movement of Kentish labourers at Bossenden
Wood in 1838[31]); while the centre of attention, as Chartism is both
a forward- and a backward-looking movement, is divided between
the large and expanding cities (London, Birmingham, Manchester,
Glasgow), the new industrial districts of England–Scotland–Wales,
and the old dying centres of handloom-weaving and rural industry
in the English West Country and the West Riding of Yorkshire. But,
after this final appearance, the last of these groups drops out of the
picture; and English handloom-weavers and Welsh peasant-farmers
follow the English peasant-labourers into almost total oblivion—
while, on the old 'Celtic fringe', it is only the Scottish Highlands that
keep up their resistance: particularly in Inverness-shire, where there
were over 200 commitments for riot and assaults on the police
between 1885 and 1888, that is even after the last great episode in
the Crofters' War, the so-called 'Battle of the Braes', was fought out
on the island of Skye in 1882.[32] Meanwhile, through the 1850s and
1860s, the honours were largely shared, though in uneven proportions, between London and the manufacturing districts of South
Wales, the Midlands, and the North. So, if we look back, say from
the mid-1860s to the beginning of the French wars, we find that
a dramatic shift has taken place in protest from South to North,
and from the rural counties to the manufacturing towns, with
London appearing as an occasional, though somewhat muted,
contender. Yet, if we refer back a moment to the opening section of
this chapter, this need hardly surprise us as it broadly reflects the
social and demographic transformation that the Industrial Revolution, beginning in the eighteenth century yet not bearing its *social*
fruits until the middle of the nineteenth, had brought about.

Meanwhile, responding to the same impulses, not only the location but the nature of protest had also changed; but this will be
considered in a later chapter.

[31] P. G. Rogers, *Battle in Bossenden Wood. The Strange Story of Sir William
Courtenay* (London, 1961).

[32] 'Return of Offences Committed in Crofting Parishes of the Highlands and
Islands of *Scotland*, arising out of Disputes in regard to Right to Land, or the Rent
of Land, during and since 1874'. PP 1888, lxxxii, 2–8. See also H. J. Hanham, 'The
Problem of Highland Discontent, 1880–5', *R.H.S. Transactions*, 5th series, xix (1969),
35–58; and the chapter on 'The Crofters' Land War', in J. P. D. Dunbabin, *Rural
Discontent in Nineteenth-Century Britain* (London, 1974), pp. 181–210.

2. Ireland

To turn from Britain to Ireland in the late eighteenth and early nineteenth centuries is to turn to another world: from a rich and independent nation with an expanding economy and growing population, the centre of a large and developing Empire which was soon to become 'the workshop of the world', to one of colonial status, of persistent poverty and economic stagnation. Where the tensions in British society (outside certain regions like the Highlands of Scotland and north-west Wales) may be basically attributed to the speed of industrialization and the explosive growth of cities, Ireland's problems were entirely different. Essentially, they were twofold: her colonial status arising from what a modern Irish historian has called her 'English question'[1] and the backwardness and stagnation of her economy and, where it expanded, its lop-sided growth. The two were closely interwoven and it is not easy to disentangle the one from the other, as Ireland's dependence on a wealthy neighbour whose cultural and religious traditions were entirely different from her own, and one, moreover, whose rulers could have no possible interest in developing her national resources in competition with theirs, inevitably acted as a millstone on her political and economic evolution. But this, of course, is not the whole story; for Ireland's poverty and economic stagnation became compounded as the result of developments within Irish society itself. For the Irish landlords, particularly those in the South, had qualities that no more disposed them to be attentive to their tenants' prosperity than the absentee landlords from across the sea.

From all this, it has been argued, Ireland developed a system of agriculture and landholding that ensured and perpetuated the poverty of the greater part of her population. One of its evils was the 'middleman system', a product of the eighteenth century, which rid the landlord of all responsibility for his tenants and left them at the mercy of his agents. Another was the institution of tenancy-'at-will' and its twin, the refusal of leases (until the later nineteenth century, 'tenant right' was a privilege of Ulster alone). A third was the sub-division of land to the point where, as late as 1841, 45 per cent of all Irish holdings were under five acres and only seven per

[1] Patrick O'Farrell, *Ireland's English Question* (London, 1975).

cent over thirty, while two and a half million labourers (almost a third of her population) had little or no work. A fourth evil, which partly arose from the third, was the exclusive cultivation of the potato. The potato, in one sense, was the answer to the poor man's prayer in that a holding of one and a half acres sufficed to feed a family of six for a year, but it also had the grave disadvantage of leaving the cultivator at the perpetual mercy of the weather. The result was a recurring failure of the potato crop, culminating, after repeated failures in the 1830s, in the national disaster of the Famine of 1845.[2]

One feature of Ireland's stagnation and stunted growth was the dismal poverty of her rural population which, outside Ulster, counted among the most wretched on God's earth. The Duke of Wellington, who knew the country well, wrote that 'there never was a country in which poverty existed to the extent it did in Ireland', and a French traveller, also writing on the eve of the Famine, thought the condition of Indians in many ways superior to that of the Irish.[3] Another feature was the remarkable course of her population growth, expanding rapidly at one stage and stagnating the next. Dublin, for long her only large city with a population of 200,000 in 1800, expanded only to 250,000 by 1850 and to 300,000 in 1914; at a time when Belfast, in the more prosperous and industrial North, rose from being a small market town (with a population so insignificant that the general historian does not think it even worth a mention) to a city of 100,000 in 1850 and 400,000 in 1914. National population was equally erratic and was only consistent in that both expansion and decline appear to have reflected poverty and despair rather than prosperity and hope in the future. So, in the first phase, Ireland's population rose from 2½ million in 1767 and 5 million in 1801 to over 8 million in 1841; and then, with the disaster of famine, emigration, and disease in the mid- and late-1840s, it fell to 6½ million by 1851 and to little over 4 million on the eve of the First World War.[4]

It is against this rather dismal background that we must attempt

[2] For the above, see C. Woodham-Smith, *The Great Hunger* (London, 1974), pp. 9–200; R. D. Crotty, *The Land Question. Its Structure and Volume* (Cork, 1966); G. O'Tuathaigh, *Ireland Before the Famine 1798–1848* (Dublin, 1972), pp. 1–7; W. H. Crawford, 'Landlord–Tenant Relations in Ulster 1609–1820', *Irish Economic and Social History*, ii (1975), 5–21; and A. P. W. Malcomson, 'Absenteeism in Eighteenth Century Ireland', ibid. i (1974), 15–35.

[3] Woodham-Smith, p. 14; Nicolas Mansergh, *The Irish Question 1840–1921* (London, 1968), p. 23.

[4] O'Tuathaigh, pp. 5–6; Woodham-Smith, pp. 23–5.

to follow the course and pattern of Irish crime and protest between about 1780 and 1860 along lines similar to those we followed in the previous chapter. Unfortunately, Irish criminal statistics do not go back as far as even the 'global' statistics we noted in Britain from 1805 onwards. This is partly due to the almost total destruction of the Crown Books at Assizes and other criminal and convict records by fire in the Dublin Four Courts in 1922.[5] But, from 1826 onwards, there are a variety of returns and reports to draw on that correspond broadly (and from 1845 more exactly) to the English and Scottish returns of committals and indictments we consulted before. First, there is a table of prisoners and the offences with which they were charged compiled by the Inspectors-General of Prisons for the years 1826 to 1838.[6] This is supplemented by a 'comparative statement' of the average number of committals for the first and last three years over the same thirteen-year period and based on the same information.[7] Next there is an abstract of committals and convictions for the same period taken from reports of the Inspectors-General, this time with a breakdown into counties.[8] Following this, we have a return of 'outrages and offences' reported to the Constabulary Office from mid-1834 to mid-1838 but this time with no breakdown into counties.[9] Then, after a break, we have a detailed report and return of all 'outrages' (a term peculiarly applicable to Ireland) committed in each county in 1844, a year of rising social tension;[10] and, finally, as for England and Scotland but covering a different span of years, a county-by-county return, beginning in 1845, of committals for every sort of crime—but, in this case, including all cases brought before the courts and not only indictable offences.[11]

[5] Previously existing records are listed in H. Wood's *Guide to the Records Deposited in the Public Record Office of Ireland* (Dublin, 1919), pp. 207–8.

[6] 'Ireland: Minutes of Evidence before the Select Committee', PP 1839, xii, 228–9 (MS. copy in Bodleian Library, Oxford).

[7] 'Comparative Statement . . . 1827–1838', MS. in Bodleian Library.

[8] 'Abstract of Committals and Convictions, 1826 to 1838', MS. in Bodleian Library.

[9] 'Return of all Outrages and Offences reported to the Constabulary Office from 1st July 1834 to the last day of June 1838 from the different Counties in Ireland', MS. in Bodleian Library.

[10] 'Return of Outrages reported to the Constabulary Office during the Year 1844', Appendix to Minutes of Evidence before Commission of 1845, PP 1845, xxi, 964–5.

[11] PP 1846, xxx, 176–7; 1847, xlii, 284–5; 1847–8, lii, 456–7; 1849, xliv, 224–5; 1850, xlv, 622–3; 1851, xlvi, 196–7; 1852–3, lxxxi, 164–5, 528–9; 1854, liv, 298–9; 1854–5, xliii, 86–7; 1856, xlix, 88–9; 1857, xlii, 266–7; 1857–8, xlvii, 406–7; 1859, xix, 578–9; 1860, lvii, 738–9; 1861, lii, 224–5.

In view of the gaps in the records and changes in the classification of crimes, it is probably best to divide this thirty-five-year period into two parts: from 1826 to 1838 and (after a six-year gap and an interim report for 1844) from 1845 to 1860. In the first period the returns represent crime as tending to rise; but in fits and starts and not in steady progression as in England and Wales. Thus a total of 16,141 committals in 1826 rises to nearly 18,000 in 1827 and falls to 14,500 in 1828, rising again to a platform of 15,000 to 17,000 cases in 1829 to 1833; rising again sharply to 21,000 in 1834 and reaching a peak of 23,894 committals in 1836. We gain a better over-all picture by taking the figures from the 'comparative state-ment' of three-year averages, which shows the three-year mean of 16,145 in 1826–8 rising to one of 23,346 in 1836–8. This high ceiling appears to have been followed by a lull because the committals for the second period start at the comparatively low level of 16,696 in 1845. (Besides, the authorities were not much interested in collecting reports and returns of 'outrages' except in years when they presented a threat.) From then on they rise sharply—far more sharply than over any previous five-year period—to a peak in 1849, as illustrated by the following national figures:

1845	16,696
1846	18,492
1847	31,209
1848	38,522
1849	41,989

After this they decline, steadily at first (there are still 31,328 com-mittals in 1850) but with a gathering momentum: 15,141 committals in 1853, then continuing to fall steadily to 7,210 in 1857 and 5,386 in 1860. So, after following an erratic pattern all their own in the mid 1820s and 1830s (when crime in England was steeply on the upgrade) and reacting violently to the catastrophic conditions of the 1840s, of which there was no equal in Britain, the pattern of decline in the 1850s is broadly similar, and no doubt for broadly similar reasons, to that in England, Scotland, and Wales.

Once more, as with Britain, we may trace the geographical distri-bution of crime by breaking down the committals to a county or city level, while remembering that, in this case, we are dealing with committals as a whole and not only with cases brought before assizes and quarter sessions. As with England and Scotland, we have made a selection of a number of representative counties and cities (including two examples from the less turbulent North) and

placed them in descending order of volume of crime. The results for
the period 1826–30 are the following (figures are approximate):

City of Dublin	31,700	Co. Limerick	7,025
Co. Cork	13,250	Co. Dublin	6,950
Co. Tipperary	13,225	Co. Antrim	6,850
Co. Mayo	11,700	Co. Clare	4,750
City of Cork	7,900	Co. Tyrone	4,275
Co. Galway	7,150		

What is striking—once more similar to the English pattern—is the
predominance of urban over rural crime: with the City of Dublin
well ahead of all others in the list and eclipsing its own county with
a total of over four to one, and with the City of Cork (whose population was about one-third of Dublin's) having a total of over half that
of its county, the most 'criminal' county of all. If we now rank the
same counties and cities according to the number of committals
during the period 1845–60 (the figures for 1851 and 1852 have been
omitted), we shall note that the order is by no means the same as
before:

Co. Cork	24,597	Co. Clare	10,023
Co. Tipperary	20,853	Co. Tyrone	6,628
City of Dublin	15,263	Co. Antrim	5,771
Co. Mayo	11,582	City of Cork	4,775
Co. Limerick	11,413	Co. Dublin	3,693
Co. Galway	11,040		

We now note a considerable increase in rural crime which, unlike
the situation in Britain, has moved well ahead of the urban. The
most striking feature of this new set of figures is the fall in the volume
of crime in the City of Dublin which, having eclipsed all others
before, has now dropped to third place behind the counties of Cork
and Tipperary; another is the fall of the City of Cork to almost the
bottom of the list. The rise in the volume of rural crime is particularly
striking in the southern and western counties, such as Cork, Tipperary, and Mayo, and is no doubt a direct reflection of the devastat-
ing impact of the Famine on these rural communities.[12] But, as we
have already seen in the national figures, once these catastrophic
conditions improved and the pressure of population began to be

[12] The rising toll of thefts of sheep, horses, and cattle in certain counties may be
a useful indicator: thus, in *Clare* these rose from 2 in 1846 to 119 in 1847, 229 in
1848 and 579 in 1849 and had only fallen to 297 in 1852; in *Co. Cork*, they were: 77
in 1846, 266 in 1847, 559 in 1848, 597 in 1849, 205 in 1850.

eased by massive emigration, the volume of crime declined: a comparison of the county statistics will show that this was particularly true of the counties in the South; the pattern in the more prosperous North, which had not suffered so acutely from the Famine, was, not surprisingly, a little different.

How did protest relate to these changes in the volume and pattern of crime? First we must note that the nature of protest in Ireland at this time differed in important respects from the English. Poaching, for example, in sharp contrast with its prevalence in England, does not feature on the list of Irish crimes, whereas a number of violent crimes against property, such as robbery of arms, forcible possession of property, armed assembly, and attacks on houses and land, which play no part in the English records, are conspicuously present in the Irish.[13]

To begin with the period 1826 to 1838. Here it is impossible to present a complete or satisfactory picture, as figures given in the 'comparative statement' for 1826-38 are incomplete and no distinction is made between assaults on police officers (which feature high on the list of Irish 'protest'-crimes) and assaults of any other kind. But in so far as they indicate the *trends* in rural protest, it appears that, between the first three-year phase (1826-8) and the last (1836-8), arson decreased by one-half; cattle-maiming and oath-taking remained constant; the destruction of buildings and their forcible occupation (two separate offences) doubled; armed assembly increased by half; combinations to raise wages (a rare offence in the countryside) trebled; and the number of menacing letters fell by a half. So, by and large, there was an appreciable increase in the volume of 'outrage'—a term frequently used in relation to rural crime—but the number of cases reported to the Inspectors-General are, in some cases, so small as to carry little conviction. We may perhaps have a little more confidence in the return of 'outrages' made to the Constabulary Office between July 1834 and June 1838. They cover a far shorter period, it is true; but the figures are more complete and the recorded offences include a dozen crimes of protest (the only one missing is assaults on revenue officers), and even if, as 'cases reported', they do not strictly accord with the cases brought before the courts, they bear, as far as they go, some stamp of credi-

---

[13] In what follows 'protest'-crimes fall under the following thirteen heads: robbery of arms; forcible possession; arson; riot and destruction of buildings or machinery; attacks on houses or land; cattle-maiming; threatening letters; unlawful, armed assembly; assaults on and obstruction of police; assaults on revenue officers; unlawful oaths; combinations to raise wages; high treason (limited to 1848).

bility. Broadly, what they suggest is that, over these four years, the volume of social protest rose in 1835-6 and, with certain exceptions (cattle-maiming and robbery of arms), fell sharply in 1837-8; so the period as a whole appears to have been one of muted rather than of rising protest.[14] In fact, if we make such use as we can of the 'comparative statement' as well, we may reasonably conclude that the same may be true of the 1830s as a whole. So, at this stage at least, crime and protest seem to have followed a different course.

It is only with the 1840s, however, that we come on to safer ground in making such comparisons. Yet this is hardly the case with what at first seems a promising document, the returns of 'outrages' reported to the Constabulary Office in 1844. One is at once struck by the fact that the total number of 'outrages' is suspiciously low: only a little over 6,000, whereas nearly three times that number appear on the far more credible return for the following year. The explanation turns out to be a fairly simple one: typical urban offences, particularly larceny, are omitted altogether (presumably not rating as 'outrages'), thus tilting the balance heavily in favour of rural crime and, no doubt, of protest-crime as well. So this report does not enable us to establish any relationship between protest and crime. Yet it has the virtue of being divided into counties and principal cities and towns; so, for the first time, we are able to make some sort of distribution of 'protest' (in terms of 'outrage') as between one county and the next and to form some opinion of the degree of 'rebelliousness' of the various counties of Ireland during what appears to have been a comparatively turbulent year. From this record, Tipperary—with 907 reported cases of 'outrage'—emerges as by far the most 'rebellious' county of all; it is followed by Cork (447), Limerick (312), Clare (281), Roscommon (264), Galway (239), Sligo (215), and Longford (205); while Mayo comes half-way down the list with the comparatively low total of 181. Ulster, as might be expected, is the least 'rebellious' of the four provinces: it is headed by Tyrone with 205 cases, with Antrim and Armagh (sharing Belfast between them) trailing far behind with 137 and 127 'outrages' apiece.[15]

But, it must be insisted, this is an imperfect record not only of crime but of protest, as 'outrages' are seen to include such common-or-garden crimes as robbery, rape, infanticide, and assaults of all

[14] 'Return of all Outrages and Offences reported to the Constabulary Office' from mid-1834 to mid-1838, Bodleian Library.

[15] 'Return of Outrages in each County of Ireland, specially reported to the Constabulary Office during the Year 1844', PP 1845, xxi, 964-6.

kinds, most of which are not remotely connected with 'protest' in the
sense in which it is being used in this book. In fact, it is only with
the appearance in the following year of the annual returns of committals for every type of crime in the thirty-two counties that we
can with any degree of confidence present a comparative picture of
crime and protest in Ireland similar to the one we presented for
Britain, though over a slightly longer period, in the previous chapter.
To start with the total record of protest, both as to its annual volume
and its distribution among a selected number of counties and cities.
Beginning with a total of 2,364 committals for protest-crimes in
1845, it rises to 3,618 in 1847, to 6,830 in 1848, and a peak of 6,927
in 1849; after which it drops sharply to 4,753 committals in 1850
and further to 1,099 in 1853, 457 (the lowest point) in 1859, and 462
in 1860.[16] So for these years in Ireland, differing here from Britain,
the pattern of rise and decline of protest is similar to that of crime
in general that we noted before. In both cases the high-point is
reached in 1849 (compared with 1842 in England and Wales and
1848–9 in Scotland) and the low-point in 1859 and 1860. But the
ratio of protest to crime does not remain constant: while protest as
a percentage of crime has an average of 13·1 for the sixteen-year
period as a whole, it reaches the remarkable figure of 17·7 per cent
in 1848 and of 16·5 per cent in 1849. Then it falls progressively
through the early 1850s and reaches its lowest point, 6·5 per cent, in
1855. Not only is this pattern quite different from the British, but it
eloquently reflects, as we already noted of crime, the violent tensions
of the years of famine and disease and of the massive emigration
that followed the disaster of 1845, when crime and protest-crime
were closely linked, particularly in the rural areas of the South, and
in many cases, as with cattle-maiming and sheep- and cattle-stealing,
can hardly be told apart.

To turn to individual types of protest: arson reached its peak
around 1849, with 243 cases in that year, 152 cases in 1848, and 226
in 1850 (compared with only 69 cases in 1847 and 86 in 1853). Arson,
in fact, appeared in a common context of protest and did not, as in
England in the 1840s, follow a course of its own. Similar patterns
can be observed in the rise and fall in the numbers of cases of violent
crimes against property that were so typical of Irish protest at this
time: assaults on the police, cattle-maiming, forcible possession of
property (though here with some notable exceptions), and even the
administration of unlawful oaths that often accompanied them, all
reached their peaks around 1848 and 1849 and declined, usually

16 For details see p. 29 n. 11 above.

rapidly, in the early 1850s.[17] Threatening letters alone, apparently by now an outmoded form of protest, failed to conform to the general pattern, falling steadily through the whole period from 33 committals in 1845, to 19 and 20 in 1848 and 1849, and to one solitary case in 1860.

Some counties, of course, were more notable for some types of protest, or for protest in general, than others. Cattle-maiming, as previously in the Rebellion of 1798, was largely an affair of the West. Of 515 cases recorded in 1848, 61 took place in Clare (with a further 64 reported in 1849) while Galway had the remarkable total of 432. (In both counties, significantly it would seem, sheep- and cattle-stealing also reached their peak in 1848 and 1849.) Cork took the lead in assaults and obstructions of the police (495 cases in 1848 and 837 in 1849); it was also remarkable for acts of arson, with 49 cases in 1848, 47 in 1849, and 38 in 1850; yet Limerick, another incendiary county, had as many as 80 cases (the highest annual total of all) in 1850. There were 118 cases of forcible entry in Tipperary in 1850; and, in 1848, 127 cases in Clare and 122 in both Limerick and Cork. Attacks on buildings and machinery reached their highest point in Mayo—where protest phased out later than elsewhere in the South and the West—in 1854. By this time, as we have seen, protest-crimes were generally in steep decline in Connaught, Munster, and Leinster. In Ulster, the pattern was different. In Antrim and Armagh, the volume of protest was only slightly lower in the early 1850s than it had been in the years of crisis, 1848 and 1849. Tyrone, which had had only 12 committals for all types of protest in 1847 and 35 committals in 1848, had four times that number in 1850 and still had 81 in 1852 and 74 in 1853. (It did not fall below the 1848 figure until 1854 and rose well above it again in 1856.)

If we now add up the crude score of protest over these sixteen years in the case of eight selected counties and a couple of cities, we arrive at a picture which it is instructive to compare with the order of protest that we drew up (with reservations) for 1844:

Co. Cork	3,744	Co. Tipperary	2,031
Co. Galway	2,734	Co. Tyrone	600
Co. Clare	2,336	Co. Antrim	367
Co. Mayo	2,259	City of Dublin	217
Co. Limerick	2,130	City of Cork	92[18]

---

[17] For the general decline in crimes of violence against property in Ireland in 1848–52, see Tables in PP 1852–3, lxxxi, 433–9.

[18] If we were to 'weight' protest in the various counties and cities by taking account

So we note, with the mid 1840s, the emergence of the western counties as principal counties of protest and the relative eclipse of Tipperary; and we also note, far more emphatically than in the case of England and Scotland after the early 1840s, that protest remains an essentially rural phenomenon with its main focus in the West. The point becomes underlined when, as we did for Britain before, we present protest in these counties and cities as a percentage of crime:

Co. Galway	24·76% (39·8% in 1848)
Co. Clare	23·3% (37·4% in 1848)
Co. Mayo	19·5% (34·6% in 1850, 42·3% in 1854)
Co. Limerick	18·6% (26·2% in 1848)
Co. Cork	15·2% (23·3% in 1849)
Co. Tipperary	9·7% (14·9% in 1848)
Co. Tyrone	9·0% (14·4% in 1850, 13·2% in 1853)
Co. Antrim	6·4% (13·5% in 1856)
City of Cork	1·9% (7·4% in 1857)
City of Dublin	1·4% (4·7% in 1857, 7·7% in 1862)

But if we consider these figures as a whole (including those in parentheses), we shall note something else besides: that while, with the exception of Mayo, these principal counties of protest in the South and West had passed their peak in 1850 or before, this was not so with Ulster nor with the cities of Dublin and Cork. This suggests that *after* the critical years of 1848 and 1849 (had it something to do with emigration from the countryside?) there were the beginnings of a shift in protest, as there had been earlier in Britain, from the country to the cities and industrial towns. We shall hear more of this at the end of the section that follows.

And now, again following the model of our previous chapter, we come to the record of protest in terms not of statistics but of popular movements. They fall into half a dozen stages. First, the agrarian revolt, represented by the Defenders of Ireland, in the 1780s and 1790s; next, the nominally political Rebellion of 1798 which, with its aftermath in Dublin and Wicklow, lasted until 1803; third, the

of population, Co. Cork—with a population nearly three times that of Limerick, more than twice that of Mayo and Clare, and almost twice that of Galway—would drop to fifth place below Galway, Mayo, Clare, and Limerick; and Antrim, with a population second only to Cork among these ten, would drop to the last place among the counties. (Populations (to the nearest 1,000) in 1851 were as follows: Co. Cork 563,000; Antrim 352,000; Galway 299,000; Mayo 275,000; Clare 236,000; Limerick 209,000; Tipperary 331,000; Tyrone 256,000; City of Dublin 258,000; City of Cork 86,000.)

most protracted movement of all, the 'land-and-tithe' war of the early part of the nineteenth century which, with short interludes, extended from the end of the Napoleonic Wars to the early 1840s. This was followed by the agitation arising from the Famine and the Young Ireland movement and attempted rebellion of 1848; and, finally, there came the Fenian movement and rising of the 1860s. Apart from these, there were riots on Orange Day in Belfast in 1857, with further riots in Belfast and Londonderry in 1864. In the Irish case, as we have seen, rural protest-crimes, like cattle-maiming and arson, have no reason to be treated apart as they did not form movements of their own, as arson did in England in the 1840s and early 1850s.

The Defenders' movement, which led into the Rebellion of 1798, was one of a long series of violent movements of peasant protest led by secret societies. The first of these in the later part of the eighteenth century was that of the Whiteboys which began in Tipperary in 1761 and extended its operations against landlords into other counties of the South and (with its offshoot, the Rightboys) only ended its activities about 1787. Meanwhile, in riposte to the activities of the Catholic peasants mainly centred in the South, other movements began in the North where they soon took on a sectarian anti-Catholic bias: movements and societies like the Oakboys, Hearts of Steel, Peep o' Day Boys, and, particularly, the more 'respectable' Orange Order. It was out of this confrontation with the Protestants in Ulster that the Catholic peasants began to enrol in a new secret society, the Defenders of Ireland. The Defenders championed the Catholic farmers' and smallholders' interests against the Protestant landlords and clergy in the North and, in the South, against tithe-proctors, clergy, and landlords in general.[19] The Defenders' movement, which was going strong on the eve of the Rebellion, was taken in tow by the Society of United Irishmen, originally a non-sectarian organization committed to Ireland's freedom, founded in Belfast in 1791, and provided the shock-troops of rebellion in the South. The Rebellion started at Naas, in Co. Kildare, on 23 May 1798, spread through the midlands and southern counties (with a brief appearance in the North), and ended in a massacre at Wexford and a short French occupation of a part of the West in September. It was a strange type of rebellion—or near-revolution—in that the

---

[19] See ed. T. Desmond Williams, *Secret Societies in Ireland* (Dublin, 1973), esp. pp. 13–25, 36–40, 58–67; and Peter Gibbon, 'The Origins of the Orange Order and the United Irishmen. A Study in the Sociology of Revolution and Counter-Revolution', *Economy and Society*, i (1972), 134–63.

main body of its leaders—the United Irishmen centred in Dublin and Cork—were betrayed and rounded up before the uprising began; yet their peasant followers under local leaders (priests among them) fought on in Connaught, Leinster, and Munster and were suppressed only after savage battles and bloody reprisals on both sides. But the Rebellion revived, after the proclamation of the Union, in Wicklow, Limerick, and Carlow in 1802 and 1803 and in Robert Emmet's abortive rising in Dublin in July 1803.[20]

A lull followed the suppression. It was broken by a new and prolonged series of peasant revolts over land, tithe, and the price of potatoes, beginning with a number of incendiary fires in Roscommon in 1812.[21] Events took a more serious turn in 1813, when requests were made to the Government to apply the Insurrection Act (first adopted in 1796) by petitioners in Westmeath, Meath, Limerick, and Clare, soon to be followed by others. This first stage of the 'land-and-tithe' war was to last until 1834; but it was by no means continuous, with peaks of activity in 1815,[22] 1821-2, and 1831-4 and long periods of comparative inactivity in between: marked in 1822 by famine conditions and, in the years immediately following, by the peaceful agitation of Daniel O'Connell for Catholic Emancipation.[23] It has been noted that the high-points in the various phases of this peasant rebellion coincided with economic crises affecting wages, employment, rents, the imposition of tithe, and the rise and fall in the price of potatoes. In consequence, it was no longer the farmers but the smallholders, cottiers, and labourers who were the most affected and, with their participation, the centre of protest tended to move from the western to the southern and central counties. At this stage the movement was often led by a new secret society (or rather an amalgam of secret societies) calling itself the Ribbonmen. Ribbonism became a great force in the countryside, championing the cause of the labourers and cottiers at a time of

[20] For a brief and readable account, see Thomas Pakenham, *The Year of Liberty* (London, 1972).

[21] *Calendar of State of the Country Papers*, i (1780-1821), 187-9, 220-36. SPO Dublin.

[22] The prolonged lull of the 1820s is graphically illustrated in the prisoners' petitions in Dublin Castle for the period. Of 874 petitions in 1823-6, little more than a dozen relate to 'political' crimes such as breaking the curfew; the rest relate to common-law offences, a large number (fifty-four, arising from one single police raid at Carrick-on-Shannon in 1826) to illicit distilling. SPO Dublin, Prisoners' Petitions, nos. 1990-2863 (1823-6).

[23] We can measure the concern of the authorities from the space devoted to this year in the *State of the Country Papers* (see vol. i, pp. 404-530).

economic crisis and only finally fading out on the eve of the greater crisis of 1845.[24]

The Famine raised quite different issues, as now, for both rural and city populations, it became a matter not of securing a larger share of the cake but of sheer physical survival. The upsurge of protest that we have noted in Clare and Mayo, Cork and Tipperary in these famine-years consisted, in spite of its scale and wide diffusion, of individual acts of anger and despair rather than a part of an organized movement; nor should this surprise us as famine rarely acts as a stimulus to collective behaviour. Dr. Woodham-Smith, who records meticulously such protests as she can find in the various counties against shortage and maldistribution of food and the social evils arising from them, comments: 'Apart from these terrible acts of individual vengeance [she is referring to such activities as cattle-maiming, incendiarism, and the murder of landlords], the mass of the Irish people lay helpless and inert; indeed as blow after blow fell, they appeared too weakened to protest.'[25]

However, one organized movement of protest developed out of the 1840s—in the context of the Famine, therefore; yet it was curiously unrelated to it as it chose to ignore the conditions that the Famine engendered. The Young Ireland party, a breakaway from Daniel O'Connell's wider and more moderate Repeal Association, was a party led by urban intellectuals who had little interest in the land or the problems of the peasantry, still less in the particular problems of the Famine-years. Moreover, they bungled their preparations; so it is hardly surprising that they failed and that the rebellion they staged in 1848 was a dismal failure that ended in disaster. After a brief skirmish on the Tipperary–Kilkenny border, the leaders surrendered and, having had their death sentences commuted, were sent as convicts to Australia.[26] We shall hear more about them in a later chapter.

Young Ireland, whatever else it failed to achieve, left a legacy for other patriots to inherit. It was adopted ten years later by another secret revolutionary society—also, like the Young Irelanders, urban-based. The Irish Republican Brotherhood, better known as the Fenians, was founded by James Stephens, a Kilkenny man, who had fought with Smith O'Brien in the ill-fated skirmish of 1848.

[24] See Joseph Lee, 'The Ribbonmen', in *Secret Societies in Ireland*, pp. 26-35; and Galen Broeker, *Rural Disorder and Police Reform in Ireland, 1812-36* (London, 1970), pp. 12-13, 109-12.

[25] Woodham-Smith, p. 326.

[26] D. Gwynn, *Young Ireland and 1848* (Cork, 1944); Woodham-Smith, pp. 326-57; and (briefly) G. O'Tuathaigh, *Ireland before the Famine*, pp. 190-202.

Having gone to France and later to the United States (where an Irish Republican Union had already been formed), he returned to Ireland and with others, some of whom were also survivors of the rising of 1848, he formed the new Republican Brotherhood on St. Patrick's Day 1858. Its members were bound by an oath of loyalty to 'The Irish Republic', and it had the novelty of recruiting members among the working class in Dublin and other cities. It also recruited in Britain and set up a centre for planning a rising in Liverpool.

The rising was planned for 1865, by which time the Brotherhood claimed 80,000 members in Ireland and England. But Stephens was arrested that year, the society was riddled with police spies, and had little money and made inadequate preparations for the task. So the rising was postponed, and when it was attempted in 1867 it was almost as dismal a fiasco as that of 1848. But it left its legacy of martyrs: those executed by the British in Manchester and those— John Boyle O'Reilly among them—who were sent to Western Australia in 1867.[27] Their story, too, will be told in later sections of this book.

Looking back from the Fenian rising to the Rebellion of 1798, we see that the geographical pattern of protest in Ireland had changed, but not so dramatically as in England. In the earliest two periods, those of the 1780s and 1790s, Irish protest had been firmly based in the countryside, particularly in the southern, central, and western counties. The cities, outside Wexford and Cork, had played only a minor role in the Rebellion. It had been essentially a peasants' rising and the main centres of revolt (if we are to trust the claims made by 'loyalists' for compensation after the event) were Wexford, Mayo, Kildare, Kilkenny, Co. Dublin, Carlow, Sligo, and (briefly) Antrim and Down in the North;[28] it appears also from the records of those transported to Australia that we should add Limerick, Cork, and Tipperary to the list. So it was an extensive movement ranging over counties widely dispersed, but with its principal axis in Wexford, Wicklow, Kilkenny, and Cork.

In the land-and-tithe war of the early nineteenth century, the focus shifted to the labourers and cottiers of the central counties— above all, to Limerick and Tipperary; but this was due to particular circumstances and the focus moved back to both the central and western counties with the impact of the Famine. Meanwhile, the

[27] See Kevin B. Nowlan, 'The Fenians at Home', in *Secret Societies in Ireland*, pp. 90-9.
[28] Pakenham, p. 392.

cities continued to be only marginally affected; but this began to change with the political, patriotic movements of Young Ireland and the Fenians in the following two decades. Meanwhile, too, there had been riots in northern cities like Belfast and Londonderry[29] and wages movements, too, had been almost entirely limited to the more industrial North. But this was only a beginning and, unlike the experience of England, South Wales, and the Lowlands of Scotland, the decisive turn, in terms of protest, from country to city or industrial towns came only with the development of a labour movement and the hard-fought industrial disputes, based on Dublin and Belfast, on the eve of the First World War.

[29] See Riot Commission's Report on the Belfast Riots in PP 1857–8, xxvi, 3–322. There are further reports on the riots of 1864 and 1872.

3. Canada

THIS chapter will take a different form from the others. In the case of Canada, the only movement of protest that led to the transportation as convicts of Canadian citizens—and Americans as well—was the dual rebellion of 1837 and 1838 that engaged the two principal provinces into which Canada was then divided: Lower Canada (the present Province of Quebec) and Upper Canada (the present Ontario). So, as the only type of protest involved was armed rebellion, it would be a useless exercise to attempt to draw a general picture of protest and discuss its relation to crime, as we did in our two earlier chapters. It will be sufficient to focus our attention on the two rebellions that led to the Australian exile of fifty-eight French-Canadians and ninety-six Anglo-Canadians and citizens of the United States.

Though Canadian historians, possibly due to their lack of a common culture, language, and experience, have tended to keep the two rebellions in separate compartments, they clearly had much in common; for how else, to put the question in its simplest form, explain that both the initial outbreaks of 1837 and the renewed outbreaks of 1838 took place a few weeks apart? (One answer might be that the 'open season' for rebellion was bound to be with the *prise des glaces* in early winter; but that is only a part of the story.)

The common factors that lay behind the two rebellions were: the growing resentment in both provinces over the domination of their political, cultural, and economic life by Great Britain (all the more unacceptable after the great Reform Bill of 1832); the severe economic crisis of 1836-7; and the close proximity of the hoped-for 'liberator', the United States. The last two factors are obvious enough. The crisis of 1836-7 was common not only to the two Canadas, but to the whole of North America and Western Europe as well; besides, it was liable to hit poor farming communities with greater severity than others.[1] And the proximity of the United States, with its common border running north of Vermont, New York State, and Ohio, is evident from even a cursory glance at the map.

---

[1] For the financial crisis of 1836-7 as a factor in the Lower Canadian rebellion, see Fernand Ouellet, *Histoire économique et sociale du Québec 1760-1850: structures et conjonctures* (Montreal, 1966), pp. 417-27.

Moreover, at this time, that border was an open one and there was a continuous to-and-fro across a frontier that was fluid and virtually non-existent.

The third factor needs a little more explanation, as the forms it took in the two provinces were by no means the same. In Upper Canada, the central grievance against British rule expressed itself in growing hostility to the two visible pillars of their colonial subjection, the 'Family Compact' of Church and State: the Tory supremacy in government and the Anglican domination of Church affairs, with a monopoly in the holding of the best lands that was common to both. In Lower Canada, there was a similar resentment over the appropriation of valuable land by Britain and her allies; as when, in 1833, some 850,000 acres in the Eastern Townships, south-east of Montreal, were granted to the British-American Land Company. But they also thought of themselves not only as a dependency of Britain, but as a conquered people with a different language on whom the settlement of 1763, and its subsequent modifications, had been imposed by an alien power. So the questions of language and culture played an important part in the national question as it presented itself to French-Canadians. On the other hand, the religious issue played only a minor part, as the Catholic Church, the Church of the great majority of Lower Canadians, had been given full authority, under the Canada Act of 1774, to do as it would with the spiritual lives of the French-speaking inhabitants; so that such grievances as existed over religion and the role of the Church were directed towards the provincial Catholic hierarchy which had long since made its peace with the occupying power. There was another issue to cause resentment that was peculiar to the lower province: the survival of the seigneurial or 'feudal' system of tenure (a relic of the old French days), which was considered all the more vexatious to the farmers and smallholders (the *habitants*) when these tenures and the services and privileges that went with them had, as was often the case, been acquired by English or Scottish settlers. 'The devil you know' being 'better than the devil you don't', the foreign presence in the village compounded a problem that already existed: the resentment felt by growing numbers of *habitants* and townsmen against the *système féodal* itself, including—though this was not always mentioned—the payment of tithe to the Church.[2]

[2] There is a considerable body of literature on this question, particularly on when 'feudalism' or the seigneurial system of land-tenure, came to an end and on the degree of support for its abolition before and during the rebellion of 1837-8. For varying views, see: F. Ouellet, 'Les Insurrections de 1837-38: un phénomène social', *Histoire*

And, of course, as it cannot be too strongly insisted, all such grievances became sharpened by the impact of economic crisis on the eve of the two revolts.

As the Lower Canadian rebellion was the first to break out, let us consider it first: both the immediate background and the course of events.[3] At one level, the background may be studied in the growing political conflict between the elected Assembly (in which French-Canadians held a majority) and the appointed Legislative Council: between 1822 and 1836 the Council rejected no fewer than 224 bills passed by the Assembly. It also gave short shrift to the '92 resolutions' adopted by the Assembly in 1834. These, stimulated by the reforms that had recently taken place in Britain, now served as a programme for the French-Canadian, or 'Patriot' cause: they demanded liberal changes in the Constitution consonant with the recent changes in Britain; also an elective Legislative Council; and one of them even hinted that unless their major claims were met, they might be tempted to follow the example of the Americans in 1776, and another (more specifically) that they might be led to leave the Empire and seek support elsewhere. The 'resolutions' were followed by a supporting petition with 80,000 signatures; and, in due course, these were curtly rejected at Westminster. But worse was to come when Lord John Russell, the British Prime Minister, authorized the Governor to dispose of the province's revenue without the elected Assembly's consent; it was also decided, as a precautionary measure, to transfer troops from the Maritimes into the St. Lawrence valley. So, almost inevitably, though Louis-Joseph Papineau, the moderate leader of the Patriots, urged caution, matters were moving towards a showdown. It came all the closer when the Patriots set up a committee of action to co-ordinate their activities, the Central Committee at Montreal, and a semi-military defence force, *Les Fils de la Liberté*,

sociale no. 1 (1973), pp. 54–82; G. Baillargeon, 'A propos de l'abolition du régime féodal', *Revue d'histoire de l'Amérique française* (1972), pp. 365–91; J.-P. Wallot, 'Le Régime seigneurial et son abolition au Canada', in his *Un Québec qui bougeait* (Montreal, 1973), pp. 225–51.

[3] For my account of the two rebellions I have relied largely on Stanley B. Ryerson, *Unequal Union* (Toronto, 1968), which has the great virtue of placing them in a common context. Other useful accounts are (for Lower Canada) F. Ouellet, 'Les Insurrections de 1837–38 . . .', loc. cit.; and the same author's chapter 'L'Échec du mouvement insurrectionnel (1837–1839)', in his *Histoire économique et sociale du Québec 1760–1850*, pp. 413–50; and (for Upper Canada, which has been less well served in terms of authors' originality) Edwin C. Guillet, *The Lives and Times of the Patriots* (Toronto, 1938); Fred Landon, *Western Ontario and the American Frontier* (Toronto, 1967), chaps. 8–12; Aileen Dunham, *Political Unrest in Upper Canada 1815–1836* (Toronto, 1927).

which, soon after, issued a manifesto that virtually called for an independent 'Canadian nation'. A meeting at St. Charles on 23 October, which was attended by 5,000 villagers and townsmen, called for the raising of a popular militia; but there was no call to arms until the Government issued warrants for the arrest of the Patriot leaders. So it was in defence of their threatened leaders that the *habitants* gathered with such arms as they could muster in the small towns and villages in the Richelieu valley, to the north of Montreal.

The Patriots were ill armed and ill prepared and they found to their consternation that, when the shooting started in late November, Papineau, the most respected of their leaders, had already abandoned the fight. So they were at a considerable disadvantage when 6,000 Government troops advanced into the Richelieu valley to engage them. Operations took place in two small clusters of villages: the one to the north-east of Montreal, based on St. Denis and St. Charles; the other, to the north-west, at St. Benoit and St. Eustache. In the first encounters, the Patriots managed to hold on to St. Denis but had to retreat from St. Charles. It was early December before the Government force, with increased numbers, reached St. Eustache and carried it by storm; and St. Benoit, caught in a pincer-movement, decided to surrender. Vengeance was summary and the campaign ended with the razing to the ground by fire of the two rebellious villages.

Several leaders now took refuge in the United States. They included Papineau (not involved in the rebellion) and Robert Nelson and Dr. Côté, spokesmen for the Patriots' radical wing, which now planned the next round from across the American border. A preliminary foray was made in February, when Nelson led a small force of Canadian exiles into Canada and set up a 'Provisional Government' and issued a proclamation before being expelled by a superior force. The proclamation is of interest because it not only committed the Patriot movement to establish a Republic but also to abolish the whole 'feudal' and seigneurial system, including tithe. So it was around this new, more advanced, programme that 'Hunters' Lodges' were secretly formed on both sides of the frontier and that the next phase in the Lower Canadian rebellion started on the night of 3–4 November 1838. This time, not only was the American contingent no more in evidence than the last (one solitary American, Benjamin Mott, who strayed across the Vermont border, later found himself in Sydney for his pains), but the leaders either kept close to the border or did not cross it at all. So the *habitants* were left largely to fend for themselves, finding such local leaders as they could. Once more, the expected support from the two cities of Quebec and Montreal did not arrive; and it is not surprising that the Patriots' resistance, this time based on the Eastern Townships, lying close to the American border, soon crumbled when faced with 7,000 Government troops and a battery of artillery. The operation was over within a week.

In Upper Canada, too, the Reform party (as the 'Patriots' there were called) were pledged to an extension of political democracy, and a radical wing, headed by William Lyon Mackenzie, to the achievement of national independence as well. Their programme also included more limited reforms concerned with education, public health, civil liberties, and, in view of the form taken by the Family Compact, religious equality besides. In 1828, a petition, sponsored by Mackenzie and others, attracted 8,000 signatures; it called for 'religious liberty' and for the removal of the Anglican clergy from positions in government. In 1830, Mackenzie was elected to represent the new township of York in the Upper Canadian Assembly; and when the Tory majority, who won the elections that year, expelled him and continued to do so, his constituents—much as the Middlesex electors in England had done for Wilkes over sixty years before—returned him five times over. In 1834, Mackenzie became the first mayor of Toronto and was able to play a key role in the Assembly when the Reform party won the general election that year. The Reformers, no doubt inspired (like the Lower Canadians) by the Reform Act in England, now called for 'responsible government', a demand that was as curtly rejected by Westminster as the Lower Canadians' '92 resolutions' would be rejected soon after; and when the British Government ordered the seizure of the provincial revenues at Quebec, the Reformers at Toronto denounced this 'coercive' measure and pledged their support. As the political crisis developed, steps were taken (again as in Lower Canada) to organize resistance outside the Assembly itself. In July 1837, the Toronto Reformers issued a defiant declaration, recalling the Americans' example of 1774, proposing the convocation of a popularly elected convention whose task it should be to concert a common programme for the redress of grievances in the name of the two provinces.

Soon after, the authorities baited a trap to provoke the militant Reformers (the Reform party had by now become divided) into precipitate action by leaving a 4,000 stand of arms virtually unguarded at Toronto City Hall. The Reformers fell for the bait and their attempt to seize the arms became the opening shot in their rebellion—rather as the capture of the 'guns of Montmartre' was to prove the opening shot in the Parisian insurrection of 1871. The plan was to march on Toronto on the night of 7 December, seize the arms, lock up the Government in the City Hall and appoint one of their number, Dr. John Rolph, as provisional administrator pending new democratic elections. The plan was bungled—not least by the decision taken without Mackenzie's knowledge (and he was a key actor in the enterprise) to postpone the date of operation. Matters were made worse by the arrival of news of the Lower Canadians' defeat; and worse still by the failure to respond of many who had promised to give support. So the Toronto operation failed, as did, a few days later, a supporting movement led by Dr. Charles Dunscombe from London, on Western Ontario.

Once more, as with Lower Canada, such leaders as remained after the initial defeat (two of them, Samuel Lount and Peter Matthews, had been captured and were hanged a few months later, in Toronto) crossed over to the United States; and here Mackenzie, who was never to return to Canada, planned the next uprising. As in the lower province, the nucleus of the next wave of insurgents was to be provided by the Hunters' Lodges, raised and equipped initially in Vermont and later in Buffalo and Cleveland and composed of Americans and Canadians who had escaped across the frontier. But, in the event, it was the Americans who provided the manpower and the Canadians, on both sides of the border, played scarcely any part at all. (In the Lower Canadian case, of course, the opposite was true; the Canadians started the operation on their side of the border and the Americans failed to give support.)

Once more, there were preliminary expeditions to scout out the land and test the enemy's defences. There were two raids made across the Niagara in June, followed by skirmishes at Short Hills and St. Clair; and their failure may have delayed the major operation from July to late November. This unfolded in two stages and ended in the battles of Prescott and Windsor. The Prescott expedition, the first to set out, was commanded by von Schultz (or Sczoltewski), a Polish revolutionary democrat living in the United States. The force became divided and von Schultz's vanguard of 170 men alone saw battle and held the windmill, overlooking the River St. Lawrence at Prescott, for four days before being forced to surrender by British troops. The second expedition set out from Detroit and landed on the Canadian shore of Lake Erie on 4 December. It moved on to Windsor where, this force too having become divided, only one sixth of a body of 1,000 men became engaged in a struggle for their objective, the military barracks. After an initial success, they were dislodged by greatly superior numbers; most of them were taken prisoner or shot down, and only a handful straggled back to safety across the American border.[4] So both rebellions, after a number of comparatively minor engagements, had ended in failure. The causes of this failure, except in so far as they emerge from this brief narration of events, will not concern us here.[5]

But two questions remain for discussion, as they are relevant to the purposes of this book. Who were the rebels and why had they rebelled? The leaders of the Lower Canadian rebellion were lawyers (there were three notaries among a dozen executed), doctors (Wolfred Nelson and Charles Côté were both doctors), army officers, and substantial farmers. Some were men of considerable wealth; when the amnesty came in 1849, Wolfred Nelson was awarded £12,784. 3s. 8d. compensation for damage done to his estate by the rampaging Loyalists in the winter of 1837.[6] Their followers were essentially the *habitants*—small farmers, shopkeepers, and craftsmen—of the Eastern Townships and villages and hamlets of the Richelieu valley north of Montreal. Among 108 who were court-martialled after the second uprising, sixty-six were farmers and the rest blacksmiths, innkeepers, shoemakers, carpenters, a small number of doctors, and half a dozen notaries.[7] In Upper Canada, the mixture was a little different, as befitted communities where class distinctions within the farming population had become more pronounced. Of the topmost leaders, Mackenzie was a one-time shopkeeper turned politician; Rolph and Duncombe were doctors; and of the two martyrs Peter Matthews was a farmer, Samuel Lount a blacksmith-farmer and surveyor. Their followers were substantially the same as those in the other province, though the wage-earning element was higher: of 885 Canadians listed among those arrested or absconded before November 1838, 375 were farmers and 'yeomen' and 345 were labourers; and the rest were almost equally divided between crafts-

[4] For a contemporary account of the battles of Prescott (Windmill Point) and Windsor by an American participant in the rebellion, see Linus W. Miller, *Notes of an Exile to Van Diemen's Land* (New York, 1846).

[5] For a summary of the reasons for defeat in both rebellions, see Ryerson, pp. 82–3, 132–3.

[6] 'Statement of the Commission on Rebellion Losses 1849–1853', Public Archives of Canada, RG4, B37, vol. 5, pp. 72–8.

[7] Ryerson, pp. 80–1. Ouellet finds a far higher proportion of professional men among the cadres of the insurrectionary movement (few of whom were actually rebels when it came to the point) in the Montreal region and has noted among them 119 lawyers and forty-three doctors ('Les Insurrections de 1837-38 . . .', p. 371).

men and small tradesmen on the one hand and professional men—
doctors, lawyers, surveyors, and the like—on the other.[8]

As far as the Canadians were concerned, the aims of the two
rebellions were essentially the same: to free the two provinces of
the British 'connection'; for once the rebellions had started and the
moderates had been pushed aside, the achievement of 'free institutions' or 'self-government', and (in the Upper Canadian case) the
uprooting of the Family Compact, no longer went far enough. The
Lower Canadians, who had problems of their own, added another
dimension: the abolition of all traces of 'feudalism', both in landholding and in the role of the Church; yet this latter demand was not
acceptable to all. Nelson and Côté, representing the militants,
certainly made it a major plank in the programme of the 'provisional
government' they proclaimed on the eve of the second uprising; but
to others—and there were not only moderates among them—to strike
at tithe and thus undermine the Church appeared to endanger a vital
prop in the nationalist cause.[9]

But there was a third party involved in the affair: the Americans
across the border who financed and equipped a major part of the
second operation and for whom it can hardly have been merely a
matter of planting 'American liberties' on Canadian soil. This is
purely a surmise in the case of the second stage of the Lower
Canadian rebellion where any outside help that was intended hardly
showed up at all. In the Upper Canadian case it is a different matter,
and evidence heard at the trials suggests that the project was warmly
supported in 'respectable' (if not necessarily in the highest) quarters.
So we find William Reynolds, a saddler of New York State, at his
trial at Kingston, 'accusing many leading men of fomenting the
invasion' and also telling his judges that 'the families of the married
men were to be taken care of during the absence of the husbands'.
Martin Woodruff, sheriff of Salina, in New York State, who was
later hanged for his part at Windmill Point, was more explicit when
he stated that 'all the respectable people in Salina and Syracuse were
in favour of the projects'.[10]

The rank-and-file Canadians—the small farmers, craftsmen,
and shopkeepers, who provided the shock-troops of rebellion—
undoubtedly shared their leaders' nationalist (and maybe, their
Republican) views. To them (it would appear from their cross-

---

[8] Ryerson, pp. 130–1.

[9] Ouellet, 'Les Insurrections de 1837–38 . . .', pp. 362–3, 377–8.

[10] 'Rebellion. Militia Court Martial of Prisoners. Fort Henry, 1838', Pub. Arch.
Canada, RG5, B36, vol. 1.

examinations) the ending of the Family Compact or British 'connection' was not merely a matter of politics and independence, but
it spelt an end of over-population and economic crisis, and more
jobs, more acres, and more bread. But to many of the French-
Canadian rank-and-file (as to their leaders) there was a further
dimension as well: not merely the end of the British domination but
that of their own capitalists and bureaucrats—and maybe of the
Church as well. This mood was certainly evident in some of the
villages in which the *habitants* took up arms—notably in the village
and district of Beauharnois which had (to confuse matters further)
a British *seigneur*. David Normand, a local merchant and a witness
at the court martial at Montreal, when asked what the rebels' intentions were, replied that 'they wished to abolish the *lods et ventes*
[a 'feudal' levy on the sale of land], and [that] they were now for
Nelson and Papineau and were resolved to succeed or die'. Another
witness was more precise and said that the object of the rebels'
armed occupation of Beauharnois 'was to suppress the priests'
tythes, rents and *lods et ventes*'.[11] Ouellet rightly insists that such
aims were by no means universal; but he infers that they might well
have become so if the rebellion had lasted longer. For, he argues,
it was the fear that the rebellion, launched by the *élite* with the
limited aim of achieving national-liberal goals, might, had it continued, develop into a wholesale assault on 'feudalism'—with all
this would entail for property in general—that weakened many
of the leaders' resolve and caused them to pull their punches,
or even (as in the case of Papineau) to abandon the struggle
altogether.[12]

What about the rank-and-file Americans? Some of them said
(again at their later court martial) that they got caught up in the
invasion by mistake: like Thomas Stockton, of Jefferson County,
who claimed that he was on his way to Montreal to look for work
and was 'forced to take a gun and bayonet by the people at the Mill';
or Asa Priest, from Auburn, Massachusetts, who said he came to
Oswego to get money he was owed for a cow, followed his debtor
on to the schooner that was taking Patriots over to Canada, fell
asleep on board and was forced to land! Others certainly believed
that they came to Canada to champion the cause of freedom; men
like John Gillman, from New York State (as most of them were),
who told the court that he 'expected he was rendering a service to

---

[11] *Report of the State Trials before a General Court Martial held at Montreal in
1838-9* (2 vols., Montreal, 1839), i, 376; ii, 286.
[12] Ouellet, 'Les Insurrections de 1837-38 . . .', pp. 377-8.

mankind in assisting the people of Canada to obtain a free Government'; or 'Captain Barnett' (possibly Henry Barnum, a Canadian by birth), who said on landing with a party near Windsor that they had come over 'to give sums and liberty to Canada, and to free the People from the oppression of the damned Tories'. Others were devout Methodists, Presbyterians, or Baptists—there are several of these among those later brought to trial—(men like Elijah Woodman, of whom we shall hear more in a later chapter) who sincerely believed that their fellow dissenters in Canada, as victims of the Family Compact, were in need of their help.[13]

But there were others, too, of a more freebooting and mercenary disposition for whom the adventure was a means of acquiring land and money. There are plenty of such examples among the prisoners brought to trial at Kingston and London. There was John Morisette, a Lower Canadian by birth and a self-confessed mercenary, who was 'hired at Louisburg [in Acadia] by a Yankee at $10 a month'. John Berry, a ploughman of Columbia County, did better: he was engaged for $16 a month by a Captain Benedick to help fortify an island as winter quarters for the Patriots prior to their assault. John Gutridge, another New Yorker, said he had been promised $8 or $9 a month and also 300 acres of land. One hundred and sixty acres was a more common figure: this was the amount promised to Elizar Stevens, Orlan Blodgett, and Daniel Liskum (or Liscombe), all three of New York State; Stevens was to have, in addition, $8 a month, Liskum a bounty of $80, and Blodgett (the most fortunate of the three) both an $80 bounty and a wage of £10 a month. (Was it significant that Liskum's payment was to be made 'after the *conquest* of the country'?) Luther Darby, another New Yorker, merely stated that he 'expected to be paid'. Orin Smith and Nelson Griggs, both labourers (the one of Vermont, the other of New York State), evidently had similar expectations but thought they had been cheated; for they both told their judges that they had been 'induced' to join the invasion of Canada 'by false representations'.[14]

We shall return to some of these men, both leaders and followers, in the context of repression and transportation in later chapters.

[13] Linus Miller believed that the distressed Canadians had 'turned their eyes to the United States, studied our glorious and peaceful institutions until they imbibed the spirit of the heroes of the American Revolution, and felt the God-like divinity of liberty stirring within their souls' (*Notes of an Exile*, p. 2).

[14] For John Gutridge, see 'General Court Martial at London, December 1838–January 1839', Pub. Arch. Canada, RG5, B41, vol. 3, file 3. For all other cases see 'Rebellion. Militia Court Martial of Prisoners. Fort Henry, 1838'.

4. The Changing Face of Protest

IN an earlier chapter, we noted that protest in Britain turned from south to north and from villages to cities as the century went on; and we suggested that this had a lot to do with the two great formative influences on Britain's social history at this time: industrial revolution and urban growth. The pattern in Ireland, as we saw, was quite a different one.

But it was not only the *location* of protest that tended to change; there was a change in the forms and nature of protest as well. Here, too, as industrialization proceeded and as modern industrial society —with its factories, railways, and national trade unions—began to take shape, the face of protest correspondingly changed. We may, in this sense, speak broadly of protest being at a 'pre-industrial' and an 'industrial' stage each with characteristic features of its own.[1] At its earlier, 'pre-industrial', stage, one of the most distinctive of these features was the 'direct-action' method and violent destruction of property (though rarely attended by violence to persons). This was true of the machine-breaking activities of the Luddites towards the end of the Napoleonic Wars; it was also true of the labourers who, nearly twenty years later, smashed threshing machines in the southern counties; as it was of the Reform Bill rioters of 1831, of 'Rebecca's Daughters' in Wales and the most violent phase of Chartism in the pottery towns in 1842. A second feature, common to all these movements and to many others that we have mentioned, was the careful selection of targets. This, of course, does not accord with the view of many historians and writers in the social and political sciences that the 'mob' is as fickle and irrational as it is violent and destructive.[2] Yet the hard core of evidence relating to these movements disproves such notions. Luddites, Rebeccaites, Reform Bill rioters at Bristol, Derby, and Carmarthen, and Chartist potters and miners who 'pulled down' houses and wrecked machinery in Staffordshire towns were all scrupulously discriminating in selecting their targets; and the 'Swing' labourers confounded the fears of the authorities

[1] See my 'The "Pre-Industrial" Crowd', in *Paris and London in the Eighteenth Century. Studies in Popular Protest* (London, 1970), pp. 17–34.

[2] For the classical exposition of this view, see G. LeBon, *The Crowd* (London, 1909), esp. pp. 16–17, 42, 73.

that they might cause a more general upheaval by extending their activities into the industrial western region of Wiltshire.[3]

A third feature, and one that is perhaps less liable to be disputed, is the tendency for protest at this stage to be spontaneous, unstructured, and to possess a minimum of organization. Again, we may cite as typical the 'Swing' and Luddite movements: in both there was a nucleus of organization; but, in spite of the complexity of its operations, which ranged over several counties, it never extended beyond the level of the village or of a group of villages at most.[4] A closely related feature is that of leadership. At this stage, it might take a number of forms, depending on whether the movement was promoted, in the first place, from without or within the rioters' or protesters' own ranks. In the first case, it was usual to find the 'crowd' responding to the direction, or believed direction, of a leader from a higher social group like John Wilkes or Lord George Gordon in London in the 1760s to 1780s. In the second case, it might vary between the small-time leaders-from-within (common to short-term local movements) and, in the case of wider and more protracted operations, the 'composite', almost mythical, leader as the personification of the group: men (or women) like Ned Ludd, Rebecca, or Captain Swing. (In extreme cases, as a variant of the local leader, primitive egalitarianism or fear of exposure might determine, as on at least two occasions in the 'Swing' movement, that there should be no 'captain' as 'we are all as one'.)[5] And, finally, the most complex of all these common features: the outlook or ideology of the protesters. At this stage, it tended to be backward-looking: that is, it was inclined to look for redress of grievance not through reform but through a restoration of a happier, 'golden', past. This looking to the past was typical of the food-rioters, machine-breakers, and 'direct-action' rioters in cities at this time; and even certain Chartist leaders, such as Feargus O'Connor, believed that they could solve the evils of industrial society by opting out of city life and putting unemployed factory workers back on the land.

But, of course, there was no sudden change from this older style of protest to one better adjusted to the values and outlook of an advanced industrial society. This, when it came, would include more organized and structured and (generally) less violent forms of protest; and leaders would tend to come from within the ranks of the popular protesters themselves, not only as a short-term phenomenon

[3] Hobsbawm and Rudé, pp. 126–7.
[4] Ibid., p. 209.
[5] Ibid., p. 106.

whose authority was strictly limited to a particular event, but as professionals, or near-professionals, of proven ability or experience. And, perhaps the most striking change of all, protest became forward-looking, no longer yearning nostalgically for the past but seeking its solutions through reforms and even a total change in society by socialism or other means.

As I say, there were no sudden changes and there is no exact point at which one can say with any confidence that the old 'pre-industrial' stage of protest had completed its course; yet we may for expediency place the period of transition in the case of England and the Scottish Lowlands somewhere in the 1840s or 1850s; that is, during the last phase of the transportation of convicts to Australia. One way of charting the course of this transition from the 'pre-industrial' to the 'industrial' stage is to note the phasing-out of certain types of protest and the phasing-in of others. As we have seen, a typical 'pre-industrial' form of activity was the food riot, which was still a frequent phenomenon during the lean war years of the 1790s but began to phase out soon after the wars ended and, in southern England, virtually came to a stop with the agricultural riots in East Anglia in 1816. After that, it continued only on Britain's 'Celtic fringe': in Cornwall until the early 1830s and, in the Scottish Highlands, until 1847 at least. Why this was so has a great deal to do with the pace of industrialization and improved facilities for marketing flour and grain. More particularly, in the case of southern England, we must note the fall in wheat-prices at the end of the wars and the remarkable levelling-out of prices between one decade and the next. To illustrate the last two points: the annual average price of a quarter of wheat between 1805 and 1820 was 85s. 3d., with a maximum of 106s. 6d. (in 1813) and a minimum of 63s. 8d. (in 1815); whereas the annual average price in the decade 1821-30 was 58s. 3d., with a maximum of 66s. 6d. (in 1825) and a minimum of 43s. 3d. in 1822.[6]

Similarly, as more and more workers adapted to the new methods of production, industrial machine-breaking virtually ended with the burning of Beck's steam factory at Coventry in 1831; and, in country districts, half a dozen years after 'Swing', with the last recorded committal for breaking a threshing machine in Leicestershire in 1837. The old-style urban riot, characterized by the widespread 'pulling-down' of houses, as witnessed most conspicuously in the Gordon Riots in London in the century before, was staged on a grand scale for the last time in the West of England at Bristol in 1831 and,

[6] William Hoyle, pp. 14, 25.

in the Potteries, in 1842; and, outside the Highlands, the old-style destruction of tolls and turnpikes ended with the final phase of the Rebecca riots in Wales the following year. Of 'marginal' forms of protest, poaching and cattle-maiming had their heyday (in England) in the 1830s and 1840s and were phasing out by the mid-1850s. After this, only arson remained as a survivor from the more conspicuous of the 'direct-action' methods of the past; but this, too, was beginning to phase out, even in England where it was always more prevalent than in Scotland or Wales; yet there were waves of rural incendiarism extending into the 1860s as is evident from the number of arsonists still being transported to Western Australia in 1866 and beyond.

Meanwhile, the newer-style 'industrial' protest which had begun to emerge many generations before was gradually taking over. As a substitute for riots and machine-breaking, peaceful marches, public rallies, and petitions were already a common feature of industrial disputes in London in the 1760s and, generally, became more frequent in political protest after the end of the wars. At that time, there was the perfectly peaceful march of the unemployed 'Blanketeers' and, four years later, the peaceful open-air meeting of radical weavers in St. Peter's Fields in Manchester, that led to the massacre of 'Peterloo'; and, later still (around 1828–30), Manchester and other cotton-spinning towns were the scene of a new style in workers' industrial activity that depended on organization and numbers and hardly at all on the spontaneous guerrilla type of reprisal of the past. But even now (as in Staffordshire Chartism in 1842), there was always the chance that organized and more structured protest of this kind might spill over into older-type 'direct-action' forms; and it needed a further growth in the development of factory towns and a further forward-leap in the creation of a national working class, ready to look to the future instead of the past, before the new style of protest, both in industrial and political action, could really come into its own.

In this sense, Chartism, which was both a social and a political movement of the working classes, may be seen as a watershed between the old and the new. On the one hand, the workers' claim to the vote was still seen as the restoration of a right that had been lost to the 'free-born Englishman', like so much else, with the imposition of the 'Norman Yoke'. There was the widespread refusal, most often expressed in the centres of handloom-weaving and other dying trades, to come to terms with industrial society that appeared to many to have little beneficial to offer. And we have noted the survival of 'direct-action' methods of protest in such dramatic episodes as the armed attack on Newport in 1839 and—on the fringe of the Lancashire Plug-Plot Riots—the old-style machine-breaking and 'pulling-down' of houses in the Staffordshire pottery towns. Yet, on the other hand, Chartism was the first independent political—and national—movement in working-class history; it saw the emergence in the National Charter Association of the first nucleus of a workers' party; and the campaign for a People's Charter was conducted—at the top level at least—by means of a series of massive petitions to Parliament. Meanwhile, the old 'riot-captains' and mythical-'composite' leaders had bowed out and given way to new forward-looking and more 'permanent' leaders: here we may perhaps mark the transition with the appearance of George Loveless, a Tolpuddle Martyr transported to Australia in 1834, who returned to England and became a Chartist three years later.

So, even in English cities and industrial districts, it was a long haul from the old 'pre-industrial' style of protest to the new. In English villages (in spite of the brief and untypical interlude of Tolpuddle) it took much longer: there is nothing remotely resembling these newer forms in the agricultural workers' movement of 1830, and trade unionism in the countryside, with all that this implies in terms of activity and organization, did not become firmly grounded until 1872. In the rural parts of Wales, it took longer still (we have noted the strange primitive episode of Rebecca in the 1840s[7]); and even longer in the Highlands of Scotland, the last bastion in Britain of a 'pre-industrial' society. Here, as we saw in an earlier chapter, the crofting parishes of Inverness-shire (including the Isle of Skye) remained as a solitary outpost of the 'direct-action' method of protest—though attended by remarkably little physical violence—until the 1880s. In Ireland—south of Ulster at least—resistance to change was even more prolonged; in fact, it will be more realistic to treat Irish protest as a case on its own rather than to see it—as with Scotland and Wales—as a variation on what was happening in England. There were, it is true, certain similarities between the 'direct-action' forms of protest in Ireland and those in 'pre-industrial' Britain. For example, arson, cattle-maiming, and assaults on peace

---

[7] But, to put the score straight, we also have to take note in England of that strange millenarian movement of Kentish farm-workers of 1838 that ended in a last-ditch battle with the military in Bossenden Wood. (See P. G. Rogers, *Battle in Bossenden Wood. The Strange Story of Sir William Courtenay* (London, 1961); and also Kent Archives Office, U951. C37/40, 53.)

and revenue officers were common to both, though even here there were significant differences. While, in Britain, rural incendiarism more than held its own, cattle-maiming, as we have seen, was never on the scale that it attained in Ireland, particularly in the West. Food-rioting, on the other hand, was more of an English than an Irish phenomenon; in fact, in Ireland it played little part until the minor-famine years of 1829–31 and the greater famine of the 1840s, by which time in England it was already a thing of the past.[8] Urban rioting on the grand scale was also little known in Ireland until the Belfast riots of the 1850s; and even these lacked the destructive fury of the Gordon Riots in London and later riots in Birmingham, Bristol, and the pottery towns. Machine-breaking, too, the most costly and destructive of all forms of popular violence experienced in England, played virtually no part at all in the record of Irish protest. In short, in Ireland, there was nothing remotely similar to the activities of Ned Ludd or Captain Swing, no more than she had any experience at all of movements like Chartism in England's industrial towns.

In most types of rural riot, however, the boot was on the other foot. In Britain, there was nothing that remotely resembled the Irish rural secret societies or the nightly visitations and 'outrages' of Defenders, Peep o' Day Boys, Rockites, Ribbonmen, Terry Alts, Caravats, or Molly Maguires. In fact, compared with Ireland, rural protest in England—even with the occasional violent outbreaks of machine-breaking and arson—was far more muted and restrained; and it is perhaps not surprising that that most typical of all English forms of 'marginal' rural protest, poaching, should have left not a ripple on the Irish country scene. For, in Ireland, it was armed assault or assembly that was most typical of the farmer's, cottier's, or labourer's mode of settling accounts with the rack-renting landlord, wage-cutting farmer, or rival claimant to a house or a piece of land; and such assaults might take the form of forcible possession, shoot-outs between opposing factions, the wholesale slaughter of cattle, or the murder of the landlord or his bailiff.[9] Such acts of 'outrage', so common in Ireland up to the end of the 1840s and again

[8] For a comparatively rare example from the earlier period, see the petition of John Hogan, carpenter, who was arrested on 15 Apr. 1822 and put in Maryborough jail for taking part in a riot. He claimed to have been on the road in pursuit of his lawful business on the day Mr. Dunn's corn was 'rescued'. The soldiers escorting the convoy, however, said Hogan had been one of a crowd of 400 which had attacked them and seized the corn. SPO Dublin, Prisoners' Petitions, no. 1707.

[9] For Irish agrarian disturbance, see Kevin B. Nowlan, 'Agrarian Unrest in Ireland 1800–1845', *University Review*, iv (1967).

in the Land War in 1879–82, had had no equivalent in England or Scotland since the days of peasant revolt under Richard II or the Tudor Kings. (Even the Scottish crofters, for all the tenacity with which they clung to their traditional modes of resistance to 'clearance', were rarely given to physical violence of any kind.)[10]

After 1850, as we have seen, there was in Ireland, as in England and Scotland, a steep decline in the volume of protest; and here, too, there was a tendency for such protest as there was to move away from the countryside and become centred on the towns. But this was only a temporary appeasement, as the 'blood-letting' of famine and emigration had done nothing to solve the long-term disabilities of the Irish tenants of the centre, South, and West. So rural protest revived in 1879 and, in the three-year Land War in Kerry, Galway, and Mayo, attained a volume and a degree of violence almost equalling those of the 1840s: in Kerry alone, 298 cases of rural crime were reported where there had been only five a couple of years before.[11] In short, in Ireland as a whole, there had come with the mid-century, as in Britain (outside the Scottish Highlands), a certain refocusing of protest in the direction of the towns; but, south of Ulster, the face of rural protest for the present remained virtually unchanged.

[10] See E. Richards, 'Patterns of Highland Discontent, 1790–1860', in *Popular Protest and Public Order*, pp. 104–9.

[11] Joseph Lee, *The Modernisation of Irish Society 1848–1918* (Dublin, 1973), p. 80.

PART TWO

PUNISHMENT

1. In Britain

AFTER protest came punishment and retribution. This took a number of forms and, in the case of protest, as it often involved larger numbers acting in unison, the variables were greater than with other crimes; for, at the initial stage, it might not be merely a matter of rounding up individual suspects but of pacifying whole districts by the army, militia, yeomanry, or police. In the eighteenth century, for lack of a professional police force, the pacifying role was played by troops, either of the militia or regular army; and the violence of the crowd was generally outmatched by the violence of authority. This might have gruesome results, as in the Gordon Riots (1780) when 285 rioters were shot dead or later died of wounds, or at Bristol where 110 people were killed or wounded in the tollgate riots of 1793.

In the nineteenth century troops continued to be used to repress disorders; in fact, it was argued that this was a major reason for keeping a large army on foot;[1] but blood-letting was never quite on the earlier scale. In the Luddite disturbances of 1811–12, the army mounted a large-scale military operation, and over 12,000 troops, a larger force than Wellington's in the initial stage of the Peninsular War, occupied the rebellious districts between Leicester and York;[2] but only eight rioters were killed. The number of victims was greater in the 'Peterloo' affair in Manchester in 1819, when the Lancashire yeomanry cavalry sabred eleven demonstrators to death and wounded a further 400 or more; and this, as is well known, caused a general outcry which far greater slaughters of civilians in the previous century (or, for that matter, in contemporary Ireland) had not. Up to now, it had been usual, at moments of widespread protest, to declare an emergency, suspend habeas corpus, and virtually wage war on the local population. This had been done in 1812; it was still done in the East Anglian riots of 1816; and, in Ireland, it continued to be done under the Insurrection and White Boy Acts; but it was no longer done in Britain after the consolidation of the penal code by Peel in 1827.[3] Thus the 'Swing' riots of 1830 were

---

[1] L. Radzinowicz, *A History of English Criminal Law*, iv, 123–4.

[2] F. O. Darvall, *Popular Disturbance and Public Order in Regency England*, pp. 259–60.

[3] Richard Hawkins, review of *Captain Swing*, *The Historical Journal* (1969), p. 717.

dealt with under the ordinary criminal law: the army was deployed in a number of military districts; but there was no military occupation of the disaffected districts and the army was reinforced by a far larger number of yeomanry cavalry, special and voluntary constables, and even semi-feudal levies of gentry, tenants, and labourers, as enrolled by the Dukes of Buckingham and Wellington on their estates in Hampshire; and, in Wiltshire, the most disturbed of all the counties, it was the yeomanry cavalry and not the army that claimed the only victim.[4]

Yet, after this comparatively peaceful interlude, there were some bloody encounters in the 1830s: troops killed a dozen rioters at Bristol (but contrast this with the 285 killed in London in 1780!) and at least sixteen striking and riotous ironworkers were killed and seventy wounded at Merthyr Tydfil in 1831; eleven Kentish labourers were shot dead in the Battle of Bossenden Wood in 1838; and maybe as many as twenty-four Monmouthshire ironworkers and miners were killed in the Newport rising in 1839. But this was really the last blood-bath of its kind. Even at the height of the 'Plug-Plot' riots in August 1842, which, as has already been said, were the most violent outbreak in Chartism, the number of victims of police or military was comparatively small. Troops were ordered to shoot that month at Preston, Burslem, Blackburn, and other northern towns, leading to three deaths at Burslem, four at Preston, while twenty more were wounded in these and other towns. But, by this time, the 'new' police, armed with staves but not with firearms, had been brought in to support the military as the main line of defence; and Sir Charles Napier, who commanded the Northern (military) District, was a humane and intelligent officer who appears to have had a genuine distaste for shedding civilian blood.[5]

The big change, by the 1840s, had been the institution of a professional police and the consequent removal of the military as the major pacifying force. The need for such a measure had been urged by property owners from the time of the Gordon Riots; but, for several decades, the arguments in favour of a more efficient system of law and order and crowd control had been drowned by the voices of liberals, city corporations, and others who, on the one hand, pointed to the dreadful example of 'tyranny' in France and, on the other, warned of the danger of further encroachments of the

---

[4] Hobsbawm and Rudé, *Captain Swing*, pp. 253–7.

[5] For the above, see D. Jones, *Before Rebecca*, p. 186; G. Rudé, *The Crowd in History*, pp. 255–8; and F. B. Smith, 'The Plug Plot Prisoners and the Chartists', *ANU Historical Journal*, no. 7 (Nov. 1970), p. 5.

Executive at the local authorities' expense.[6] It appears that the decisive factor that tipped the balance in favour of the 'proposers' was the alarm caused by the new wave of civil commotion starting about 1829; so the report of the Royal Commission on the Establishment of a Constabulary Force used arguments similar to those used earlier in favour of the retention of a standing army: that law and order imperatively required it.[7] It came about in four main stages, beginning with Peel's Metropolitan Police Act of 1829; followed by its extension to first boroughs and then counties in 1835 and 1839, and ending with the Police Act of 1856, which co-ordinated the activities of the various local constabularies under the Home Office in London. Soon after, the special constable had become redundant and the military ceased to be called in. So, by now, the means of repression at street level had become dramatically changed, as much, no doubt, in response to the continuous call for a more efficient method of policing the new and expanding cities as to the change in the nature of protest itself, which (as we saw in our last chapter) had by now abandoned its more violent 'direct-action' methods of confrontation.[8] Yet, as we have also noted, to the workers in the industrial cities a more 'efficient' police appeared to be an uncertain blessing and 'police-bashing' continued into the 1860s, though without quite the vigour of the 1830s and 1840s. But, whatever the motives that inspired the introduction of the police and whatever the misgivings of those most immediately concerned — the working classes of the cities and manufacturing towns — it had the great merit of eliminating the use of troops and, as in the most violent phase of Chartism, of pacifying civil disorder with a relatively minor effusion of blood.[9]

The next stage, after pacification by troops or police, was the judicial reckoning as applied by the courts. By the time of the Regency and before Peel's reforms of the 1820s, there were some 225 capital crimes on the Statute Book, including such social or protest-crimes as treason, arson, frame-breaking, sending threatening letters, rioting, 'pulling down' houses, shooting at a revenue officer or a gamekeeper, destroying turnpikes or silk in the loom, malicious maiming, killing cattle, certain types of smuggling, and

[6] Radzinowicz, iii, *passim.*

[7] D. Philips, 'Riots in the Black Country, 1835–1860', in *Popular Protest and Public Order*, pp. 141–2.

[8] See D. Philips, pp. 169–73; and (in the same volume) R. Quinault, 'The Warwickshire County Magistrates and Public Order, c. 1830–1870', pp. 210–11.

[9] F. C. Mather, *Public Order in the Age of the Chartists* (Manchester, 1959), pp. 90–187.

cutting down trees in an avenue (useful for Liberty Trees as well as for firewood). In fact, to protest was, almost by definition, to commit a felony and, in theory at least, all felonies were punishable by death. So it is hardly surprising that so many of these early outbreaks of popular protest ended in executions. Among them were thirty Luddites who were hanged in the various Luddite districts between 1811 and 1817; five of the East Anglian rioters were hanged in 1817; three of the Pentrich rebels of 1817; three of the Scottish Radicals and five of the Cato Street conspirators of 1820 whom we spoke of in an earlier chapter. After the Bristol riots of 1831 four were hanged (out of fifty that were originally sentenced to death) and nineteen of the rebellious 'Swing' labourers were put to death in the same year. After this, the hangman took a rest and, for those found guilty of protest-crimes, prison or transportation took over. Next to death, the most severe and dreaded punishment was to be sent as a convict to Australia, nominally for life or for a term of fourteen or ten or seven years; but the term made little difference to those wishing to come back, for, as we shall see in greater detail in a later chapter, remarkably few were able to return after serving their sentence. The numbers of those sentenced to be transported accounted for a considerable proportion of all convictions in the higher criminal courts: about one in three in England and Wales between 1811 and 1834, a little over one in four between 1835 and 1837 and falling to less than one in seven when transportation was beginning to phase out in 1847–8.[10] (In Scotland, the proportion was always much lower.) But, among these, the British protesters, as we have seen before, formed a relatively insignificant minority: even including all poachers and arsonists, only about 1·5 per cent of the whole.

But this is an over-all picture covering a period of more than sixty years. Yet punishment, like protest, changed its face so that, by the 1840s, it looked very different from what it had looked at the end of the Napoleonic Wars. We have seen how the police took over the role of the army as the major pacifying force in civil unrest. But, meanwhile, the criminal law, which basically determined what went on in the courts, had been progressively amended as well. From 1808 onwards, expediency and humanitarian motives had combined

---

[10] A. G. L. Shaw, *Convicts and the Colonies*, p. 150. The number actually transported was considerably lower than those sentenced: Shaw puts the proportion at about 30 per cent in 1811–17, 60 per cent in 1818–24, 65–75 per cent between 1825 and 1846, and 40 per cent in 1847–8—i.e., allowing for the greater numbers in the 1830s, an average of about two in three in all.

to scale down the number of capital crimes. Thus, by 1820, the death penalty was no longer invoked for picking pockets or for robbing dwelling-houses of amounts less than £15; in 1823, it ceased to be a capital offence to send threatening letters or to destroy silk or cloth in a loom or frame,[11] and the Black Act, which for long had imposed the death-sentence for almost every imaginable crime against property, was repealed;[12] and, in 1825, it ceased to be a capital offence to assault or obstruct a revenue officer, thus making smuggling a less hazardous trade. The process was carried further by Peel's revision of the penal code in 1827, which abolished the death penalty in cases in which it was rarely imposed, and by the transfer the same year of minor crimes against property (such as damaging trees or fences and various offences against the Game Laws) to the summary jurisdiction of the justices in petty sessions.[13] But Peel was prompted by a desire for efficiency rather than to make the law more humane, and new acts were passed defining the death penalty more precisely in the case of other property-crimes. So it was still possible in 1830 and 1831, as appeared in the riots of those years, for a man to be put to death for breaking machinery (other than threshing machines), for destroying barns or buildings, for burning a haystack, for extorting money with threats, for cattle-maiming, or simple riot.

Bigger changes came with the Whig governments of the 1830s. Capital punishment was abolished for sheep- and cattle-stealing (and maiming) in 1832 and for housebreaking in 1833; and more capital offences were abolished by Lord John Russell's reforms of 1834, with simple 'riot' following in 1841. So that, by 1849, only eight capital crimes remained, including murder, treason, piracy, burglary and robbery with violence, and arson of dwelling-houses with persons therein; and, by then, neither machine-breaking nor rick-burning, nor cattle-maiming, nor robbery with threats, nor non-lethal assaults (including those on peace and revenue officers)— some of the principal crimes for which protesters had been sentenced or put to death in the past—rated as capital offences. In fact, among the more obvious 'protest-crimes' previously carrying the death penalty (if we discount the doubtful category of 'riot and felony') only two remained: high treason and arson endangering human life; and it was for committing one or other of these that fifteen

---

[11] Radzinowicz, i, 580-2.

[12] See E. P. Thompson, *Whigs and Hunters: The Origin of the Black Act* (London, 1975).

[13] J. Tobias, *Crime and Industrial Society in the 19th Century*, pp. 227-8.

persons (all but one of them arsonists) were sentenced to death
between 1842 and 1848.[14]

The scaling-down of capital crimes naturally had the effect of
increasing the number of sentences to prison and transportation.
Peel's reforms of 1827 alone have been held responsible for doubling
the number of convicts shipped overseas from an annual average of
2,149 between 1824 and 1826 to one of 4,160 between 1828 and 1830;
and, in the 1830s, there was a sharp upward swing in the number of
transported sheep-stealers and burglars.[15] Numbers were further
inflated by the numerous death sentences that, in cases of reprieve,
were commuted to transportation for life. But, to offset this tendency, there were counteracting factors whose influence began to
be felt after 1835: among them the growing hostility of Australians
to the jailer's role for which they had been cast; and the removal of
several minor crimes (including 'protest'-crimes) from the list of
transportable offences. (Poaching, for example, having already,
by a law of 1816, been struck from the list, except in the case of
night-time operations, by a further law of 1828 ceased to be a transportable offence except for third offenders and where violence was
used against gamekeepers.)[16]

But this is not the whole story. The law was one thing, its application was something else. This might be lenient or severe according
to the state of the law or the occasion, or as the pressure of government or public opinion demanded. Early in the century the severity
of the law was such that, in cases of capital crimes, juries tended to
give the criminals the benefit of the doubt and were reluctant to find
them guilty. (This, as we shall see, was less likely to apply in times
of civil commotion.) Moreover, even if he were convicted, there was
a twelve to one chance (this was, in fact, the average for the seventeen
years 1811 to 1827)[17] that the sentence would not be carried out:
in the case of 'protest'-crimes the odds in favour of execution appear
to have been rather higher.[18] There were, in addition, several other
hurdles to be jumped between the commission of the crime, its
detection and expiation, all of which in the common run of such
cases lengthened the odds considerably in favour of the guilty.
Fowell Buxton, the penal reformer, in a speech to the House of

[14] PP 1849, xliv, 58.
[15] L. Evans and P. J. Pledger, *Contemporary Sources in Modern British History*
(2 vols., Melbourne, 1966–7), ii, 90.
[16] Shaw, p. 157.
[17] Evans and Pledger, ii, 90.
[18] Between 1820 and 1827, 9 arsonists were executed out of 48 condemned to death;
also 5 out of 33 condemned for high treason. PP 1847, xlvii, 290.

Commons in 1819, actually put them as high as a thousand to one.[19] However far-fetched the calculation, it was evident that the law was both savage and unworkable and had fallen into disrepute; and it was this consideration more than any other that prompted Peel to rationalize the penal code in 1827—and no doubt, to improve the policing of cities as well. The results are hard to assess as Peel's new laws were rapidly eclipsed by others; but it appears that, in the years immediately following, severity and leniency were nicely balanced or applied in varying and vacillating doses. On the one hand, the chances in favour of the average convicted felon increased further, as only one in twenty death sentences were carried out between 1828 and 1834 and fewer still in 1836.[20] On the other hand, judges continued (for this was nothing new) to interpret the law with far greater severity when occasion appeared to demand it.

Such occasions, of course, included times of national emergency and others when property appeared to be in danger. At such times, protesters were liable to get a rougher deal from the courts than they would do at others. In the various Luddite trials, for example, the number of executions that followed a sentence of death was remarkably high: the Special Commission at York sentenced twenty-four out of sixty-four prisoners to death and of these seventeen were hanged; the other seven were sent as convicts to Australia.[21] The Scottish Courts of Judiciary at this time had an even more unenviable reputation than the Commissions of Gaol Delivery in England: it was twenty years earlier that, before sentencing Thomas Muir, a Scottish Jacobin, to transportation, Lord Braxfield, the Lord Justice Clerk, is reported to have whispered to one of the jurors, 'Come awa' and help us to hang one o' thae damned scoondrels'.[22] Though the proceedings were more decorous, justice appears to have been equally harsh in the case of the thirty Scottish Radicals tried for treason at Glasgow, Dumbarton, and Stirling in July and August 1820. Three were executed out of twenty-five who were sentenced to death; seven of these were transported for life and twelve for a term of fourteen years. After being sentenced to be hanged, drawn, and disembowelled, James Wilson, a veteran stocking weaver and recognized leader of the group, denounced what he called 'this

[19] Evans and Pledger, ii, 97–8. It is doubtful, however, if this had much relevance to the case of protesters.

[20] Tobias, pp. 199–220. Yet it is notable that within the same period (1828–33) 54 out of 87 sentences to death for arson were carried out. PP 1847, xlvii, 290.

[21] *Proceedings of the York Special Commission, Jan. 1813* (London, n.d. [1814?]).

[22] P. A. Brown, *The French Revolution in English History* (London, 1918), pp. 95–6.

mummery of a trial'.[23] The 'Swing' trials followed in England eleven years later; but the Special Commissioners who conducted them (especially those in Winchester and Salisbury) were no less severe: of 1,976 persons brought before ninety courts, nineteen were hanged and nearly 500 sent with varying terms as convicts to Australia.[24]

It was not the last occasion when judges stretched their powers to the limit to impose harsh sentences on political and social protesters. In 1834, the six men of Dorset—the Tolpuddle Martyrs—were condemned to seven years' transportation, nominally for 'administering unlawful oaths' but, actually, for having organized a union—in itself no longer a crime since the repeal of the Combination Acts in 1824. But, by now, the pendulum was swinging back to leniency both in the making and the application of the law. In fact, by the 1840s, though murder, as we saw, was not the only remaining capital crime, it was the only one for which a man was likely to be hanged; and of the nineteen death sentences imposed for high treason and arson between 1842 and 1849 not one was carried out.[25] (Compare this with the forty-seven arsonists hanged out of eighty-seven sentenced between 1830 and 1834).[26]

The new leniency was also reflected in the trials of Chartists in 1839–40, 1842, and 1848. In the first group of trials, sixty Monmouth Chartists were charged with conspiracy and riot following the armed attack on Newport. Eight were condemned to death but had their sentences commuted to prison or transportation; the rest were either discharged or imprisoned; no one was hanged. At Lancaster, of fifty-four persons tried for conspiracy and sedition and seditious conspiracy in the same year, twenty-five were sent to prison for a few months or weeks, none were sentenced to death or transported.[27] At Stafford, where 245 persons were brought to trial after the 'Plug-Plot' riots of 1842, there were also no death sentences or hangings but the judgements were more severe: 146 were sent to prison with hard labour and fifty-four to be transported for terms varying from seven years to life.[28] (Yet it was a great step forward from the executions—not to mention the shootings—that followed the riots in London in 1780 and in Bristol in 1831.) That this greater leniency in the administration of justice was part of official policy is evident from a report of the Criminal Register in 1847, which speaks, in the unpalatable jargon of officialdom, not only of the 'diminished

[23] Ellis and Mac A'Ghobbainn, *The Scottish Insurrection of 1820*, p. 255.
[24] Hobsbawm and Rudé, pp. 101, 258–63.
[25] Radzinowicz, iv, 320.   [26] PP 1847, xlvii, 290.
[27] HO 27/61.   [28] *Ann. Reg.* lxxxiv (1842), 157–9.

severity of the law' but of the decrease, over a wide range of common crimes, in the numbers transported even in cases 'in which the Legislature has made no alteration in the punishments which attach to them'.[29]

So the chances of a political or social protester (whatever his offence) being sentenced to death by the middle of the century—let alone of the sentence being carried out—had become remarkably slim. Once arson, riot, and attacks on property had ceased to be capital offences, the worst he would have to face—and this was terrifying enough—was a term of transportation. It is not surprising, therefore, that the most serious crimes for which protesters were transported in the 1840s—the Chartists or Rebecca's Daughters, for example—were for former capital offences like arson, demolishing turnpikes, pulling down houses, sedition, 'cutting and maiming', 'mobbing and rioting', assaults on the police, and 'attempted murder'. After this, the 'marginals' took over. The last few ships bringing convicts to Tasmania carried several hundred arsonists; and when Tasmania closed its doors in 1852 as Sydney had done a dozen years before, penal servitude at home began to replace transportation as the usual method of punishment for the more serious crimes. But transportation continued in Western Australia, where the settlers, finding themselves short of labour, petitioned to have further shiploads of convicts sent out. So, between 1854 and 1868, another 7,065 convicts (all men and few Irish or Scots) arrived on the Swan River in twenty-six ships. The protesters (whether actual or 'marginal') among them were nearly all arsonists (338), with a handful of poachers (10), cattle-maimers (5), and sixty-two Irish Fenians (who belong to the next chapter). After this, such protesters as remained to be sentenced, like the Highland crofters of the 1870s and 1880s, were confined to the jails at home; and, as we noted before, indictments for such offences were, by the 1860s, in fairly steady decline.

So if we once more look back from the mid 1860s, we shall note the radical changes in repression that had taken place in Britain as we noted them in the case of protest before. The most noteworthy perhaps were the emergence of a professional police; the removal of many hitherto indictable offences from the assizes and quarter sessions to the summary jurisdiction of the magistrates' courts; the drastic scaling-down of capital crimes and executions; the ending of transportation to Australia; and the greater flexibility of the courts in interpreting the law. Here, too, the changes were gradual;

[29] PP 1847, xviii, 10.

but, once more, the great leap forward came around the mid-thirties and 1840s.

Why did these changes come about? A short answer might be that as protest changed, so punishment, responding to that change, underwent a similar transformation. There is some truth in this as, though the numbers of protesters might be relatively small, their impact might be great and at moments of high social tension (as in 1812, 1830, and 1842) protest appeared to eclipse all other crimes and probably appeared as a greater threat to the State and to men of property than all other crimes combined; and, conversely, as protest became more muted and lost its thrust, the army, the hangman, and the penal colony could, without much danger, be phased out in turn. But, obviously, this is an over-simplistic explanation that begs half the questions. Punishment, while adapted to meet such changes, was responsive to a wide range of other pressures as well—to the growth of urban and industrial society; to the demands of an increasingly omnicompetent State; to the work of humanitarians and penal reformers; to changes in public opinion; and to the demands for freer institutions in the old penal settlements in Australia. And all this was further complicated by the resistance to change from other quarters—like the resistance put up to the 'new' police by the old corporate municipal interests (the City of London, for example) and (for quite different reasons) by Radicals and the working-class population of the towns.

2. Ireland

As with protest, the pattern of repression in Ireland followed a different course from the one we noted in Britain. Where in Britain the pacifying role of the army was already phasing out and the periodical states of emergency, which entailed a suspension of normal civil rights, ended in the 1820s, in Ireland such means of repression merely changed their forms. Though the army lost its role as the main support of the civil power, the new police or constabulary that replaced it was a para-military force, amply provided with weapons, and whole districts of Ireland remained for periods under something equivalent to martial law.

Ireland's English rulers, even the most level-headed among them, were inclined to believe that the Irish common people were beyond redemption and that she was not only chronically lawless but ungovernable as well. Peel, who had reason to believe that he knew her well, spoke at one time of her 'national predilection for outrage and a lawless life which I believe nothing can control'; and, at another, of the 'wretched depravity and sanguinary disposition of the lower orders'.[1] Such views were shared by the 'country gentlemen' who formed the Irish magistracy and had an unenviable reputation for venality and a supreme contempt for the less privileged of their fellow subjects. It was not surprising, therefore, that the Rebellion of 1798 should have shown them, and the administration of justice in general, at their worst. In 1796, long before the Rebellion broke out, it was reported to the Irish House of Commons that 'certain magistrates had privately conferred together, and without any information on oath or good evidence of any kind, at their own pleasure and without any Form of Law, did lay their hands on several of their fellow subjects and transport them'.[2] To procure their victims, ample use was made of informers, who were even in more plentiful supply in Ireland than in England at this time. They were often recruited among the suspects themselves; and a letter of the same year, addressed to Under-Secretary Cooke at the Castle, tells of the convicts of Kildare—evidently Defenders—'now waiting at the Cove of Cork for transportation to Botany Bay', who had

[1] Quoted by G. Broeker, *Rural Disorder and Police Reform in Ireland 1812-36*, pp. 2–3, 96.　　　　[2] Quoted by Shaw, *Convicts and the Colonies*, p. 169.

offered 'to make discoveries of various Descriptions, particularly
of the Depots of Arms belonging to the Defenders'—in return, it
was supposed, for a free pardon or for being allowed to join the
Navy.[3] It was through such services, no doubt, that several hundred
United Irishmen—or those reputed to be such—were rounded up
and brought to trial at assizes in the thirty-two counties in 1797–9.
Of these, 357 were ordered for execution and 237 respited over the
three years; 508 were sentenced to transportation (though, as we
shall see, many of them were later offered other options); and, in
January 1798, 1,186 Crown prisoners were held in custody (many
in Dublin); and of these all but twenty were still held in custody,
uncertain of their fate, a couple of years later.[4]

These were the comparatively fortunate ones; for once the
Rebellion started—in the summer of 1798—panicky or vindictive
magistrates and the army took over and little regard was shown for
the niceties of the law. Even earlier, the first of the Insurrection Acts
—that of 1796, soon to be followed by a second in 1799—authorized
the Lord-Lieutenant to proclaim disturbed counties, impose a
curfew, ban meetings, execute persons administering unlawful oaths,
and transport for life those taking them; it also made persons who
were out at night or suspected of other crimes liable to a summary
sentence of transportation for life. But even before a district, reputed
to be disturbed, came under the Act, the army might be in occupation
and military justice, by means of the court martial, anticipate that
of the magistrate's summary court. The rather scanty records of the
courts martial have survived (or a certain part of them); in them
I have counted 432 sentences to exile or transportation, but these
are obviously incomplete and lop-sided (Ulster is over-represented
and known rebellious counties in the South, such as Wicklow,
Mayo, and Kildare, hardly figure at all);[5] and there is only the barest
indication of the numbers of those summarily executed and shot out
of hand. In fact, the judgement of Governor King of New South
Wales regarding the difficulties of accounting for the number of
rebels—many of whom were due to be committed to his care—is

[3] SPO Dublin, 620/26/114.

[4] Summaries in *Journal of the House of Commons* (Ireland), xvii, Pt. 2 (1798),
682–3; xviii (1799), 348–9; xix, Pt. 2 (1800), 848–9. For denunciations of United Irishmen in Belfast, see 191 names in the 'Black Book of the North of Ireland during the
Rebellion', PRO Northern Ireland, D 272/1.

[5] SPO Dublin, Rebellion Papers 620/73–97. Even this imperfect record gives a
larger number than the 418 said by Lord Castlereagh to have been 'banished or
transported by sentence of Court Martial' between June 1798 and Sept. 1798. Shaw,
p. 170; Pakenham, *The Year of Liberty*, p. 392.

accurate enough as far as it goes. They had been convicted (he wrote) 'mostly by Courts-Martial prior to the time when the proceedings of such Courts were sanctioned by Law', or summarily 'before magistrates who exercised their powers under the Insurrection Acts, and whose proceedings were, in the disturbed state of the country, not recorded'.[6] There were others, later appearing in Sydney after being herded on to convict-ships at Cobh, who either had had no trial at all, either by court martial or other summary means, or had already been tried and pardoned or released on bail and been sent to Australia by mistake. In fact, such was the haphazard way of accounting and compiling, there was a considerable element of chance involved in whether a man believed to be a rebel or a United Irishman was brought to trial or not and, if he was, whether his eventual fate was to go scot-free, to be put in a prison-ship in Dublin Bay, left to rot in a country jail, pressed into military service, or shipped to Sydney Cove. Such hazards are reflected in the often anguished appeals in the prisoners' petitions in Dublin Castle, which include more than one case of a man transported in mistake for another or whose pardon arrived at the dockside at Cobh after his ship had already sailed.[7]

In the event, it is quite impossible to arrive at any reasonably accurate conclusion as to how many men were executed or shot out of hand; and it is still a highly debatable question as to how many, having been sentenced to transportation, actually arrived in Australia. About 1,000 appear to have been so sentenced by courts martial and courts of assize; but, as we have seen, the courts-martial records are defective and, besides, many others must have been added (perfectly legally in this case) from those whose death sentence had been commuted. But against this figure of possibly 1,200 to 1,500 we have to set the 318 men sent to Emden on board three ships to serve in the King of Prussia's army;[8] the smaller number who were allowed to go into self-exile in America; and many others who were given the option of serving His Britannic Majesty either on land or at sea. So the final figure is debatable, though it is not likely to fall below 325 or to rise above 500: these were the men that more particularly concern us: those who arrived in Sydney on half a dozen ships between 1800 and 1806.[9]

[6] Quoted by Shaw, p. 169.
[7] See SPO Dublin, Prisoners' Petitions, nos. 427-9 and 1140 (cases of Robert and Rowland Goodman and William Orr); and Shaw, p. 169 (case of John Temple).
[8] Pakenham, p. 399.
[9] For my own estimate of 325 and the higher estimates of T. J. Kiernan and A. G. L.

So the justice meted out to the rebels—or reputed rebels—of 1798 and 1803 was savage, arbitrary, and vindictive; but it was tempered with a confusion that at times was so grotesque as to turn the tragedy of the event into a comedy of errors. When Peel came to Dublin as chief secretary in 1812, he was determined to put an end to all that. In his view, even allowing for the breakdown of justice during the years of rebellion, the traditional Irish system of maintaining order by an uncertain combination of magistrates, constables, and military without defined responsibilities had proved a dismal failure. Moreover, he had as hearty a contempt for the Irish magistracy as he had for the yeomanry, both of which he considered to be partisan and corrupt; and he determined to clip their wings. Nor could the army be fully relied on as a supporting force, as its effectives were being continually drained by claims on its services from other quarters (from 50,000 in 1800–5 it fell to 35,000 in 1813 and to 18,000 in 1818). But, with Peel's extraordinarily poor opinion of the Irish and his belief in their propensity for rebellion, he was firmly convinced that a strong hand was required, and one that could be continually brought into play, so that the Government should never be caught unprepared.[10] So he decided to make Ireland a testing-ground for ideas that were already germinating in his mind for the better policing of Britain. Ireland thus became a guinea-pig for England (she had already had imposed on her the first Government-controlled police force with the Dublin Police Act of 1796[11]); and, on Peel's initiative, a number of measures were introduced that, to some extent, anticipated the later Police Acts adopted in England. Yet, in spite of certain similarities, the differences were more significant. In both cases, the Government's authority was strengthened at the expense of the local magistrates or urban corporations; and, therefore, in both the most stubborn resistance to the change came from these and their supporters in Parliament. But there the similarities ended; for the British police were a civilian force armed with staves and used to detect every manner of crime, whereas the Irish constabulary evolved as a semi-military body, armed and intended from the start to subdue a rebellious population with far greater efficiency than the old combination of magistrates, yeomanry, and militia had been able to do before.

Shaw, see G. Rudé, 'Early Irish Rebels in Australia', *Hist. Stud.*, xvi, no. 62 (Apr. 1974), 17–23.

[10] For this and much that follows, see Broeker, *Rural Disorder and Police Reform in Ireland, passim.*

[11] Radzinowicz, *A History of English Criminal Law*, iii, 131–3.

Peel's first measure was to introduce a Peace Preservation Force and a number of stipendiary magistrates; and to provide such intelligence as he could command, he continued to rely on the old army of paid informers. These original 'peelers' were a body of armed policemen, trained to quell subversion and operating as mobile units, under the Government's direction, in the counties to which they were sent out. They were used as occasion required: in response to the appeal of the magistrates of a district that had been proclaimed as 'disturbed'. (The rub was that, in the earlier stages of the scheme, any district that appealed for the Force's aid had to pay the full cost of its operation.) The 'proclamation' was a relic of the Rebellion with its Insurrection Acts of 1796 and 1799. A third Act had followed in 1807 and a fourth soon after Peel took office in 1814; the fifth and final Act was in 1822. This retention of a part of the old machinery of pacification was not entirely to Peel's liking; but it was a concession he was bound to make to the magistrates whom such procedures, by leaving the initiative if not the direction in their hands, assured of a certain measure of control.[12] The Peace Preservation Force proved on the whole successful in serving the purposes for which it was set up; but it was always a bone of contention with the magistrates who saw it, with good reason, as an attempt to undermine their authority. But long before the Force was disbanded (in 1836), it was supplemented by the County Constabulary, created by the Constable Act of 1822, which won the magistrates' approval as they were given a share in administration and full control over the constables' operations. It was a compromise and one that the Government (Peel was by now at the Home Office), having been forced to accept it, were eager to undermine by engaging in a drawn-out duel with the magistrates over the control of appointments. The two forces—the Constabulary and the Peace Preservation Force—continued in uneasy alliance until Grey's Whig Government in 1836 carried Peel's reforms a stage further by disbanding the Peace Preservation Force and County Constabulary and merging their functions by the Constabulary Act of 1836. This created the Irish Constabulary, a far more effective and more highly centralized body, headed by a single official, the inspector-general, who was vested by the chief secretary with full authority over his men and empowered to direct their operations when they were used to reinforce the local police in districts which had been 'proclaimed', not on the initiative of the magistrates but on that of the Lord-Lieutenant himself. (The last of the Insurrection Acts had expired—

[12] Broeker, pp. 55-104.

and was not renewed—in 1825.) Another feature, that also accorded with Peel's long-term intentions, was that members of the new Constabulary were required to take an oath barring them from membership of any political or 'secret' organization. (Meanwhile, the Orange Order, a major bone of contention with the Roman Catholic majority, had been suppressed in 1825.)[13]

It was this succession of police systems initiated or created by Peel —and, more particularly, the first two of them—that was called upon to deal with the various stages of the 'land-and-tithe' war with its peaks in 1815-16, 1822-3, and 1831-4. How successful were they and how many rebels or *banditti* (a word commonly used to define the rural protesters) did they help to bring to justice? It is quite impossible, from the available evidence, to tell anything like the full story; but as the second stage—that of 1822-3—appears to be better documented than the others let us consider it for a while. The curtain-raiser to the proclamation of the Insurrection Act of 1822 was the so-called 'war' in Munster which, led by Whiteboys, began in 1821 and extended its activities over Cork, Kerry, Limerick, and Tipperary. In February 1822, 300 persons were awaiting trial before special assizes and quarter sessions in these counties but most of them in Limerick and Cork. Thirty-six death sentences followed, of which twenty-two were respited after the Lieutenant-Governor had intervened leaving the remaining fourteen (after what appears to have been a somewhat arbitrary method of selection) for execution.[14] The records are not precise on the point, but it seems that about eighty of those convicted of 'insurrectionary' activities (some with life-sentences, others with seven-year terms) were among the 190 who sailed on the *Mangles* in late June of that year.[15]

Meanwhile, the Insurrection Act had been applied to these counties in the spring of 1822 and to the Cities of Limerick and Cork and Counties Westmeath, Clare, Kildare, King's County, and Kilkenny in addition. Under the terms of the Act (which were not identical with those of the Acts of 1796 and 1799), a total curfew was imposed from sunset to sunrise and persons found away from home at night or in possession of arms and ammunition were liable to be transported for seven years. Persons arrested on these non-capital charges were to be brought for summary trial before courts of general sessions, presided over by a barrister assisted by as many magistrates as could be persuaded to attend. More serious offences

[13] Ibid., pp. 219-39.
[14] Quoted by Broeker, pp. 135-6.
[15] Arch. NSW, MSS. 4/4008 (convict indents).

of a capital nature were to be tried by courts of criminal assize; but, in all cases, whether capital or not, trial by jury was suspended. We have a record of the number of prisoners, convictions and acquittals, and sentences to transportation in these 'disturbed' counties between mid 1822 and early 1824. The charges brought against them (all non-capital charges) in addition to absence from home and the possession of arms, were tendering or taking oaths, unlawful assembly, and posting or delivering a threatening notice. The record, based on returns to the Castle published in Parliamentary Papers for 1823 and 1824, is as follows:

Committals and Convictions under the Insurrection Act, 1822-4

Counties and Cities	Committals	Convictions	Transporta-tions	% Convictions
Clare	441	15	15	3·4
Co. Cork	282 (1822–3 only)	118	80	41·8 (1822–3 only)
Cork City	47	2	2	4·3
Kerry	151	33	33	21·9
Kildare	85	21	6	24·7
Kilkenny	40	1	1	2·5
King's Co.	60	15	15	25·0
Co. Limerick	785	173	173	22·0
Limerick City	28	8	6	28·6
Tipperary	1,815	121	121	6·7
Totals	3,940 (approx.)	507	452	12·9[16]

There are two striking features about these figures: one is the comparatively large number of persons sentenced to transportation (452 in all), compared with the number that eventually arrived in Australia. In March 1824 the Castle published a list of seventy-five names: they were of those who had been tried in half a dozen of these counties between 1 January 1823 and 1 February 1824 and had, by that time, already sailed for Sydney.[17] Unfortunately, this first instalment was never followed by another; but we may reckon, on

[16] PP 1823, xvi, 687–95; xxii, 212–15, 230–9. There is no figure given for committals in Co. Cork for 1823–4. I have therefore added 206 as an 'allowance' for Co. Cork in the combined total in the left-hand column and taken account of this in the '% Convictions' column at the end.

[17] PP 1824, xxii, 190.

the strength of this list and the shipping lists in Australia, that about 330 convicts, sentenced under the Insurrection Act in these counties, arrived in Sydney in a dozen ships between November 1822 and September 1825.[18] So, presumably, the remaining 120 were later pardoned, given short jail sentences, or left on the hulks.

The second feature is the small proportion of convictions: a little under 13 per cent of all committals. How does this compare with other occasions? One authority has argued that before the police reforms of the 1820s, at least, the rate of convictions to committals in Ireland was one-half the rate in England: roughly 30–40 per cent in the first case compared with 60–70 per cent in the second; and he ascribes the difference to poorer intelligence in Ireland and the obstruction of justice by gang-warfare or terrorism.[19] This, in the case of Ireland, appears a high figure compared with those we have just noted in the ten most rebellious counties of 1822–3. But if we look at the published returns of the period 1825 to 1834, which are about the only ones from which it is possible to make a direct comparison between Ireland and England and Wales, we find that it is true enough that the proportion of convictions is far higher in England and Wales than in Ireland; but also that the Irish proportion is both higher than that suggested by Dr. Palmer and considerably higher than it was in the eighteen months of the Insurrection Act in Munster. The figures for 1825–31 and 1828–34 (for this is how they appear in the records) are as follows:

Convictions as a Percentage of Committals (yearly averages) 1825–31 and 1828–34[20]

	(a) 1825–31	(b) 1828–34
England and Wales	79·5	80·8
Ireland	61·8	57·6

A further complication is that whereas the English proportion remains reasonably constant for other years (79·12 per cent for 1811–27), the Irish fluctuate wildly: 54 per cent in 1826, 66·5 per cent in 1833–4, 75·8 per cent (well up to the English standard) in

[18] Arch. NSW, MSS. 4/4008–10 (indents). This is rather more than half the total number of persons transported under the Insurrection Acts between 1814 and 1825 (see Introduction).

[19] Stanley Palmer, 'Police in England and Ireland, 1780–1840: a Study in Contrasts', paper read to American Historical Assoc., New York (28 Dec. 1971), pp. 6–7.

[20] Based on PP 1831–2, xxxiii, 135; 1835, xlv, 24–5 (England and Wales); 1835, xlv, 343; 1839, xlvii, 288 (Ireland).

1836, and down to a mean of a little over 43 per cent in the early and middle 1840s. So, as far as Ireland is concerned, the pattern is distinctly erratic.[21] As for the ratio of reprieves to executions, which we discussed at some length in relation to Britain, there appear to be no figures for Ireland to make any comparison possible.

And, finally, how did Peel's reforms and those of his successors affect the protest movements from the mid-1820s to the 1860s? During the years 1823 to 1829, the time of Daniel O'Connell's movement for Catholic Emancipation, the troubles in Munster were over and rural protest became muted for the time being and lost its violence, and the Insurrection Act was not invoked after 1824. And this, it appears, was due far more to the pacifying role of the Catholic Association than to the activities of the forces of law and order.[22] After a revival of rural unrest in the 'tithe-war' of the early 1830s, the new Irish Constabulary, the creation of the Whigs, had little time to prove its worth in the new lull that followed in 1837. But they came into their own in the 1840s in dealing with the rural violence in the western counties that followed the Famine. The new Irish Constabulary were also involved, and won greater renown, in the crushing of the Young Ireland rising of 1848: the Lord Chief Justice of Ireland even went so far as to declare that they had 'saved the country'. (It might perhaps be added that the leaders of the rising had made the job comparatively easy for them.) Twenty years later, they were also praised for their part in meeting the far more serious challenge of the Fenian Rising of 1867, for which they were rewarded with the thanks of Parliament and permitted to bear the title of 'Royal Irish Constabulary'. They survived into the next century to provide a training-base for Britain's colonial police.[23]

Meanwhile, the courts were not inactive either. They continued into the early 1850s to sentence country labourers found guilty of robbery of arms, of assembling riotously, or of assaulting habitations (the most common change of all) to varying terms of transportation as they had done in the 1820s and 1830s when the 'land-and-tithe' war was at its height. The last convict ship to sail into Hobart

---

[21] It would be nice to be able to explain the high proportion of convictions to committals in Ireland in some years (e.g. 1833-4, 1836-7) in terms of periods of rising tension. But it does not work out that way: *vide* (in addition to the low figures for 1822-4 that we have noted) the low percentage of convictions to committals in the assizes of 1797-9 (the most turbulent period of all): 1797, 24%; 1798, 31%; 1799, 33%. Part of the explanation for these fluctuations, no doubt, must be sought in the unreliability of many of the returns (as we noted already in relation to the Rebellion).

[22] Broeker, pp. 160-88.

[23] Ibid., pp. 241-2.

(the *Rodney* in February 1853) brought to Tasmania half a dozen Irishmen sentenced for assaulting a dwelling under arms;[24] while the last ship of all to sail from an Irish port—the *Phoebe Dan*—brought eight cattle-maimers and one solitary arsonist to Fremantle, in Western Australia, in August 1853.[25]

The two uprisings of 1848 and 1867 were, like the Rebellion of 1798, rather special cases as high treason and sedition were involved. Of the Young Irelanders, the principal leaders—Smith O'Brien, Terence McManus, Patrick O'Donoghoe, and Thomas Meagher—were brought to trial and charged with high treason at Clonmel, in Tipperary, in October 1848. John Mitchel, who had played no direct part in the rebellion, was charged with felony and sedition at Dublin City where John Martin, the only Ulsterman among them, was also charged with high treason for writing seditious articles in the *Irish Felon*; and Kevin O'Dogherty, a medical student, was indicted on the same charge for articles he had written for the *Tribune*. All these men, except O'Dogherty and Mitchel, were condemned (according to custom) to be hanged, drawn, and quartered, though this gruesome sentence was later commuted (after Parliament had passed a special Bill) to transportation for life. O'Dogherty was given a ten-year and Mitchel a fourteen-year sentence. Another leader of the movement, Charles Gavin Duffy, was in prison in Dublin during the rising, but was later tried, like most of the others, under the Treason Felony Act and was five times acquitted before the case against him was dropped. Finally, half a dozen others were tried at Waterford at various times in 1849 and 1850 for taking part in an attack on the police barracks at Cappoquin under Smith O'Brien and James Finlan Lalor. Lalor escaped and two others were acquitted; but four of them—Cornelius Keeffe, Edmund Sheafy, Thomas Wall, and John Walsh—were sent to Australia on three ships, of which the last, the *Lord Dalhousie*, did not arrive in Hobart until August 1852.[26]

The Fenian Rising, as we have seen, was, after several adjournments, planned for March 1867. It was based on Dublin but with supporting movements from such widely scattered centres as Cork, Tipperary, Louth, Limerick, Waterford, and Clare. But, as on the eve of the Rebellion of 1798, the rounding-up of Brotherhood members by the Constabulary began before the Rising broke out. Some of these were soldiers who were tried for desertion and mutiny

---

[24] Tas. Arch., CON 33/113.
[25] Arch. WA, R.18.
[26] Tas. Arch., CON 33/100, 104, 109.

in Dublin and Cork in 1865 and 1866. But most of those arrested were tried and sentenced for Treason Felony by a dozen courts beginning in February 1867: mainly at Dublin, Cork, and Limerick but also at Clonmel, Dundalk, Menagh, and Tralee. Twelve were sentenced to death and had their sentences commuted to transportation for life; others were given various terms in Western Australia ranging between five and twenty years. Sixty-two of them sailed from London in October 1867 and arrived, on the *Hougomont*, in Fremantle, Western Australia, on 9 January 1868. It was the last shipload of convicts, whether protesters or others, to arrive in an Australian port.[27]

[27] Arch. WA, R.16, V.10.

3. Canada

WE have seen that the two Canadian rebellions were crushed by superior military force. In the Lower Canadian rebellion of 1837, the Patriots of St. Eustache and St. Benoit, and their companions at St. Denis and St. Charles, were forced to surrender by a regular army: the 32nd, 83rd, and Royal regiments commanded by Colonels Gore and Wetherall under the supreme command of Sir John Colborne. It was more, however, than a purely military operation; as the troops went on the rampage and two of the rebellious villages were burned to the ground, earning Colborne the invidious title among the *habitants* of 'le vieux Brûlot' ('old Firebrand') and involving the Government, once the crisis had passed, in considerable claims for damages: over £102,000 in all, of which £45,417 had been paid by September 1850.[1] On the second outbreak a year later, Colborne (now Governor-General of Canada) proclaimed martial law, put 7,000 troops in the field, and crushed the rebels in the Eastern Townships without much trouble. It was all over in a matter of days and there was no repetition of the excesses committed against the defeated Patriots the year before.

In the case of the Upper Canadian rebellion, both the regular army and the militia were engaged: the militia only in the first confrontation as Colborne had already dispatched regular units to Quebec and Montreal. In the second, the successive invasions from the United States, culminating in the battles of Prescott and Windsor, were met by a combination of regulars and militia; it was the militia, supported by regulars of the Coburg Rifles, that defeated the Americans at Windsor and, by order of the notorious Colonel Price (later put on trial), followed up their victory by shooting some of their prisoners in cold blood.[2]

Subsequent to the military operations in both provinces, large numbers of rebels and suspects—about 2,200 in all—were rounded up by the regulars or militia and lodged in jails in Montreal, Quebec, Sherbrooke, and Three Rivers in the one case and Toronto, Windsor, and London in the other and left there to await trial by courts martial

---

[1] 'Commission on Rebellion Losses, 1849–53', Pub. Arch. Canada, RG4, B37, vols. 5–9.
[2] For Colonel Price's trial by court martial, see ibid., B39–40.

or civil courts on charges of insurrection, sedition, or treason. Following the first outbreak in Lower Canada in November 1837, 501 persons were arrested, between November and June, at Montreal and five in the town of Quebec. So when Lord Durham arrived from England in May, he found the prisons full, and with little precedence to guide him as to what should be done about it. To meet the situation, he issued an 'Ordinance to provide for the security of Lower Canada'. Under the Ordinance, a dozen Patriot leaders who were already in the United States (including Papineau, T. S. Brown, and Georges-Étienne Cartier) were declared guilty of high treason and condemned to execution should they return to Canada. Eight others —including Wolfred Nelson, Henri Gauvin, and Bonaventure Viger—were to be deported to Bermuda. The rest of the prisoners were set free, either unconditionally or on securities ranging from £100 to £5,000.[3] So, in terms of the large numbers acquitted and discharged, Durham had behaved with commendable moderation; but he had sentenced eight men to deportation without trial; and for this there was no authority other than the Ordinance he had proclaimed without reference to his superiors in London. So, when the Bermuda authorities refused to accept their prisoners and the news reached London, the British Government disallowed the Ordinance, ordered the eight to be returned and to be given the option of self-exile in America; and Durham resigned his post and was succeeded by Colborne.

So Colborne was in charge of the next stage of the judicial retribution that followed the outbreak of November 1838. This time, 855 prisoners were taken and charged with treason—18 at Quebec (one of whom, Alexandre Dumont, was a Frenchman), 19 at Sherbrooke (St. Francis), 2 at Three Rivers, and 816 at Montreal. The handful of prisoners at Quebec, Sherbrooke, and Three Rivers were discharged unconditionally or admitted to bail. Of the far greater number in Montreal, 700 were discharged or (in a small minority of cases) released on bail. The remaining 108 were tried by court martial in the Court House in Montreal.[4]

The court martial remained in session from 21 November 1838 to 6 May 1839. One of the accused, Louis-Léandre Ducharme, from Montreal, described as a 'gentleman' in one report and as a 'clerk' in another, later wrote a journal of his experiences, including his impressions of the trial. He describes how the prisoners awaiting

[3] PP 1840, xxxii: 'A Return of the Names of Persons imprisoned in Lower Canada, charged with Treason . . . since 1st November 1837', pp. 395-415.
[4] Ibid., pp. 3-14.

court martial were put together in a separate ward of the prison where they were allowed to consult with two lawyers who had been appointed to defend them. Ducharme was one of the first to be tried and he was brought to court with eleven others when the court opened on 21 November. That day, he relates, the prisoners were brought into court shackled in pairs, and the chains were only removed an hour later after they had been carefully searched. But they were kept standing, as there was nowhere for them to sit, until the court adjourned at 5 p.m., when they were shackled again and taken back to prison under military escort, and kept there in chains until the middle of the night. Some of the prisoners had handcuffs so tight that their wrists became swollen. This went on for three weeks, after which Ducharme and his companions were left in prison all day to await the result. It was announced a few days later when the judgment of the court was read out to them, sentencing ten of the twelve prisoners (including himself) to be hanged; but this was later commuted to transportation for life.[5] This was also the fate of half a dozen of his comrades, including the brothers Thibert, farm labourers of Châteauguay, described as quiet, peaceable family men, one of them a churchwarden. But some were less fortunate. Two of Ducharme's group—Joseph-Narcisse Cardinal, a notary, and Joseph Duquette, a 20-year-old student, both of Châteauguay— were taken from the prison to be hanged a few days later. As the trials went on, ten others—five farmers among them—followed them to the scaffold.

When the court martial finished its work a little over five months after it had begun, it had ordered twelve executions; while 27 had been released on bail or on condition of leaving the province; and 58, found guilty of treason, were transported to Australia for life. Yet, savage as some of the sentences were, the punishment meted out to the Lower Canadian rebels of 1838 was relatively mild, though it did not equal the leniency shown by Durham the year before. Even if we include those sentenced to exile in Bermuda, whose sentences were later quashed, the proportion of convictions to committals after the 1837 outbreak was a little under one in 100; in 1838 it was about one in nine; in both years combined it was one in thirteen, or 7·5 per cent.

The Upper Canadian rebellion was, from the point of view of authority, not so simple a matter. It was complicated by the eventual participation of large numbers of Americans, the citizens of a foreign power. The case did not arise, of course, until the second stage of the rebellion; but it had been anticipated, and in January 1838 a special Act had been passed 'to protect the inhabitants of this province against lawless aggression from subjects of foreign countries at peace with her Majesty'; and it provided that such persons (meaning Americans) should be tried, like Canadians, before courts martial or the regular courts.[6] So the Act was already in operation when, in March 1838, Sir George Arthur, after long experience in Tasmania, arrived to take over the lieutenant-governorship from the ineffectual Sir Francis Bond Head. By August 1838 there were 885 persons in jail; their names appear on a long list and report that Arthur sent to the Colonial Office in London in December.[7] They came from eight districts, including 422 from the Home District (Toronto), 163 from London, 90 from Gore (Hamilton), 75 from Midland, and 43 from Niagara. Among the Niagara prisoners were 15 Americans and Canadians captured at the battle of Short Hills in June of that year. In addition, there is a list of 61 persons, charged with high treason, who had absconded to the United States and were now threatened with outlawry unless they returned: they include the names of William Lyon Mackenzie and three members of the Provincial Parliament: John Rolph, Charles Dunscombe, and David Gibson. Of the remainder, the great majority were discharged or acquitted, granted bail, or pardoned on giving security to keep the peace. A handful were sentenced to prison or banished from the province. One man was sent to hospital, where he died. Two innkeepers of Toronto, John Anderson and John Montgomery, were among fifteen who were ordered for transportation but escaped, most of them from Fort Henry at Kingston. Twenty-seven others were also sentenced to transportation; of these, eleven never sailed (being presumably pardoned at a later stage), while all but two of the remainder were Short Hills prisoners whose sentence of death had been commuted. It appears that Arthur had earlier visited the Canadians among them in jail: Benjamin Wait, of York near Toronto, claimed he had come to see him three times; and James Gemmel, a Scot, said on arrival in Tasmania that Arthur had promised him his freedom, and he added: 'I should have got my liberty had the rebellion not broken out again.'[8]

But in three cases the death sentence was carried out. The first two

---

[6] Edwin C. Guillet, *The Lives and Times of the Patriots*, p. 195.
[7] PP 1840, xxxi: 'Correspondence relative to the Affairs of Canada', pt. 2, pp. 197–213.
[8] Tas. Arch. CON 18/5, 16.

to be executed were Samuel Lount and Peter Matthews, captured after Mackenzie's Toronto disaster, who were hanged at the corner of King and Toronto Streets and later buried in Potters' Field (where Bloor and Yonge Streets meet today). The third was James Morrow, a tanner of the Niagara District, captured at the time of the Short Hills invasion, who was hanged at the end of July.

In the last stage of the rebellion, 184 prisoners were taken after the battles of Windmill Point (12 November) and Windsor (4 December). Of the 140 captured at Windmill Point all but nineteen were Americans: the minority included four Germans, three Canadians, four Poles, two Frenchmen, a Spaniard, two Englishmen, two Irishmen, and a Scot. They were tried by court martial at Fort Henry, Kingston, between late-November and January and charged, as befitted the occasion, with the 'piratical invasion' of Canada. Only five men— four Americans and a Canadian—were acquitted. All the rest were found guilty and sentenced to death. Of these, nine were hanged: a printer from Connecticut, a teacher who acted as paymaster for the 'invading' force, six New Yorkers, and von Schultz (alias Sczoltewski), a native of Poland and commander of the 'Patriot army' at Windmill Point. Half a dozen others who had been recommended to mercy were either released or spent a term in prison. Finally, in the case of sixty, the death sentence was commuted to one of transportation for life.[9] One of them—Leonard Delino, of Jefferson County, New York—later described how he had been reprieved at the very last moment after the order had been given for his execution.[10]

Meanwhile, the forty-four prisoners from the battle of Windsor were being tried at London (in present-day Ontario). In this case, there were six Canadians, three Scots, and two Englishmen; while the rest—once more the great majority—were Americans. Only one man was acquitted; the remaining forty-three were convicted of 'hostile invasion of the province' and sentenced to death. Five were executed: three Americans—Albert Clark, Thomas Perley, and Hiram Lynn—and two Canadians, Daniel Bedford and Joshua Doan, who had fought with Dunscombe at London a year before. The Canadians were hanged at Windsor and the Americans at London gaol. Two Americans, who had turned Queen's Evidence, were recommended to mercy and allowed to go free. Several of the rest were presumably pardoned (though there is no official record

[9] 'Correspondence relative to the Affairs of Canada', pt. 2, pp. 274–89.
[10] Mitchell Lib. Sydney, *Convicts landed in the Colony of New South Wales 1830–1842* (11 vols., Sydney, 1832–43), 1840.

to the effect) as only eighteen of those whose death sentence had been commuted to transportation (an Englishman, two Canadians, and fifteen Americans) were eventually put on transports bound for Australia.[11]

In April, after the trials had long been over, those destined for transportation were taken in wagons to prison in Toronto. One of the Windsor prisoners, Elijah Woodman, a Canadian and a devout Presbyterian, who, at his trial, had resigned himself to his fate with the thought that 'maybe God had willed it that way', wrote in his diary: 'Very early this morning we were unlocked and bread served to each man with a small piece of meat, with orders to be ready immediately to take our departure . . . We started and passed along Dundas Street, getting a nod of the head from a few true friends, who took an interest in our fate . . . I thought, why should I be cast down, for I am only in the hands of men and am able to stand all the trials that are put upon me, so with William Stevens I struck up *Pretty Susan* and continued singing for some time.'[12] A fellow prisoner, Robert Marsh, who also kept a journal, feelingly describes the conditions they had to suffer in their new jail:

> We were put in a hall that was occupied during the day by thirty or forty, and at night all locked in different cells—from five to eight in a cell. The jail was crowded full: some crazy, some for murder, some for stealing, some for desertion, and various other crimes . . . Our rations were hardly sufficient to keep us alive . . . bullock's heads, boiled with a very few peas that the rats had been among . . .[13]

After six weeks, a plan was discovered for a general prison escape; so the prisoners were moved by steamship to Kingston, where they were locked up in Fort Henry and inspected by Sir George Arthur, whom Stephen Wright, a carpenter from New York State who had been wounded at Windmill Point, quaintly described as 'the bloody Robespierre of the Canadian Revolution'. At Kingston, in the heart of this 'British Bastille', the Americans did not fail to celebrate the Fourth of July as best they could. 'The ever glorious Fourth of July', wrote Daniel Heustis, another diarist, 'we celebrated as well as circumstances would permit. Out of several pocket handkerchiefs a flag was manufactured, as nearly representing the "star-spangled banner"' as we could conveniently make it . . . We had faced the enemy as did the heroes of Bunker Hill, and we saw no cause for self-reproach.'[14]

[11] 'Correspondence relative to the Affairs of Canada', pt. 2, pp. 290–4.
[12] Cit. Guillet, p. 196.   [13] Loc. cit.
[14] Cit. Guillet, p. 197.

On 22 September 1839 the prisoners were marched out of Port Henry 'attached by pairs to a long chain', and so on to the convict ship, the *Buffalo*, lying in dock at Quebec. Here the seventy-eight prisoners of Windsor and Prescott (or Windmill Point), were joined by the fifty-eight Lower Canadians (they included an American, Benjamin Mott). They sailed together on the *Buffalo* on 27 September and reached Hobart on 12 February 1840. They were one man short as Asa Priest, one of the Americans, had died on the way. At Hobart the two groups divided; the Americans left the ship, which sailed on to Sydney with the French Canadians a few days later. Meanwhile, the Short Hills prisoners, who had been among the first to be sentenced, had already sailed, eight on the *Marquis of Hastings*, and four on the *Canton*, both destined for Van Diemen's Land, the first arriving in Hobart on 18 July 1839 and the second on 12 January 1840. So, with the arrival of the *Buffalo* in Sydney as its second port of call, all the transported prisoners from the Canadian rebellion (save one) had reached the shores of their Australian exile.

PART THREE

THE PROTESTERS

1. Political Rebels

WE now turn from the general to the particular: from a general discussion of protest and punishment in the three homelands to the individual protesters, or rather to those whose activities led them into exile in Australia. Let us start with the most dramatic and bloody episode of all: the Irish Rebellion of 1798-1803. We have seen that the Rebellion was fought with virtually no leaders, except those who could be locally recruited (and even forced into service) and that the initiators of rebellion—the leading United Irishmen—had already been rounded up and were being held as State prisoners in Dublin or London or (like Lord Edward Fitzgerald) had been killed in a preliminary skirmish, before the real shooting began. Few therefore of the topmost leaders, whether of 1798 or 1803, were shipped to Australia. Those transported were rather of the second rank or such as became leaders (some of considerable stature) as the Rebellion went on: men like Joseph ('General') Holt and Michael Dwyer, the 'Wicklow Captain'. Although Holt came to play an important role in the operations in Wicklow, he was one of those rebels—and they are not infrequent in rebellions and revolutions—who became a rebel, and a leader, against his will. Holt was born at Ballydaniel, County Wicklow, in 1756. He was one of the six sons of a Protestant farmer, and his wife Hester (whom he married in 1782) was the daughter of a Protestant farmer from Roundwood, at the foot of the Wicklow mountains. He settled in the same district as a Protestant farmer himself and, as a member of the local establishment, he held various offices, including those of sub-constable and sheriff, until the eve of rebellion. But, in May 1798, in the course of a private quarrel, his house was burned down by a company of militia. So Holt took the oath of the United Irishmen and fled to the mountains, where, after some weeks of inactivity in the early summer, he emerged in June as a rebel captain, commanding 960 Wicklowmen, with the rank of colonel, under the supreme command of 'General' Edward Roche, leader of a rebel army 11,000 strong.

But, gradually, Roche lost favour and authority and, in early July, Holt was drafted into the command of all the forces in Wicklow in his place. He fought successful actions, like one at Ballyellis, and at one time, as other rebels defeated at Vinegar Hill and elsewhere drifted into the Wicklow mountains, he commanded a force of 13,000 men. But, as the Rebellion lost its momentum, Holt was compelled to rely on a smaller force and organize guerrilla resistance. He continued these operations for several months after the Rebellion had been crushed in other counties and for long he was hunted by government forces with a price on his head. But it was only on 10 November that he chose to surrender, on his own terms, to Lord Powersmount, at Powersmount House in County Wicklow. In accordance with these terms, he was not put on trial but allowed to go into 'voluntary' exile, accompanied by his family, to New South Wales. He was confined briefly at Dublin Castle and, for several months awaiting a ship, at Cobh. He sailed with his wife and two sons on the *Minerva* on 24 August 1799, reaching Sydney on 11 January 1800.[1]

Michael Dwyer was born in about 1772 at Donoghmore, in the Glen of Imail, in County Wicklow, the oldest of four brothers and three sisters. His father was a farmer at Canragh and moved, when Michael was twelve, to a thirty-acre farm in the township of Eadestown. When the Rebellion started, he joined the rebels of Wexford and, after their defeat on the Boyne, he was one of 400 men from Wicklow and Wexford who retreated to the Wicklow hills where, for a time, he served under Joseph Holt and rose to the rank of captain. He then went into hiding for several months, appearing at different times in Leitrim, Carlow, and Wexford and paying frequent visits to his father's house in the Glen of Imail. In 1803 he was invited through a former lieutenant, Arthur Devlin, to give support from Wicklow to Robert Emmet's projected rising in Dublin; and he was supplied with arms for the purpose. When the rising failed in July 1803 he retreated once more to the Wicklow hills with a price of £500 on his head. Meanwhile, his old father and his numerous household (including Michael's wife and children) were being harried and threatened by the authorities; and it was partly to save them from further persecution that he offered to surrender with his closest associates—Hugh Byrne, Martin Burke, John Mernagh, and Arthur Devlin—on condition that they should be pardoned and allowed to go to America at the Government's expense. The negotiations were protracted and continued after Dwyer and most of his companions were put in prison and charged with high treason in Dublin in December 1803. They were still in Newgate prison in late January 1804; and, presumably, they remained there until 13 July 1805,

---

[1] *ADB*, i, 550; *Memoirs of Joseph Holt, General of the Irish Rebels in 1798*, ed. T. C. Croker (2 vols., London, 1838), i, *passim*.

when the Dublin *Evening Post* reported that, on 11 July, Dwyer and four of his companions, 'who were said to have surrendered on condition of emigrating to America, had received orders to go on board a transport destined for Botany Bay'. Recriminations followed as Dwyer claimed he had been double-crossed; but the Government held firm and the five prisoners (recently joined by Mernagh) were put on board the *Tellicherry*, lying in harbour at Cobh, in mid-July; but—important concessions—they were privileged not to have their heads shaven, to have separate quarters on the ship and (like Holt) to bring their families with them. The *Tellicherry*, the last of the 'rebel' ships to sail, left Cobh on 31 August and reached Sydney on 15 February 1806.[2]

There were many others less eminent among the transported rebels, of which the following is a small sample. There was Richard Dry, born in 1771, the son of a Protestant gentleman farmer of Wexford, who moved to Dublin, where he became a woollen draper and joined the United Irishmen. In the course of his travels he was first committed and tried in Roscommon; but, through the intervention of an accomplice in court, he was allowed to enlist in the army. He went to Cork on a visit and was recognized and tried at assizes and sentenced, in September 1797, to transportation for life. Like Joseph Holt, he sailed on the *Minerva* in August 1799. (A Thomas Dry, possibly a brother of Richard, a clothier of Windy Harbour, Dublin, appears among the ninety State prisoners held in Newgate jail in Dublin in October 1798, who petitioned to be sent as exiles to America.) Another prisoner who petitioned to be sent to America in 1798 was Farrel Cuff, of Edenderry, King's County, a schoolmaster, aged 24 when brought to trial in August 1797 and sentenced to a seven-year term. His petition failed, but he was allowed to go into 'voluntary' exile in Australia instead; his name appears, with Holt's, among seven *Minerva* men who had voluntarily surrendered to transportation. And, finally, there was James Lyons, a labourer, of County Longford, aged 25 and a private in the Longford Militia at the time of the Rebellion. Like many other Longford men, he was accused of joining the French army of 'liberation' which had recently landed, under General Humbert, in the West; and, in August 1798, he was sentenced by court martial at Ballinamuck, in County Longford, to be transported for life. He exercised the option offered him of life-service in a regiment abroad

---

[2] *Insurgent Wicklow 1798*, ed. M. V. Ronan (Dublin, 1948), pp. 48–50, 112–33; Arch. NSW, 4/4004, 2/8283, pp. 35–42; SPO Dublin, Prisoners' Petitions, nos. 864, 875–6, 935, 1144, 1190.

and was sent by way of Mullingar (Co. Meath) to the New Geneva Barracks at Waterford in late November of that year. Yet, like many others, he was put on a convict ship in Cork harbour instead and sailed on *Friendship II*, which left Cobh at the same time as the *Minerva* on 24 August 1799.[3]

The nearest thing to an armed rebellion at this stage of England's history was the Pentrich 'Revolution' or Derbyshire 'Rising' of June 1817. The affair in itself was not very impressive: it was the episode in which Jeremiah Brandreth, the 'Nottingham Captain', armed a small group of farm-workers from the villages of Pentrich and South Wingfield, in Derbyshire, and led them in an ill-fated attempt (betrayed by a spy before they even set out) to seize Nottingham Castle. It ended in disaster: thirty-five men were arrested and brought to trial at Derby City Hall charged with high treason. Half of them were set free, but Brandreth and his two principal lieutenants were hanged as traitors and fourteen others were sentenced to transportation for life. Among those transported were stocking-weavers, framework-knitters, miners, ironfounders, stonemasons, and labourers. One man, John MacKesswick, was a native of Ayrshire; the rest were either born or bred in the Derbyshire villages of Pentrich, South Wingfield, and Alfreton. Most of them were young men, whose ages ranged between 21 and 37; but there were also four 'elders' with ages from 49 to 64. The youngest was Joseph Turner (known as 'Manchester' Turner), 21 years old, single, variously described as a 'clerk' and a 'labourer', and born in Manchester though living in South Wingfield. The oldest was Thomas Bacon, aged 64, a frame-worker of Pentrich. He had been given the name of 'the Derbyshire delegate' because he had attended a meeting in Wakefield, a month before the rising, to discuss plans for a general insurrection throughout the Midlands and North and brought them back to Brandreth and his 'North Midlands Committee' at Pentrich. His brother, John Bacon, a stocking-weaver, twelve years his junior but an 'elder' none the less, was also among those transported on the *Tottenham* (one of three ships involved), which arrived in Sydney in October 1818.[4]

It was three years later that there occurred in Scotland the episode of the radical weavers of Bonnymuir (of which some mention has been made in an earlier chapter). This was when eighty-eight

[3] For these cases, see G. Rudé, 'Early Irish Rebels in Australia', *Hist. Stud.*, xvi, no. 62 (Apr. 1974), 30–5; and (for Richard Dry) see also Dr. Madden, *Antrim and Down in '98* (Glasgow, n.d.), pp. 114–15, 173; and *ADB*, i, 328–9.

[4] John Neal, *The Pentrich Rebellion*; Arch. NSW, 4/4006.

Scottish weavers, shoemakers, and nailers—many from Glasgow, more from Bonnymuir—were charged before the Court of Judiciary, meeting alternately at Glasgow, Dumbarton, Paisley, Stirling, and Ayr, with high treason or, more specifically, with conspiring to subvert the Constitution. It was claimed that a radical conspiracy of Scottish working men extended over five counties in the manufacturing districts, and that there had been demonstrations in favour of Reform at Bonnymuir and Glasgow in April of that year. There is no evidence that any rising was contemplated along the lines of that attempted in Derbyshire three years before. But, in Scotland as in England, talk of treason and revolution was in the air. It was the year that the Cato Street conspirators plotted to blow up the Government in London; and the year that thirteen Yorkshire weavers, shoemakers, and nailers—men of similar occupations and dispositions to those at Glasgow and Bonnymuir—were sentenced to death at York Castle and subsequently, after commutation, transported to Tasmania. So, the authorities being as nervous as they were, it is hardly surprising that the Scottish judges should have dispensed equally stern justice to the thirty prisoners (fifty-eight had made their escape) who stood before them in the dock. Three men were hanged (as we noted in an earlier chapter) and of twenty-two others who were capitally convicted, nineteen were sent to Australia for life or for a term of fourteen years. Most were young men (their average age was 28), but there were three veterans of 35 or more. The oldest was Thomas McFarlane, a 45-year-old widower, Glasgow-born but now working as a weaver in Condorrat village in Dunbartonshire. Next in seniority was Andrew Dawson, 38, a nailer, married without children, living at Camelon, near Falkirk, in Stirlingshire. (Evidently he had some instruction as, ten years later, he wrote a letter applying for a character reference in New South Wales.) The two youngest were Alexander (or Andrew) Johnston, a 16-year-old Lanarkshire weaver, now living in Glasgow; and Andrew White, 17, a bookbinder from Glasgow. Both of these, like most of the younger men and a couple of the older, were given a shorter sentence of 14 years.[5]

Of the English Reform Bill rioters of the early 1830s comparatively few were sentenced to transportation: I have counted twenty-seven among a hundred or more tried and sentenced for riot and 'demolishing houses' at the assizes in Bristol and Gloucester in 1832. They came to Tasmania on half a dozen ships. They were very young, far

[5] Ellis and Mac A'Ghobbainn, *The Scottish Insurrection of 1820*, pp. 252-67; Arch. NSW, 4/4007, 4/2167.

younger than the rebels we have considered up to now: their average age was 25. As is common in urban riots, they came from a variety of occupations: there were bakers, butchers, blacksmiths, brick-makers, carpenters, cabinet-makers, drapers, gardeners, grooms, brewers, ploughmen, shoemakers, stonemasons, sailors, domestic servants, and jacks-of-all-trades. A typical case was William Spokes, 22, Bristol-born, married with two children and claiming to be not only a carpenter, but also a wheelwright, a potter, and a bargeman. Among the sailors, there was Henry Green, 31, single, born in Dorset; and there was Joseph Keates, a Roman Catholic (the only one), 25, Bristol-born, and sentenced for 'larceny' in the course of the riots. Another 'marginal' protester was John Neagle (alias Cunningham), 25, Bristol-born, married with one child, described as a gentleman's servant, who was transported to Australia for 14 years for 'stealing 120 lbs. butter value £4. 10s.'[6]

The contrast between these young urban rioters of the 1830s and the fifty-eight Lower Canadians of 1838 could hardly be greater. Unlike the Upper Canadians, there were no mercenaries among them, no soldiers of fortune or vagrants: they were all men of settled residence and occupation and *habitants*—townsmen and villagers— of the Eastern Townships and villages on the southern outskirts of Montreal. There were no 'outsiders' among them—with the solitary exception of Benjamin Mott, an American who had the misfortune to be picked up across the border by Government troops. Most of them were married and (being Catholics) had large families, and their average age was 38 (compared with the Anglo-Canadians' 34, the Americans' 28, and the Bristol rioters' 25). About half of them were tenant farmers, with a sprinkling of farmworkers (variously described as 'yeomen' and *cultivateurs*); others were innkeepers, blacksmiths, joiners, bakers, carriage-makers, with a smaller number of bailiffs, notaries, clerks, doctors, and merchants. As villagers, it is not surprising to find among them men closely related: brothers, fathers and sons, uncles and nephews—such as the brothers Louis and Joseph Dumouchelle, Jean-Louis and Jean-Marie Thibert, David and Hubert Leblanc, and Edouard, Toussaint, and Jérémie Rochon; or the two Lonctins and two Morins who were father and son; and the two Goyettes and the three Roys who were uncles and nephews; while the two Héberts, and three Pinsonnaults were probably related as well. Some were relatively prosperous as farmers, businessmen, and tradesmen: such as Louis Pinsonnault,

<hr>

[6] HO 27/43; Arch. NSW, 4/4109, 4148, 4151; Tas. Arch., CON 31/2, 4, 7, 16, 20, 26, 35, 36-9, 43-4.

whose two plots of land in the parish of St. Rémi were put up for auction after his trial and sentence and sold for £255; Théodore Béchard, farmer and veterinary surgeon of the parish of Ste. Marguerite de Blairfindie, whose three lots of 56 acres in all were sold for £176; and Ignace Chèvrefils, farmer of Ste. Martine, in the *seigneurie* of Beauharnois, whose land was sold for £155, leaving his wife and six children (so it was locally reported) in penury. There were also those who, while they left no land for sale (or whose friends or relatives blocked its sale by filing counter-claims for its possession), left goods for sale instead. These were generally sold for quite trivial amounts—varying in most cases from £3 to £12; but Edouard-Pascal Rochon, a carriage-maker and painter of Terrebonne, had his goods sold for what was then the relatively large sum of £155. 13s. 4d. Rochon may, in fact, have been the most prosperous of them all, as he owned twelve plots of land dispersed over the parish of Terrebonne, of which one alone fetched £20. 5s., the rest being blocked by the opposition of other claimants. There may have been others the value of whose property is hidden, in the records of sales of the goods distrained, behind such phrases as 'no land', 'no goods', or 'unsold by reason of opposition'; and it must be remembered that several had had their properties destroyed and their houses burned to the ground by soldiers and volunteers during the holocaust that followed the rebels' earlier defeat in December 1837.[7]

To take a few case histories selected from both rich and poor. Charles Bergevin (alias Langevin), a farmer of Ste. Martine, in the *seigneurie* of Beauharnois, was 52 years old at the time of his arrest. He was married with seven boys; we cannot tell what properties he held, as his goods had been pillaged and destroyed by volunteers and the sale of his land—three lots of about 50 acres—was contested after his trial. He was involved in the armed occupation of Beauharnois, whose *seigneur* was Robert Ellice, an Englishman, in November 1838, was charged with high treason in the following March, and sentenced to death by court martial at Montreal; but his sentence, like that of most of his companions, was commuted to transportation for life. François Bigonnesse (known as Beaucaire) was a well-to-do farmer of St. Cyprien-de-Napierville (part of his land was sold for £100. 10s. in 1839), aged 47 at the time of his trial.

---

[7] Indents in *Convicts landed in the Colony of NSW*, 1840. Details of land and goods distrained and sold in 'Statement of the Confiscations . . . Lower Canada (1837–38). List of Persons Exiled to V.D.L. (*sic.*)', Pub. Arch. Canada, RG4, B37, vol. 10.

He was married with seven children—three boys and four girls—
and met with a formidable list of accusations when he faced his
judges in January 1839. He was charged with having helped to
destroy a part of the railway track between Laprairie and St.
Jean to arrest the movement of troops; it was easily proved that he had
held the rank of captain in the operations at Napierville and that
later he had a leading role in the engagement at Odelltown. He
pleaded innocence and appealed to his reputation as a citizen with
an unblemished record; but it was all to no avail. Désiré Bour-
bonnais was a young blacksmith, aged 19 at the time of his arrest,
single and working for a Mr. Brown, agent of Mr. Ellice, *seigneur*
of Beauharnois. At his trial at Montreal, witnesses claimed to have
seen him armed and mounted on a horse, carrying messages between
St. Clément and Châteauguay during the events of November 1838,
and (later) drilling with the Patriots who were about to set out for
the camp at Napierville. Not only that; but he had also been seen
in charge of forty prisoners, captured on the steamship *Brougham*
and being brought to the presbytery of a local vicar (the *curé*
Quintal). He was sentenced to death but recommended to mercy;
so he found himself with the others on board the *Buffalo* in September
1839. Charles Huot was a notary public at Napierville, 52 and unmarried at the time of his court martial. He was then described by
witnesses as being a 'peaceful, honest and inoffensive man of an
exemplary character', also timid and liable to be imposed upon
by Patriot leaders. He had, in fact, been arrested by the rebels in
1837. Yet, in the November following, he appears as quarter-master
of the rebel army of 4,000–5,000 men at Napierville. He denied it;
but his claim to have been forced to act as he did and to have been
a 'loyalist' at heart, while it may have saved his life, did not save
him from transportation. Another lawyer was Hyppolite Lanctot,
a 22-year-old notary of St. Rémi, who had only been articled a year
before. He was married with two boys and held 25 poles of land that
were later sold for £69. It appears from a statement he made after
his arrest in November 1838 that he had been enrolled as a *frère
chasseur* ('Huntsman') and, though he denied ever having taken the
oath of initiation, that as an officer of the Brotherhood he had
attended a meeting at St. Constant in early November, which had
led to the uprising at Napierville a few days later. It seems, too, that
he had been one of 600 men who, on 8 November, set out for Lacolle
and Odelltown (both near the border) on Robert Nelson's orders;
but he claimed in his defence that, at Lacolle, he had left the force
that was marching on Odelltown to return to Napierville and had

surrendered to a company of volunteers a couple of miles from the line of battle.

Among these French-Canadian rebels, there were also the two Morins. Pierre-Hector Morin, the elder of the two, was a merchant sailor, born in 1784; the son of a captain in the merchant marine, he had fought in the American war in 1813 and was successively captain of the *Swiftsure* and the *Aigle canadien*, which carried passengers and merchandise between Quebec and Montreal. He was arrested after the battle of Odelltown with his second son, Lucien, as they were trying to cross the border to the United States. At this time, he was 53 years old, married and with three sons. During his trial, it was said by some witnesses that he was a respectable citizen and a good husband and father, who 'detested the revolutionary opinions so often expressed in Canada'. But others claimed that he had played a leading part in the camp at Napierville; and it was also held against him that he had married an elder sister of Dr. Côté, the rebel leader (yet it appears that this had happened some years before Côté was born!); and—a more serious charge—that he had been seen in the company of Robert Nelson and Charles Hindenlang (one of the executed leaders). Morin's son, Achille-Gabriel, is variously described as a clerk, a merchant, and a *cultivateur*; and he may have been something of each. Aged 24, he lived with his father at Napierville; so he was readily thought to be implicated, whether he actually was or not, in the occupation of that town by rebels in early November. Moreover, being found with a leg-wound soon after the battle of Odelltown, it was reasonable enough that he should be charged with involvement in that affair as well. So he was arrested—by Sir John Colborne in person, he claimed later—a day before his father and younger brother, on 10 November. Thus father and son were tried together and together condemned to death in January 1839; and, having had their sentences commuted, they sailed together on the *Buffalo* to New South Wales in September. And they would return together, after eight years of exile, in 1847.[8]

So we return to Ireland—this time to the romantic insurgents of 1848. As we have seen, this was a rebellion of a very different stamp and on a far more limited scale than those in Ireland in 1798 and in Canada in 1837-8; and a mere dozen Young Irelanders were sent as convicts to Australia. These prisoners fall into two groups. On the one hand, there were the leaders: William Smith O'Brien and his lieutenants, Terence McManus, John Mitchel, Patrick O'Donaghoe,

<hr />

[8] See *Convicts landed in the Colony of NSW*, 1840; and, more particularly, A. Fauteux, *Patriotes de 1837-1838* (Montreal, 1950), pp. 85-338.

and Thomas Francis Meagher; and, somewhat on the fringe of leadership, the two journalists given 10-year sentences for treason by a Dublin court: John Martin, farmer and former medical student at Trinity College, a close friend of Mitchel and editor of the *Irish Felon*; and Kevin O'Dogherty, also a Dublin medical student and publisher of *Tribune*. These are they whose names are recorded in the history books and in the pages of Dictionaries of National Biography. Among them, if Smith O'Brien is the father-figure and acknowledged political leader and Mitchel the publicist and man of ideas, Meagher is the spinner of words and romantic-in-chief. He was born at Waterford in 1823, the son of a prosperous merchant, mayor of the city and its member of Parliament for several years. He was educated by Irish Jesuits at Clongowes-Wood, in Kildare, and at Stonyhurst College, in Lancashire. Returning to Dublin in 1843, he became a law student, joined Daniel O'Connell's Repeal Association, and won a reputation for silver-tongued oratory in the Association's debates at Conciliation Hall. In 1845 he joined the militant Young Ireland wing of the Association and in the critical disputes of 1846-7 consorted with Mitchel and O'Brien in breaking with the older and more conservative 'moral force' leaders. In the spring of 1848, Meagher accompanied O'Brien to Paris to present a congratulatory address to the newly formed French Republic—the product of the revolution of 1848—and, as a challenge to authority, brought back an Irish tricolour flag to Dublin. He was appointed to the committee of five that directed the abortive insurrection that followed. After its defeat, as we have noted before, Meagher was tried with O'Brien and others at Clonmel and, in October, was sentenced to death and later to transportation for life for his part in the affair. With O'Brien, McManus, and O'Donaghoe he sailed on the *Swift* and arrived in Hobart Town in October 1849.[9]

On the other hand, there were the followers who responded to the leaders' call to arms: such were the five men sentenced to various terms of transportation (some to seven years, others to fourteen) at Waterford in 1849 and 1850 for taking part in successive attacks on the police barracks under the command or direction of Smith O'Brien. Unlike the leaders, they were ordinary working men: John Walsh and Thomas Donovan, both farm labourers; Cornelius Keeffe, a waterman; Thomas Wall, a top-sawyer; and Edmund Sheafy, a painter—all born and bred in the city and county of Waterford.

[9] *DNB* (1909), xii, 194-6; *ADB*, ii, 217-18; D. R. Gwynn, *Thomas Francis Meagher* (Dublin, 1961); Tas. Arch., CON 37/5.

Their average age was 29; two could read and write, one could only read, and two could do neither.[10]

And, finally, the last group of convicted protesters of all: the sixty-two Fenians who sailed from London to Western Australia in October 1867. They were a mixed bag and had been sentenced for different offences (but mainly for 'treason felony' and mutinous conduct) to varying terms of transportation: 12 for life, 2 for twenty years, 2 for fifteen years, and the rest (the majority) for terms of seven years and less. Their birthplaces were scattered all over Ireland: some were from Tyrone, others from Down, Louth, Wicklow, Waterford, Tipperary, Limerick, Kerry, and Dublin; but more came from Cork than from any other county. Their trades were even more numerous than their places of birth: there were 10 labourers among them, 8 clerks, 7 farmers, 4 carpenters, 3 bakers, 2 butchers, 2 drapers, 2 shoemakers, 2 painters, 2 masons, 2 coachmen, 2 building contractors, 2 schoolmasters, a shipsmith, a fitter, a boilermaker, a spinning master, a horse-trainer, a tailor, a weaver, a journalist, a compositor, a gardener, and a regular soldier. Sixteen others had served in the British Army: six in the Dragoon Guards and three in the 61st Foot, with half a dozen spread over the 24th and 53rd Foot, the 68th Rifles, and the Queen's and the 10th Hussars. None was among the most prominent of the Fenians in Ireland: these had either been put in jail (like John Devoy) or had escaped to the Unites States.

One, however, was later to win a reputation in America, though not so much for purely Fenian activities. He was John Boyle O'Reilly, the son of a schoolmaster, born in Drogheda, County Louth, on 24 June 1844. Having received his early education from his father, he was apprenticed as a compositor to the *Drogheda Argus* and, at fifteen, went to England to become a reporter with the *Guardian* at Preston. It was here that he joined the Fenian movement; and, returning to Ireland in 1863, he enlisted in the 10th Hussars and engaged in revolutionary propaganda among the troops; with such success, it later emerged, that the 'treasonable songs and ballads' that he taught them were sung throughout the Regiment. However, it was not until February 1866 that O'Reilly was denounced by an informer; and, in June, he was court martialled at the Royal Barracks, Dublin, and ordered to be shot for having withheld knowledge of an 'intended mutiny'. But the sentence was commuted, first to penal servitude for life and, subsequently, to a term of twenty years. After a few days in Mountjoy prison, he was removed in succession to Chatham, Dartmoor, and other English

[10] Tas. Arch., CON 33/100, 104, 109.

jails; and it was from Dartmoor that, over two years after his trial, he was put aboard the *Hougomont* to join the sixty-one other Fenians waiting to be transported to Fremantle, in Western Australia.[11]

O'Reilly's later story, like that of several of the other rebels mentioned in this chapter, will be told in a subsequent section of the book.

[11] Arch. WA, R.16; J. S. Moynihan, 'Fenian Prisoners in Western Australia', *Éire-Ireland*, iii, no. 3 (1968–9), 6–13; *ADB*, v, 370–1.

2. Irish Rural Protesters

THE forms and issues of Irish rural protest are so confused that it is hard to tell one movement or one type of protest from another. The 'land-and-tithe war', as we noted, extended into the 1840s and had four main phases: 1813–16, 1821–24, the early 1830s, and the greater part of the 1840s, the first two being marked by the application of the Insurrection Acts to the more turbulent counties and districts.

In the first phase, following the end of the wars, the number transported for protest-crimes was comparatively small, but the offences committed ranged over a wide variety of armed assaults often masquerading behind the labels of Carding, Whiteboyism, and Ribbonism, none of which gave as precise a description as Defenderism and Peep o'Dayism (let alone Orangeism) had in the past. To take a few examples of protesters of this period who found their way to New South Wales (virtually no Irish came to Tasmania until after 1840). John Cormican, a ploughman, and Patrick Carrol, a blacksmith, were sentenced to death at the Galway assizes in March 1816 for 'carding' (or violently assaulting) a farmer. The Bishop of Clonfert and a number of local magistrates and priests intervened and petitioned for a mitigation of the sentence. The result was that both men were reprieved with Carrol spending a term in jail and Cormican being transported for life to Australia on board the *Surrey*.[1] Lacky Commins, a labourer of County Mayo, married with six children, was sentenced to be hanged at the spring assizes in Castlebar in 1820 for an offence that was variously described as 'seditious practices' and 'Ribbon business'. In petitioning on his behalf, his wife pleaded for mercy both for her own sake and for that of her 'six helpless children' and secured a reprieve. So his sentence, like Cormican's, was commuted to one of transportation for life and he sailed from Cork on the *Lord Sidmouth* in November 1820.[2] A more unusual case was that of James (or John) Leary, a 19-year-old boy, who was capitally convicted at Waterford in 1816 for his part in a case of abduction which, according to witnesses, involved the use of firearms. Leary pleaded in his defence that he was merely

[1] SPO Dublin, Prisoners' Petitions, no. 1325 (6 Apr. 1816).
[2] Ibid., no. 1451 (8 Aug. 1820).

helping a schoolmate to elope with his girlfriend; and the combined efforts of his defence counsel and his widowed mother won him a reprieve and a commuted sentence of transportation to Australia.[3] An older man, who sailed on the same ship as Leary—the *Mangles*— in June 1822, was Denis Croneen, a 45-year-old labourer with a wife and nine children. He was sentenced to death at the spring assizes in County Cork that year for having been a member of an armed gang which had attacked Lord Bantry and a party of country gentlemen in a glen. He denied the charge and swore that he was merely on his way to his father's house near by when the soldiers picked him up; moreover, it was pleaded on his behalf that he was subject to epilepsy and had a large family to support. Even Lord Bantry, the principal victim of the assault, spoke in his favour; so he was given a life-term in Australia instead.[4]

In this earlier period, it was comparatively rare (although the Insurrection Act of 1814 was in force in certain counties) for a man to be transported on the simple charge of having been away from his house at night. One of the few cases where it happened is that of Philip Dwyer, 42, a labourer of Tipperary, who was sentenced to seven years' transportation at the March sessions at Clonmel in 1816 for this offence, or—more specifically—for 'sedition—being out at night'. Dwyer claimed that he was 'falsely charged', and the Dean of Clogheen petitioned on his behalf; but to no avail, and he sailed on the *Chapman* for Sydney in March 1817.[5]

As we saw in an earlier chapter, the enactment of a new Insurrection Act in 1822 made a big difference; and now—in the two years that followed—it was quite a frequent occurrence for persons who had been away from home at night—and, in addition, those who had been found with arms or had administered or taken unlawful oaths—to be transported for seven years. One of the many unfortunates who suffered this penalty—all the more unfortunate as he was caught on the very first night that the new Act was put into force—was William Nix, a 31-year-old Limerick man, a labourer with a wife and six children. Nix was sentenced at the special quarter sessions held at Limerick in March 1822 for being out of his house between seven and eight o'clock at night; and it was not until he was already on board the *Mangles* in Cobh harbour awaiting transportation that he found time to tell his own story in petitioning for his release. According to his account, he had been ordered by a

---

[3] SPO Dublin, Prisoners' Petitions, no. 1367 (4 Apr. 1816).
[4] Ibid., no. 1633 (July 1822).
[5] Ibid., no. 1343 (10 May 1816).

magistrate, in conformity with the law, to put his name up on his door; and not being able to write it himself, he had gone to a neighbour's house to have him write it for him.[6] On the same ship with Nix were twenty-five other Limerick men who had been sentenced for the same offence by the same court in March 1822. Their names, and those of four others (who appear to have been released), are on a petition addressed to Dublin Castle on 17 June of that year. The thirty petitioners—most of them country labourers, with a sprinkling of tradesmen (carpenters, weavers, shoemakers, tailors)— pleaded their innocence; they claimed to have been convicted 'more by accident than otherwise' and pledged that, if given a pardon, they 'will take an oath of allegiance and become loyal subjects' of the King.[7] It appears—except, presumably, in the case of the 'missing' four—to have done them no good.

In the next couple of years there were others arriving in Sydney— notably from Cork, Kilkenny, Limerick, and Kildare—whose only recorded offence was to have been away from home at night. There was Cornelius Healy, a tailor, aged 28, sentenced for the usual seven-year term at Cork City sessions in September 1823; he pleaded ill health (but to no effect) when he petitioned for mercy on the convict-hulk *Surprise* in Cobh harbour prior to sailing on the *Ann and Amelia* in January 1825.[8] There were also John and Thomas Hicky, ploughmen of Dunmurry, County Kildare, and probably father and son, who sailed on the same ship and for the same crime as Healy. They were sentenced by special sessions at Naas for breaking the curfew and failed (through ignorance of the law, they claimed) to produce evidence of being men of good character.[9] And, on *Hooghly I*, a few months later, there was James Callaghan, a 25-year-old groom from County Cork, tried at the special sessions at Marlow in October 1824, who pleaded in his defence that he had been denounced by an 'abandoned character' who was only after the reward.[10] With others the charge under the Insurrection Act was often one of having administered an oath, concealed arms, or engaged in Whiteboy activities. Another Cork man, John Clifford, a 40-year-old bootmaker, was sentenced at Fermoy in September 1823 for tendering an illegal oath; he, too, pleaded false evidence in a letter he wrote from the convict-hulk *Surprise* at Cobh.[11] Daniel Ahern, a 25-year-old labourer of Castle Harrison, County Cork, was convicted and sentenced to transportation at Limerick on 29 April

[6] Ibid., no. 1754 (10 June 1822).   [7] Ibid., no. 1771 (17 June 1822).
[8] Ibid., no. 2321 (10 July 1824).   [9] Ibid., no. 2327 (3 Apr. 1824).
[10] Ibid., no. 2212 (late 1824).   [11] Ibid., no. 2227 (18 Jan. 1824).

1823. According to the petition he sent to the court, he was convicted of firing at the police on the night of 11 March 1823; but, officially, his offence was simply stated as 'Insurrection: absent from dwelling house'. He denied the charge on two counts: first, that it was so dark that the police could not possibly have recognized him behind the high wall they spoke of in the indictment; and, second, that he had not left his bed that night anyway. Ahern's master, Henry Harrison, a local squire, testified to his excellent character and other signed recommendations in his favour were produced; their effect, however, was a little deflated by another witness, a Captain Carter of Doneraile, who said that two of the signatures had been forged and that 'Daniel Ahern is a most notorious *Whiteboy*'.[12] Others whose offence is not clearly and specifically stated include Michael Cunningham, a young labourer of Mayo, sentenced at Castlebar to transportation for life on a charge of 'unlawful oaths'—alternately, of 'Ribbonism'—on 23 May 1824. He pleaded in mitigation that he was less than 18 years old and the 'only support of six orphaned boys'. There were, in addition, supporting recommendations from three magistrates and a chaplain; all to no avail, and he was shipped to Australia on *Asia I* which sailed out of Cork on 29 October.[13] Another young man who was given a seven-year sentence under the Insurrection Act for an unspecified crime was George Reynolds, 25, a labourer of County Cork. When he came up for trial at Mallow, his father-in-law, John Cahill, a shopkeeper and farmer of Castletownroche, pretty well wrecked any chances he might have had of a pardon by saying that he did not believe he was innocent, though he would agree to go surety for his future good conduct if he were released.[14] In the case of Daniel Neville, a 32-year-old blacksmith of Limerick, sentenced to fourteen years' transportation, the charge was clear enough: he had administered unlawful oaths; and, to make matters worse for him, the public prosecutor accused him, more precisely, of going through the villages of the barony in which he lived, 'swearing the people to a test or oath of a horrid description'.[15]

The so-called 'tithe war' of the early 1830s came, as we have seen, in the wake of the serious economic depression, with its attendant misery, of the years 1829 to 1831. These were, therefore, inevitably

---

[12] SPO Dublin, Prisoners' Petitions, nos. 1802–3 (26 Nov., 19 Dec. 1823) (my italics).
[13] Ibid., no. 2245 (24 May 1824).
[14] Ibid., no. 4146 (11 Mar. 1825).
[15] Ibid., no. 3033 (16 Mar. 1826).

years when Whiteboyism and Ribbonism flared up again to heights they had hardly ever reached in the years of comparatively muted protest in the 1820s. This new upsurge is reflected in the large number of cases of transportation for carrying firearms, administering oaths, and what is often vaguely called 'Whiteboy activity'. To cite some examples from 1831 and 1832. At the Castlebar assizes in March 1831, two labourers of County Mayo, Edmund Gildea (aged 40) and Patrick Mally (30), were given a life-sentence for 'unlawful oaths' — described in another record as 'illegal assembly'. Through their petitions for a mitigation of sentence we learn more precisely what these 'oaths' and 'assembly' were all about. Both claimed that they had been stopped on the road by a 'mob' of strangers who had compelled them with threats to go with them to attend a public meeting. Its purpose (according to Gildea) was 'to petition landlords for time to pay rent until the distressed season would pass over'. More explicitly, Mally describes the nature of the oath which was that 'they should all go to Westport next day, when the justices were meeting to petition them for a reduction of rents'. Both petitioners prayed for mitigation. Gildea's argument is of some interest, though its terms may not have been best chosen to dispose the court in his favour: if (he wrote) he were to be transported, his family of two boys and four girls 'in all probability will be compelled to resort to dishonest practices to procure a subsistence'. Having failed to move their judges, both men duly sailed to Sydney on the *Norfolk* in October 1831.[16]

Two cases of Whiteboyism — also leading to transportation for life — belong to the following year. One concerned Patrick Carey, a 30-year-old house carpenter of Killimore, in Co. Galway, who was sentenced as a Whiteboy at the Galway assizes in March 1832. Once more, the petition addressed to the authorities on his behalf throws more light on the actual nature of his crime. This was, it appears, to have demanded the 'increasing of hire-wages and decreasing of the rent of land'. Carey was extremely well supported. The petition presented in his favour was signed by half a dozen gentlemen and inhabitants of Killimore who, while deploring the excesses of the 'misguided peasantry', insisted on the prisoner's 'gentle character and peaceful non-violent disposition' and (more generally) on his 'irreproachable character' to date. The jury entered a recommendation for mercy and even the prosecutor added his name to the petition; but to no effect, and he sailed on the *Eliza* in May 1832.[17]

[16] Ibid., nos. 3567, 3590 (— 1831, 11 Apr. 1831).
[17] Ibid., no. 3634 (7 May 1832).

The other case was that of James Boland, a farm servant (or tenant farmer?), of the parish of Feakle, in County Clare. He, too, was sentenced to a similar term for 'Whiteboyism' at the Galway March assizes; but the offence committed was by no means the same as Carey's. He was accused of attacking the house of one Patrick Glynn, who lived ten miles out of Feakle. But his father, who petitioned against the sentence, maintained that his son was building a house for himself on a piece of land that belonged to him but had excited the jealousy of some of his neighbours. His innocence was further pleaded by a number of witnesses for the defence, including his landlord, who supported the father's story and described the prisoner as an 'honest, quiet, industrious young man', punctual in paying his rent. But again to no avail; and Boland sailed in the *Roslin Castle* in October.[18] They were not the only two Whiteboys to sail to Australia that year. On Carey's ship—the *Eliza*—there were twenty-five others sentenced as Whiteboys, besides ten convicted of 'unlawful oaths', four of carrying firearms, and one of riotous assembly; and on the *Roslin Castle* (on which far fewer protesters sailed) there was one other Whiteboy (also sentenced in Galway) and three who had been convicted of assaulting habitations.[19]

Following the prolonged lull of the middle and later 1830s, we come to the rural protesters of the 1840s. The types of crime for which they were transported now changed again. Whiteboyism (in name at least) now almost disappears; unlawful oaths and threatening letters continue as before; but now it is Ribbonism and, above all, assaults on habitations that come into their own. The *Egyptian*, which sailed from Dublin for Hobart in August 1840, had on board some thirty prisoners who had been sentenced for rural protest-crimes: some had been convicted of stealing or hiding arms, others of Ribbonism, or administering oaths or 'attempting to compel to quit'; but the most common crime of all was to have made an armed assault on a farm or other habitation. This was the case with nine men of Limerick, most of them farm labourers, who had been tried and convicted by the Limerick assizes in July of that year (and originally sentenced to death) for attacking two houses in the county. Three men—Patrick Murphy and Dennis and Owen Carrol, father and son—had assaulted the house of Patrick Kennedy and attempted

[18] SPO Dublin, Prisoners' Petitions, no. 3628 (28 Apr. 1832).
[19] Arch. NSW, 4/4165, 4163. An unusual case at this time was that of John (Richard) Hartnet, 54, a Catholic priest and schoolmaster, from Co. Limerick, sentenced for life at Clare assizes in Feb. 1832 for 'unlawful oaths'. He arrived on the *Java* in July 1833. (Ibid., 4/4164.)

to compel him to take an unlawful oath (what its purpose was we do not know). The other six—the brothers Madigan and Whelan, John Daly, and Patrick Roche—had been sentenced for 'taking arms and attacking the house of Mr. John Rice of Ballinverick, in Co. Limerick'. Most of them were married men, including Francis Whelen, at 23 one of the youngest, a carpenter of Kilmovee, near Kildimo; but both the Madigans, who were labourers from the village of Kilmulty—the one aged 23, the other 25—were unmarried; as was also Owen Carrol, 19 years old and the youngest of the nine.[20] On the next ship to sail from an Irish port—the *British Sovereign*, which reached Sydney in March 1841—there were several others who had been given a seven-year term for tendering unlawful oaths or assaulting habitations, and some (like Murphy and the Carrols whom we mentioned before) for a combination of the two. One such person was Patrick Keoghan, a 20-year-old labourer who lived with his widowed mother and seven younger brothers and sisters at Corbetstown, Co. Westmeath; he was also, it appears, a tenant of one John D'Arcy of that town. And it was in the neighbourhood of Corbetstown that he was alleged to have assaulted the house of Brian O'Hara Mayo and to have tendered him an unlawful oath. He was tried at the county assizes at Mullingar in July 1840 and transported for seven years.[21] Another case of assault involves rent collectors and landlords and is perhaps significant of the times. The brothers James and Joseph Dwyer, farm labourers of Co. Tipperary, were tried for manslaughter at assizes in Clonmel in March 1841 and sentenced to transportation, one for seven years and the other for ten. It appears from statements they made when they arrived in Tasmania that the victim was Timothy Kelly, a rent collector for their landlord, Mr. Hamilton. Kelly (they claimed) had already been paid but had omitted to hand over the money to Hamilton and asked for it again. In James Dwyer's words: 'He had received the rent once and applied for it again. We then beat him.'[22]

In the early 1840s, Ribbonism was probably as flourishing as it was at any other time; and, at this time, too, if not aggravated by murder, it carried the comparatively lenient penalty of transportation for seven years. Like Whiteboyism in the 1820s and 1830s, it had become a sort of catch-as-catch-can and had almost as many facets as the number of 'outrages' committed in its name. Basically, to be a Ribbonman meant to be a member of a secret society, but

---

[20] Tas. Arch., CON 33/3; Petitions 1840 (O'Farrell).
[21] Tas. Arch., CON 33/18.
[22] Ibid., CON 33/7; Petitions 1841 (O'Farrell).

what kind of society and what that society stood for is usually left to the imagination. On the same ship *Egyptian* that we mentioned above there were three men sentenced for Ribbonism. In no case is it at all clear what the offender had actually done, or if he was being sentenced for holding certain opinions what those opinions were. One of them, John Clarke, a 30-year-old farm labourer of Fermanagh, had been sentenced in Cavan for 'being a member of a secret society', and he himself (on arrival in Hobart) added the further information that 'papers had been found on [my] person by the police'. Another, Michael McGrath, a 56-year-old shoemaker of King's County, who had been convicted of 'Ribbonism' at assizes in Longford, added, in similar terms, that the police had found 'papers about me'. The third, Patrick McEntire, also a shoemaker, of Tullyvin, Co. Clare, was sentenced for 'being a member of a secret society'—to which someone in authority had added the phrase 'illegal conspiracy', while in his own words he later explained it equally enigmatically as 'Ribbonism—prosecuted by the Queen'.[23] Ribbonism might also (again like Whiteboyism) be combined with 'robbery'; as in the case of Francis McCanna, a roadmaker of Co. Longford who, having been sentenced for 'Ribbonism and robbery' at the Longford assizes in July 1842, explained on his arrival on the *North Briton* in the following April that he had stolen '£2 and a hat from Patrick Smith'.[24] So, in none of these cases are we left any the wiser as to what Ribbonism really was.

One prisoner, at least, Richard Jones a Dublin clerk, sentenced for 'being a member of a secret society' by a Dublin court in June 1840, helps us to get nearer to the truth. He had been convicted, he said on arrival in Hobart, of 'Ribbonism, or forming an illegal society for the purpose of protecting men of our own persuasion against the Orangemen'. And he added: 'I was imprisoned on a charge of murder, at first, of an Orangeman. No Bill was found. I was next charged with having broken out of gaol while confined on a charge of Ribbonism in the month of Aug. 1840.'[25] Eight months later, when Francis McCanna, the Longford roadmaker arrived on the *North Briton*, the authorities, in a long note appended to his record, also tried their hand at giving a more exact definition. It runs as follows:

Ribbon societies are illegal combinations, sworn to obey their chiefs to take the arms of protestants and turn them out of the country. Country delegates

[23] Tas. Arch., CON 33/3; Petitions 1840 (O'Farrell).
[24] Tas. Arch., CON 33/37.
[25] Ibid., CON 33/16.

travel all over Ireland giving the ribbon men new signs of making appointments to meet at certain times. They also travel through England and Scotland . . .[26]

After this case, Ribbonism appears, like Whiteboyism, to phase out as a transportable offence; and McCanna seems to have been the last Irishman to have been transported for what the judicial records most often describe as 'Ribbon activity'.

Meanwhile, assaulting habitations and writing threatening letters continued without respite. In the 1840s, too, when prisoners were required to answer questions about their offence on arrival in Tasmania, we can sometimes read between the lines and see what those threatening letters were about. Once more, to cite a few examples. Abraham Dekeliah, a 22-year-old schoolmaster and clerk of Queen's County, was transported from Tipperary for writing a threatening letter; he explained, on arrival in Hobart on the *Richard Webb* in March 1842, that it was addressed to a certain Duncan, a schoolmaster, who had defrauded him of his wages.[27] A year later, Denis Reilly, who arrived on the *Orator* in November 1843, explained that the threatening letter he had been convicted of posting in Co. Cavan had been addressed to Oman Holding, warning him 'that if he did not quit the land, I would provide his coffin'.[28] Similarly, John Healy posted a letter in Tipperary in the summer of 1844 warning a man 'to leave the place or he would kill him';[29] and on board the *Ratcliffe*, arriving in August 1845, there were three cases—from Westmeath, Wicklow, and Carlow—of smallholders who had been sentenced for writing threatening letters to persons they believed to be trespassing on their land; and one man—Lawrence Kelly, a labourer of Kilkenny—had written a threatening note to his landlady, Mrs. Fitzgerald.[30] One note that was particularly pointed was the 'threatening notice' served on a Mrs. Bourke by Thomas Devine, a stonemason of Co. Cavan, to the effect that 'if she did not reduce her Rent, the Molly McGuire boys would visit her; they never failed to do their duty'.[31] And on the same ship—the *Samuel Boddington* (arriving in Hobart in January 1846)—there was Patrick Kennedy, a farm labourer of Tipperary, who appears to have been engaged in a wages dispute, as he was sentenced in King's County in July 1845 for threatening to shoot Mr. Matewell 'if he did not leave his

---

[26] Ibid., CON 14/20. The note continues: 'The members of the Society choose their delegates by a polling. They assemble once every quarter. The older delegates appoint a chairman. He has the general superintendence of the delegates. Parish masters . . . are Guardians who have the power to dismiss the delegates . . .'

[27] Ibid., CON 33/18.   [28] Ibid., CON 33/47.   [29] Ibid., CON 33/65.
[30] Ibid., CON 33/67.   [31] Ibid., CON 33/75.

employment'.[32] And finally—and to close this chapter with a case of a more general relevance—towards the end of a turbulent decade there was Philip O'Reilly, a shopkeeper of Roscommon, who arrived on the *Blenheim* in February 1849 having been sentenced at Leitrim for publishing a threatening letter, or (to use his own phrase) for 'writing a seditious letter relative to bad landlords'.[33]

[32] Tas. Arch., CON 33/75.
[33] Ibid., CON 33/93.

3. English Rural Protesters

ENGLISH rural protest of the transportation period lacked the continuity of the Irish. In Ireland, as we have seen, protest took the form of a prolonged land-war extending over almost forty years, interspersed with longer or shorter periods of *détente*. In England and Wales, on the other hand, though there was a continuity of tension in the village (as instanced by the frequent waves of poaching and arson), there was no single movement but several, and these can be easily identified; and whereas in Ireland Carding, Whiteboyism, Ribbonism, and other manifestations of the kind can scarcely be told apart and pass almost imperceptibly from one to the other, in Britain there is a clear separation between the East Anglian riots of 1816, the 'Swing' riots of 1830, between Tolpuddle and Rebecca and the episode known as the 'Battle in Bossenden Wood'. It is with the transported protesters emerging from these movements and episodes that we are concerned in the present chapter. ('Marginal' protesters like poachers and arsonists will be given a chapter of their own.)

The East Anglian riots, which were centred on Ely, Littleport, and Downham Market, were the first significant outbreak of rural violence to occur in England after the Napoleonic Wars; they were concerned with wages, threshing machines, and the price of bread. A. J. Peacock, the historian of the movement, tells us that of eighty persons committed for trial at the special assizes at Ely in May 1816, twenty-four were sentenced to death; and of these five were hanged and the rest were re-cast for transportation.[1] In fact, with the usual vicissitudes separating design from realization, only seven sailed on the *Sir William Bensley* which arrived in Sydney on 10 March 1817.[2] They were youngish men with an average age of 31; they were all Cambridgeshire labourers and had all been convicted of either 'larceny in a dwelling-house' or 'robbery on the person', but had been given varying terms of transportation. One of the 'larcenists', Aaron Chevell, aged 29 and sometimes described as a tailor, played a leading part in the riot at Littleport on 22 May. In some of the operations of that day he seems to have served as a cashier, collecting

---

[1] A. J. Peacock, *Bread or Blood*, pp. 49, 127, 177.
[2] Arch. NSW, 4/4005, pp. 284–5; HO 27/12.

and counting the money that the crowds levied on shopkeepers, publicans, and farmers. One victim, Stephen Wiles, a grocer, was relieved of £8; another, Henry Tansley, Chevell's landlord, described him as 'the head of the Mob'; and at the end of the day he was seen counting out the money collected before his associates; it amounted (according to a rioter turned informer) to £43. 4s. Two other leaders at Littleport were the brothers John and Joseph Easy. John Easy, aged 28, is said to have knocked down a shopkeeper, John Mobbs, and robbed him of £3 and 'one loaf of bread worth 1s.'. The elder brother, Joseph, aged 35 and known as 'Little' (he was only 5 ft. tall), played the more prominent role of the two and received a life sentence where John was given only seven years. It was Joseph, it appears, who, in the march into Littleport, had been the first to 'blow the Horn' as a signal of the rioters' approach. He had further been accused (with Richard Jessop, also transported for life) of knocking down Joseph Dewey, a retired farmer of more than 70 years old, of sending Mrs. Dewey off to fetch money while her husband was held prisoner, and of helping to strip the house of its valuables. Later, he went on to lead the crowd that ransacked the house of Mrs. Waddelow, whose grandson, Henry Martin, a prosperous farmer and leading citizen, was one of the main targets of the crowd's hostility.[3] Another prisoner who played a conspicuous role at Ely and Littleport was Richard Rutter, a 40-year-old labourer, who owned two cows and enough property (it was said) to exclude him from receiving poor relief. Yet he told the Revd. Mr. Law, a Littleport magistrate, after most of the rioters had left the town, that 'it was nothing to him [that many of the Littleport people had gone home], he was starved and he would be damned if he would not be fed'. From Littleport, where he had led a crowd to James Horseley's house and demanded £5, he went on to the White Hart Inn in the market square at Ely and added to the popular demand for flour at 2s. 6d. and a 2s. daily wage a demand for beer at 2d. a pint. He was one of the comparatively lucky ones who was transported for fourteen years.[4]

The labourers' movement that followed in the southern counties in 1830 was a far more protracted affair, raising a far wider range of issues; more than thirty counties were involved in the revolt and more than 480 people—the largest single group in the history of transportation—were sent into exile in Australia—some to New South Wales, others (the larger number) to Tasmania. Among those

[3] Peacock, pp. 95-7, 103-4.
[4] Ibid., pp. 63-4, 102.

transported to Sydney from Hampshire were two brothers: Joseph and Robert Mason, of whom Joseph, the elder, was 31 at the time of their trial and Robert 24. They were smallholders and market gardeners at Bullington, owning a cow and three to four acres of land; and, on occasion, to make ends meet, they worked for the farmers as well. (Robert is also described as a schoolmaster, but this may be due to the role he filled on the passage to Australia.) They had Radical opinions, read Cobbett's *Register*, and had taken part in petitions for reform. One of these was a petition drawn up by the Masons and others at the Swan Inn, Sutton Scotney, in October 1830, was signed by 177 villagers of the 'working and labouring classes' and taken by Joseph Mason on foot to the King at Brighton.

So when the riots swept into Hampshire, as they did in mid-November, and involved the villages of East Stratton, Barton Stacey, and Micheldever—all close neighbours of Bullington—it was inevitable that the Masons should become implicated, though it was unlikely that they had had anything to do with 'demanding money' on behalf of the machine-breakers at East Stratton for which they were charged and sentenced by the Special Commission at Winchester. Robert Mason is reported to have told the court:

> If the learned Counsel, who had so painted my conduct to you, was present at that place and wore a smock frock instead of a gown, and a straw hat instead of a wig, he would be standing in the dock instead of being seated where he is . . .

And he maintained his Radical stance until he sailed for Australia, at least; as we know from the letters he wrote from his convict ship, the *Eleanor*, at Portsmouth. In these he protested that his opinions remained unchanged and urged his fellow parishioners, should a reformed Parliament or a 'revolution' come about, to press for the release of the transported convicts.[5]

One of these, a neighbour of the Masons at Bullington and a ship-mate on the journey to Australia, was John Silcock, a 27-year-old ploughman, who had also signed the Radical petition at Sutton Scotney in October and had, like them, been convicted of 'machine-breaking' at Winchester in December 1830.[6] Another Hampshire man who, like the Masons, held a rank above that of a common labourer, was John Boyes, a 50-year-old farmer of Owslebury, near Winchester. He and his brother William were known to hold strong views about rents and tithes and the responsibility of farmers for the

---

[5] J. L. and B. Hammond, *The Village Labourer*, ii, 86–8; Hobsbawm and Rudé, *Captain Swing*, pp. 265–6.
[6] Arch. NSW, 4/4016.

welfare of their labourers. Such opinions got them both into trouble in November 1830. John Boyes was accused of 'demanding money with menaces' (or, according to his own account, of 'conspiring to raise wages') and was sentenced by the Special Commission to be transported for seven years; he left behind him at Owslebury a wife, Faith, and ten children. William was more fortunate. He was charged twice but acquitted both times: the first time when tried with his brother at Winchester and the second time at assizes where with two fellow farmers he was charged with having conspired to compel landlords and tithe-owners to reduce tithes and rents in order that the labourers' wages might be raised.[7] Yet the accusation was plausible enough: it was common at the time, no less in Hampshire than in Sussex or Wiltshire or East Anglia, for farmers and labourers to combine to raise wages at the expense of the landlord's rent and the parson's tithe.[8]

With Hampshire the most rebellious counties of the 'Swing' movement were Wiltshire and Berkshire. In Wiltshire, where more threshing machines were destroyed than anywhere else, the charge of machine-breaking was often accompanied by one of 'robbery'. This was the case with six prisoners tried for machine-breaking in the village of West Grinstead, an incident that led to the transportation of Thomas Light, a 48-year-old ploughman, married with four children. Light was remarkably unfortunate; for when the crowd demanded that the farmer whose machine had been destroyed should pay the usual guinea for the privilege, Light, who was the farmer's tenant, drew attention to himself by offering to pay the guinea on condition it should be deducted from the reant![9] Another incident from Wiltshire related by the Hammonds concerns Isaac Looker, a well-to-do farmer, and his son Edward. Isaac Looker was tried by the Commission at Salisbury, charged with having sent a threatening letter to a fellow farmer, John Rowland of Haxford Farm, couched in the conventional blood-curdling and illiterate style: 'If you goes to sware against or a man in prison, you have here farm burned down to the ground, and thy bluddy head chopt off.' Isaac was sentenced to transportation for life; but he was rescued by his 18-year-old son who swore that he was in the habit of writing such letters and (unknown to his father) had written this one in order to help a cousin who was in jail for machine-breaking. So Isaac was pardoned and Edward was sent to Tasmania for seven

---

[7] Hobsbawm and Rudé, p. 244.
[8] Ibid., pp. 232–4.
[9] Hammonds, p. 97.

years in his place. In Edward's own words, when asked the nature of his offence on arrival in Hobart: 'Sending a threatening letter. My father was convicted for life for the same offence, but was afterwards discharged on my avowing myself the author.'[10] Other Wiltshire machine-breakers and 'robbers' were Thomas Abery, a bricklayer of Tisbury, aged 32 and married to Mary, a widow with two children; Charles Pizzie, 25, a ploughman of Great Bedwyn; and William Taylor, 49, a top sawyer from Islington (but presently of Ramsbury), who had a wife and eight children. Abery was unemployed at the time, but he had recently worked for Lord Arundel, a benevolent employer, for the unusually high wage for that time of 16s. a week. When Abery was awaiting trial for machine-breaking at Salisbury in December, Lord Arundel wrote a letter to *The Times* in which he described him as a most industrious worker who, when Salisbury Cathedral was being repaired, allowed himself to be hauled up to the top in a basket.[11] Pizzie and Taylor were both convicted for 'demanding money in the riots' (a sovereign in the case of Taylor) and sailed for Tasmania on the *Proteus* in April 1831. Pizzie left his wife Sarah at Great Bedwyn; also his mother (another Sarah), five sisters and three brothers, all labourers like himself. Taylor, as we saw, had a larger family of his own; his wife Elizabeth stayed on at Ramsbury, together with six sons and a daughter, Sarah, who was married to William Blackstone, a cooper, of the same place.[12]

In Berkshire, another major centre of machine-breaking, the most remarkable episode was that in which the labourers of Kintbury, near Hungerford, went round from farm to farm breaking machines and demanding money for services rendered. Among their leaders were two village craftsmen, William Oakley, a wheelwright and carpenter (aged 24), and Francis Norris, a bricklayer (41), the one born in Bristol and the other at Marsh Benham, a Berkshire village. At one stage of their operations, the Kintbury men smashed the machinery and wrought iron at Richard Gibbons's iron foundry at Hungerford, joined forces with the local labourers and went with them to meet the magistrates at Hungerford Town Hall. The Hungerford men were soon persuaded, once promises had been made to raise wages, to go home peacefully. But the Kintbury men refused and Oakley addressed the magistrates on their behalf in the following terms:

You have not such damned flats to deal with as you had before. We will

[10] Ibid., pp. 98–9; Tas. Arch., CON 37/6, 14/36.   [11] *The Times*, 3 Dec. 1830.
[12] Tas. Arch., CON 14/3.

have 2s. a day till Ladyday and half a crown afterwards for labourers and
3s. 6d. for tradesmen, and as we are here, we will have £5 before we go out
of the place or be damned if we don't smash it . . .

By this time the Kintbury labourers had collected a considerable
sum of money (including their £5 takings at Hungerford Town Hall).
Their usual fee for smashing a threshing machine was £2 (or twice
that in Wiltshire) but sometimes it was more: Lord Craven, for
example, at Hampstead Lodge, was made to pay £10, while others
(among the wealthier farmers) paid £3 or £5. So the labourers needed
a treasurer and the man they chose was Francis Norris, who, at the
time of his arrest, was found in possession of £100 in contributions
and a couple of receipts. Norris was sentenced to transportation for
life, while Oakley was one of eleven not merely capitally convicted
(like 226 others) but actually 'left for execution'. But he was saved
by a last-minute reprieve and, like Norris, given a life sentence. They
sailed on different ships: Norris on *Eliza II* to Tasmania and Oakley
on the *Eleanor* to New South Wales.[13]

There also sailed on the *Eliza* five Essex men who had been convicted of machine-breaking at the small town of Walton-le-Soken.
They had been involved in breaking a couple of machines at Samuel
Wilson's farm on 8 December. The leader of the group, and its
youngest member, was George Davey, a 20-year-old ploughman
from Kirby, in Essex. His companions included three brothers:
James, Thomas, and John Grant, aged respectively 31, 29, and 25,
all three labourers and ploughmen of Kirby like himself. All three
were married: James with a wife and child, whom he left with
relations at Clacton; while Thomas and John both left wives (and
Thomas five children as well) on the parish at Kirby. The oldest man
in the group was William Jeffries, 45, a blacksmith and labourer of
Little Clacton (blacksmiths were in great demand among machine-
breakers) who also left a wife on the parish. All five were sentenced
at the Essex special assizes in December; George Davey and James
and Thomas Grant to fourteen years and John Grant and William
Jeffries to seven. They arrived in Hobart together on the *Eliza* in
May 1831.[14]

Among other interesting cases to emerge from the 'Swing' movement was that of Henry Williams, 21, a journeyman tailor and
'ranting' preacher of Whitney, in Herefordshire. In mid-November,
as the riots swept westwards, he wrote an anonymous letter to John

[13] Hobsbawm and Rudé, pp. 138–9, 261.
[14] Tas. Arch., CON 37/6, 14/36.

Monkhouse, a wealthy farmer of Whitney, which ran in part as follows:

> Remember in Kent that have set ('with fire') all that would not submit and you we will serve the same . . . so pull down your Thrashing Maschine or els Bread or Fire without delay. For we are 5 thousand men and will not be stopt.

Williams was tried at Hereford Epiphany sessions in January and transported for fourteen years; he arrived in Sydney on *Surrey I* in November 1831.[15] A shipmate of Williams's on the *Surrey* was another young writer of incendiary tracts. He was Thomas Cook, a 19-year-old attorney's clerk, who, it appears, had been working for four years in a solicitor's office at Shrewsbury when he was persuaded by a companion, 'more for the sake of sport', to send an anonymous letter, signed 'Captain Swing', to an auctioneer (or local landowner, according to one account). Whatever the letter's purpose, the assizes judge who heard the case took the matter seriously enough and sentenced Cook to fourteen years' transportation; his companion escaped comparatively lightly with four years in jail.[16] And, finally, one of only two women to be transported for 'Swing' activities was Elizabeth Parker, a 24-year-old labourer of Tetbury, in Gloucestershire, also said to have been a 'common prostitute' in her spare time. Hers was a strange case, as she was first sentenced at Gloucester Epiphany sessions in January 1831 for taking part in a machine-breaking operation at Bevestone in the previous November; and then (having served only four months of her term in jail), she was recommitted and tried for larceny at the Summer assizes in 1832. So, for this combination of crime and protest, she was sent to Tasmania for life; she arrived on the *Charlotte* in January 1833.[17]

There is a world of difference between the movement of the 'Swing' labourers and their still archaic forms of protest and the relative 'modernity' of that of the labourers of Dorset in 1833–4. Although premature in its attempt to organize agricultural workers, it proved to be an important landmark in the history of trade-unionism; it had, moreover, the distinction of being the only wage-earners' movement leading to transportation that was not attended by physical violence of any kind. Their leader, and the only one of the six to be sent to Tasmania, was George Loveless. Loveless was born in 1797 at Tolpuddle, near Dorchester, where he worked as a ploughman,

---

[15] Hobsbawm and Rudé, p. 131; Arch. NSW, 4/4016, 4267.
[16] *The Exile's Lamentations; or Biographical Sketch of Thomas Cook* . . . (Sydney, 1841) (I am indebted to Mr. John Earnshaw, of Lindfield, NSW, for this reference). Arch. NSW, 4/4016.
[17] Tas. Arch., CON 40/7, p. 48.

married and had three children; he was also respected, both in Tolpuddle and in neighbouring villages, as a community leader and Wesleyan preacher. It is evident from his writings and activities that he had read Robert Owen and was familiar with the efforts then being made to establish trades unions in London, Birmingham, and other centres. According to his own account of the Tolpuddle affair—*The Victims of Whiggery*—written after his return from Australia, he played no part in the agrarian disturbances of 1830, though they affected Dorset; but in the next two years he represented the Dorchester agricultural labourers in discussions with the farmers, who agreed to raise wages to 10s. a week. At Tolpuddle, however, farmers refused to pay more than 9s. and later reduced wages to 8s. and 7s. and threatened to reduce them to 6s. So, advised by Loveless and two delegates from London, the men of Tolpuddle in October 1833 formed a Friendly Society of Agricultural Labourers, which charged an entrance fee of 1s. and a subscription of 1d. a week. Since 1824 trades unions had no longer been illegal in England, but witnesses were found to testify that Loveless and his associates had bound their members by secret ('unlawful') oaths, a felony under an Act of 1797; and for this offence the labourers' six leaders— George Loveless, his brother James, their brother-in-law Thomas Standfield, their nephew John Standfield, James Hammett, and James Brine—were found guilty at the Dorchester assizes in March 1834 and transported for seven years. James Loveless, the two Standfields, Hammett, and Brine sailed on the *Surrey* to Sydney, where they arrived in August 1834; while George Loveless, separated from his comrades, arrived in Tasmania on the *William Metcalfe* in September, leaving his wife Elizabeth and their three children at Tolpuddle.[18]

The next incident in England's rural history—one seldom recorded by historians—was the strange encounter in Bossenden Wood in Kent, in which forty or fifty armed villagers from Boughton-under-Blean, near Canterbury, fought a pitched battle with the military in support of their leader, John Nicholl Thom, whom they knew as Sir William Courtenay and acknowledged as their Saviour. So, on the surface, it was an old-style millenarial movement of Kentish peasants more suited to the Middle Ages than to the Age of Chartism; but there was more to it than that, as several of Thom's followers were unemployed labourers whom he had promised to save not only from all mortal ills but from the New Poor Law in particular. The battle in Bossenden Wood took place on 31 May 1838 near Boughton

    18 *ABD*, ii, 132–3; Tas. Arch., CON 23/2, 18/22.

Hill. It lasted only a few minutes, but Thom (alias Courtenay) and eight of his followers were killed (or died later of wounds), also an army officer and a constable. Fourteen of the survivors were brought to trial and nine (out of an original eighteen) were charged with murder. Six were sent to prison for a year and three, having at first been capitally convicted, were transported to Australia. Thom's followers were drawn from a typical Kentish village community of the time, a time of acute economic depression. We know something about its complexion from a list drawn up by the vicar of Herne Hill of the forty-five persons believed to have been the spurious Courtenay's most devoted disciples. There were thirty labourers among them, about half of them unemployed or 'distressed'; five jobbing craftsmen; three petty tradesmen; a bailiff; a freeholder, with a cottage and four acres; and five small farmers and farmers' sons, owning seven to twenty acres of land. On the whole, they were men of middling years but with a wide range between old and young: the oldest (the twenty-acre farmer) was 62 and the youngest 17; the average age was 37, and over two in three were married. Their state of literacy was low (well below the Kentish average, if we may trust the first official return published in the following year[19]): of thirty-seven whose literacy is noted, three could read and write, eighteen could only read and sixteen could do neither. We are, of course, more particularly concerned with the three men sent to Australia. The oldest, William Wills, frequently appears in accounts as Courtenay's right-hand man and standard-bearer, and it was at his cottage, near Fairbrook, that the master and his disciples met and planned 'the fatal blow'. He was 47 years old, the son of a small farmer and had been a small farmer himself until he was reduced to distress (so runs the vicar's account) by 'dissolute and drunken habits'. He was now a ploughman, living with his wife Lucy and their two children at Boughton-under-Blean. The vicar further describes him as being 'literate, can read and write, and leader of the Church singers and played the flute'. (He was carrying his flute, according to a witness, on the day of the 'battle'.) The youngest was Thomas Mears, 30 and unmarried, also one of Courtenay's close lieutenants. On the vicar's list he appears as a freeholder with a cottage and four acres of land; whereas his indent records him, more humbly, as a farm labourer of Herne Hill (though he may well have been both). The third man, another intimate of Courtenay's, was William Price, aged 35, illiterate, married with a child, and a farm

---

[19] Cited by Hobsbawm and Rudé, p. 64. Male illiteracy for Kent is here given as only 29 per cent.

labourer and hop-grower of Boughton. Price was given a ten-year term where the others were transported for life. They sailed together on the *Pyramus* (carrying ten men and 160 boys) and arrived in Hobart in March 1839.[20]

The Rebecca riots in Wales, which followed soon after, were a far more destructive and protracted affair: they spread over three counties, led to widespread demolition of turnpikes and tollgates and lasted, with intermissions, between January 1839 and the late summer of 1843. Yet the yield in terms of arrests and convictions was remarkably small. Sixty prisoners, it is true, were taken after the daylight assault on the Carmarthen workhouse in June 1843, but only six were convicted and sentenced to short terms in prison. The nocturnal raids on tollgates, which were the essence of Rebecca's activities, led to a further half-dozen convictions by assizes in Glamorgan and Carmarthen; and these all arose from the last phase of the riots when they were becoming more 'professional', violent, and indiscriminate and the farmers, who had played a leading part up to now, were beginning to have second thoughts and leave the movement—where they did not actually help to repress it—to the labourers and village poor. From among these, five men were sentenced to transportation; and of these the two that had won the greatest notoriety as strong-arm men were David Davies (known in Welsh as Dai'r Cantwr, or David the Singer) and John Jones (known as Shoni Sgubor Fawr, Johnny of the Big Barn). They had both been involved in a number of nocturnal raids but were specifically charged at the Carmarthen special assizes of December 1843 with demolishing turnpike gates and shooting with intent to do bodily harm. David Davies, who explained that his Welsh name 'Dai'r Cantwr' arose from his earlier days as a cantor when (as he said) he 'taught them to sing at Church', was 30 years old at the time of his trial, unmarried, a regular chapel-goer and a labourer in Glamorgan. He claimed, on arrival in Hobart, that he had been one of a party of 190 men who had demolished a turnpike gate in Carmarthenshire, known as 'Spudders Bridge'. He was transported for twenty years and left a mother, two brothers, and five sisters in his native town. John Jones was 33, a shaft-sinker at Merthyr Tydfil, in Glamorgan; he was married and had a brother, Solomon, in America. He explained his offence as having been to riot and to fire at Walter Reece at Pontyberem (which he described as 'a Rebecca affair'); and for this he was transported for life. The other three

[20] Kent Arch. Office, U951 C37/53 and 40; HO 27/55; Tas. Arch., CON 31/36; Rogers, *Battle in Bossenden Wood*, esp. pp. 92–146.

prisoners to be sent to Australia were tried together at the Glamorgan special assizes in October and were charged with demolishing turnpike gates and adjoining houses at Pontarddulais on 6 September 1843. The apparent leader, John Jones, was a 25-year-old labourer, the son of a farmer of Llan-non, in Carmarthen, unmarried and living with his parents and two brothers and four sisters. Jones was at one time considered a possible candidate for the role of 'Rebecca'[21] and received a twenty-year sentence. His two companions, John Hugh (aged 26) and David Jones (21) were let off more lightly with seven. Hugh had a wife, Susannah, and a child, also two brothers and five sisters. David Jones, the youngest of the five, was also a ploughman and labourer, who lived at home with his mother, Letitia, a brother, Thomas, and two sisters, Mary and Margaret. These three, and also Davies (Dai'r Cantwr) sailed to Tasmania on the *London*, arriving in Hobart in January 1844. John Jones (alias Shoni), who had received a life-sentence, was sent on a more circuitous voyage: he travelled on the *Blundell* to Norfolk Island, and from there (nearly three years later) on the *Pestongee Bomanjee* to Tasmania, where he eventually disembarked at Maria Island on 8 April 1847.[22]

All the movements of protest to which reference has been made in this chapter (with the possible exception of Tolpuddle) have, however distinctive in other respects, one thing in common: that they marked in England and Wales (but not yet in the Highlands of Scotland) a final desperate upsurge of the old village community against the dissolution of old social ties and the new values that capitalist commercialism brought in its train. The next struggle in the village would be of a different order. What became known as the 'Revolt of the Field' (of which the Tolpuddle episode had given a foretaste) was the assertion of the claim of the labouring part of that community to organize in defence of its own particular rights. For the villagers this belonged essentially to the period after transportation; for the urban and manufacturing workers, as the next chapter will show, it was already—though not quite in its modern form—well under way.

[21] David Williams, *The Rebecca Riots*, pp. 185–293.
[22] Tas. Arch., CON 14/281, 33/56, 33/78; HO 27/69.

4. Industrial Protesters

Up to the mid-nineteenth century at least, the most characteristic form of workers' bargaining or industrial action was to destroy the employer's property—generally his machinery, but it might be his house or (to quote the legal jargon) cloth 'in the loom' or goods 'in the process of manufacture'. This—to repeat an often-quoted phrase—is what Eric Hobsbawm has called 'collective bargaining by riot'; and this is precisely the offence that brought many British industrial protesters to exile in Australia.

Machine-breaking was not the only form that this kind of 'collective bargaining' took; but, until the end of the 1820s at least, it was by far the most common; and of all the machine-breaking movements of the century by far the best known, though by no means the most extensive or the most effective,[1] was that associated with the name of Ned Ludd, which broke out in Regency England in the hosiery- and textile-manufacturing districts of the Midlands and North. Yet though Luddism and machine-breaking have often (though quite wrongly) been used as almost synonymous terms, Luddism, like other movements of its kind, was not confined to the single activity of destroying machines: it was attended, perhaps inevitably, by other activities as well, such as arson, food riots, assaults, oath-taking, 'robbery', 'larceny', forcible extortion of money (remember the farm-workers of 1830), and sundry types of riot. The main phase of Luddism (from February 1811 to summer 1812) ended in a series of trials at assizes and special commission before which many hundreds of persons were charged with a wide variety of offences ranging over all these activities and others besides. The main trials were held at Nottingham and Derby (March 1812), Chester (May 1812), Lancaster (May–June 1812), and York (January 1813). Seventeen of those convicted at Nottingham were sentenced to transportation, eight at Chester, seventeen at Lancaster, and seven at York. Altogether, it would appear that apart from thirty who were hanged, about sixty persons associated with the Luddite movement were convicted and eventually sentenced by half a dozen courts to transportation to Australia for varying terms. Of these, a dozen or more were sentenced for purely criminal

---

[1] See Hobsbawm and Rudé, *Captain Swing*, pp. 298–9.

activities like robbery and larceny (without qualification) and have, therefore, though they sailed on 'Luddite' ships, been omitted from our count; and another ten or twelve (including six Radicals sentenced at York for administering illegal oaths) were, for one reason or another, not put aboard the ships. This leaves a total of thirty-seven presumed Luddites who came to Australia following the 'Luddite' trials of 1812 and 1813. Five of these arrived in Hobart on the *Indefatigable* in October 1812, and thirty-two were evenly distributed between the *Fortune* and the *Earl Spencer*, which arrived in Sydney in June and October 1813.[2] Among them only a dozen had been sentenced for breaking looms and frames and other machines, and the rest for food-rioting, extorting money, or tendering or taking oaths.

Of the machine-breakers, six were young lads who had been convicted at Nottingham assizes of smashing stocking-frames at Sutton's at Ashfield, near Nottingham. The three oldest were 22 and the two youngest 16; their average age was 19. One of them, Gervase Marshall, an 18-year-old hosier of Nottingham—and the only one whose occupation is stated—admitted his guilt, told the court that he was contrite, and was transported for seven years. Another machine-breaker was John Heywood, aged 20, a Cheshire cotton-spinner, who was given a fourteen-year sentence for destroying a machine at Messrs. Sidebotham's factory near Chester; and the oldest prisoner to arrive, James Crossland, aged 54, a shoemaker born in York, was convicted of smashing tools and threatening the life of Robert Thomily, a cotton manufacturer at Entwistle, in Cheshire. Those extorting money included John Henschall and Richard Lowndes of Cheshire, the first a weaver and the second a shoemaker. Both men had been convicted at the special assizes at Chester of riot and extorting 'several sums of money' with violence at the factory of Pownell Fee and Styall; they sailed together on the *Earl Spencer* to Sydney. Others had been sentenced at the Chester assizes for extorting money—a mere 7s. in this case—from John Parker at Etchell, near Stockport. They included Collin Linden, aged 16 (though one account gives 46!), a cotton-weaver from County Down; and William Thompson, a 25-year-old weaver from Cheshire. The food-rioters were mainly convicted of stealing flour.

[2] HO 27/8; Tas. Arch., CON 13/12, 31/13, 18, 29, 34; Arch. NSW, 4/4004; J. L. and B. Hammond, *The Skilled Labourer* (London, 1936), pp. 268–9, 323–32. These calculations do not claim to be strictly accurate. The reader will appreciate the difficulty of exactly pinpointing each Luddite convict at a time when the nature of the crime committed did not yet appear on the prisoner's indent (see Introduction).

There was James Radcliff, a 24-year-old Lancaster hatter, sentenced at Chester for rioting at Joseph Clay's cotton mill, where 1,000 bushels of flour were either stolen or destroyed; there was Edward Redfern, a 30-year-old labourer, transported for seven years (this was the current penalty for the offence) for stealing and destroying about 1,000 bushels of flour and meal in the granary of the Huddersfield Canal Company at Staley; and William Greenhaugh, a 49-year-old Cheshire weaver who, having first been acquitted of destroying Robert Thomily's cotton machinery at Entwistle, went down on a second charge of stealing flour from Alice Berry in the same town.

Finally, there were the oath-givers. They included Thomas Holden, aged 21, a Bolton weaver, and Thomas Whittaker, a 44-year-old joiner, born in Lancashire but convicted in Cheshire; they were both transported for seven years for administering unlawful oaths, Holden sailing on the *Fortune* and Whittaker on the *Earl Spencer*. Holden, while waiting on the *Portland* in Langstone Harbour for his ship to sail, wrote several letters to his wife and his parents at Bolton, describing his journey from Lancaster jail ('Eight days and nights without having my cloath of my back'), inquiring after the safety of his precious looms, requesting money and paper, depicting his close confinement and meagre rations, and hoping that his wife would be willing and able to join him when the occasion arose. He fell sick from yellow jaundice and was transferred to the *Fortune* about three weeks before she sailed for Sydney on 12 December 1812. While we know more of Holden's private life owing to the survival of his family correspondence, in Whittaker's case we know more of the precise nature of his offence; for (he tells us) he was accused of administering the oath to '18 to 20 men in order to destroy steam-looms'. We are also told (in a Home Office report) that he was 'a man of superior ability and education'; so it comes as no great surprise that the New South Wales census should record him fifteen years later as teaching mathematics at Richard Cooper's establishment in George Street, Sydney.[3]

Industrial machine-breaking, after minor flurries in 1813–15, revived briefly in 1817 and again, on a larger scale, in 1826 and only finally collapsed as a systematic and organized means of settling accounts with employers around 1831. In 1817, there was a renewal of frame-breaking in the hosiery trade in Leicestershire, notably at J. Heathcoat's lace factory at Loughborough. For taking part in the Loughborough outbreak five men were transported for life to New

[3] HO 27/8, 42/123; Hammonds, pp. 323–32; Lancs. RO, BDX/140/7; ML, Census of 1828 (transcript).

South Wales, one arriving on the *Larkins* (in November 1817) and four on *Ocean II* (January 1818). They were all stocking-weavers or framework knitters in their twenties or thirties, who had been convicted of assaulting a watchman, the charge being, in some cases, supplemented by one of 'burglary' or 'receiving stolen goods'. The youngest of them was James Watson, a 21-year-old stocking-weaver of Basford, Notts.; and the oldest (and the only one to come on the *Larkins*) was John Slater, 37, a framework knitter from Nottingham. There were also two Leicester men among them: John Culley (35) and Charles Hadden (32), both described as stocking-makers and both from Hinckley, Leics.[4] The larger outbreak was in 1826, when extensive riots occurred in the Lancashire cotton-towns and in the Yorkshire woollen-manufacturing centres of Huddersfield and Bradford. There were a number of machine-breakers sentenced at the York summer assizes in July 1826; but none of these were put on convict-ships for Hobart or Sydney. Many more were tried and sentenced for machine-breaking, demolishing looms, and simple riot at the summer assizes at Lancaster and Manchester that year. Sixty-six persons—including six women—appeared for trial; half of them were sent to prison for three to eighteen months and ten were capitally convicted and of these eight were eventually transported with a life-sentence to New South Wales. They sailed on three ships—the *Guildford*, *Manlius*, and *Harmony*—arriving in Sydney respectively in July, August, and September 1827. Six of the eight were men and two (unusual for such an offence) were women. The machinery destroyed must have included machinery used for farming, as all but one of the men are described as farmer's men (one combining farming with weaving and another with quarrying). The exception was Joseph Clayton, a 30-year-old wheelwright from Rochdale, who, with two other *Manlius*-men, was given a life-sentence at Manchester. But neither in this case nor in that of the other men transported do we know the exact nature of the offence: 'rioting' is the only indication given. It is only in the case of the two women that the Criminal Register in London gives us a more precise description. Ann Entwistle, a Lancashire woman, 46, married with three children and only 4 ft. 3 in. in height, is described as a laundress and weaver; and her offence (according to the Home Office record) was to have broken into a factory and demolished machinery, for which she was sentenced to death (and later reprieved and commuted) by the summer assizes at Lancaster. The other woman was Mary Hindle, aged 28, who was convicted of the same

---

[4] HO 27/14, 42/168-9; Arch. NSW, 4/4005, 3497, 3078 (pp. 307-8).

offence and sailed with Ann Entwistle on the *Harmony* in May 1827.[5]

The next—and final—wave of industrial machine-breaking began towards the end of 1829. In Suffolk, Thomas Fobister was sentenced to seven-years' transportation at assizes in January 1830 for cutting and destroying silk in a loom.[6] A few months later, at the Lent assizes at York, William Ashton and Francis Mirfield—the latter described as a flax-draper and crippled in both legs—both in their late twenties, were given a fourteen-year sentence for destroying linen yarn; of seven others indicted on the same charge, two turned King's Evidence and five were acquitted.[7] Later in the year, in December 1830, 1,000 pitmen assembled at the Waldridge colliery, in Durham, where (according to a Home Office informant) they 'stopped the Engine necessarily kept going in order to pump out the Water, and then threw large Iron Tubs, Wooden Cisterns, Corves, and other Articles, down the Shaft';[8] but this riot, too, did not lead to any sentences of transportation. The last important incident of the kind took place a year later at Coventry, when Beck's steam factory was burned down, and its new labour-saving machinery destroyed, by weavers threatened with unemployment. Beck himself was caught by the weavers while trying to escape over a wall and paraded through the streets seated back to front on a donkey 'amidst the yells and execrations of the crowd'. There were others as well as weavers among the half-dozen committed for trial for 'demolishing and pulling down machinery' at the Warwick Lent assizes in March 1832. Three were found not guilty and the others were initially sentenced to death before their sentences were commuted to transportation for life. They sailed on different ships to Australia. The youngest, Alfred Toogood, was an 18-year-old 'labouring boy', who arrived in Hobart on the *Georgiana* in February 1833. A second, and the first to sail, was Benjamin Sparks, a 22-year-old whitesmith of Coventry, who was sent to Sydney on the *Planter*, arriving in New South Wales in October 1832. And the oldest, though only 23, was Thomas Burbury, described as a cattle-dealer and doctor and the only one of the three who was neither a worker nor likely to have had any direct connection with the factory. Burbury was born in Warwickshire in 1809 (it is supposed), the son of Captain William Burbury, a member of the Duke of Wellington's

[5] HO 27/31; Arch. NSW, 4/4012, 4443; Hammonds, p. 128; *Leeds Mercury*, 12, 19 Aug., 14 Oct. 1826.

[6] Tas. Arch., CON 31/14.

[7] Ibid., CON 31/2, 31; HO 27/40.   [8] HO 52/12.

staff at the battle of Waterloo. He arrived in Hobart on the *York* in December 1832 and, as we shall see in a later chapter, he was one of the comparatively few protesters who made a distinguished and prosperous career for himself in the colony.[9]

Yet this incident, though the last of its kind to be of any great significance, was not the last to bring industrial machine-breakers to Australia. In October 1832, Thomas Heart, a 19-year-old lace-maker, was sentenced at assizes to fourteen years' transportation for destroying property at Nottingham—and came to New South Wales on board the *Heroine* in September 1833. David Bland, an 18-year-old house servant of Leicester, was given a ten-year sentence at the Leicester Borough assizes in March 1833 for breaking stocking-frames and came to Hobart on the *Southworth* in January 1834; while John Grimes, a 19-year-old labourer, was sent to New South Wales for seven years for machine-breaking at Gloucester in March 1837. Finally, in 1840, two brothers, John and Samuel Norris, both engineers in their early twenties and born at Leicester, were given a life-term at the Stafford Lent assizes for damaging a steam-engine in a coal mine; they arrived in Sydney on the *Eden* in November 1840.[10] And that, the fashion in both law and protest having changed, was the last of transportation for machine-breaking.

Yet industrial violence by other means continued and brought further batches of industrial protesters to Australia, and none in such large numbers as one of the most explosive outbursts in Britain's industrial history: that of the summer of 1842. But this is to jump the gun. Meanwhile, there were two minor wages disturbances in Glasgow and York in 1823 and 1829, both leading to sentences to transportation. More important were the major riots in London in 1834 and (even more) those in South Wales in 1831 and 1835. The London riot arose from a wages dispute in Stepney. This was the issue, though the charge on which three workers— a brickmaker, a labourer, and a kitchen gardener—were capitally convicted at the Old Bailey in February 1834, before being transported for life, was variously stated as 'riot', 'destroying houses', and 'beginning to demolish a house'. What the riot was really about emerges, as so often in these cases, from the prisoners' own statements. Thus Thomas Batt, the brickmaker, tells us that he was 'rioting to raise the price of wages'; and Nicholas Donoghue, a

---

[9] HO 27/44; Tas. Arch., CON 31/5, 43; Arch. NSW, 4/4153; J. Prest, *The Industrial Revolution in Coventry* (London, 1960), pp. 30, 48 (quoting *Coventry Herald*, 11 Nov. 1831); *ADB*, i, 178–9.

[10] HO 27/42, 45, 53, 62; Arch. NSW, 4/4018; Tas. Arch., CON 31/5.

labourer and the youngest of the three, adds to the official charge that he was 'riotously demolishing a house' the words: 'in Stepney in consequence of a combination'. The two men were sent to Tasmania: Donoghue on the *Lady Kennaway* and Batt on the *Aurora*, arriving in February and October 1835. The third man, George Kippin, the kitchen gardener, convicted of destroying a house in the riots, sailed later on the *Strathfieldsay* for New South Wales and arrived in Sydney in June 1836.[11]

The Welsh riots of 1831 and 1835 were more violent affrays, particularly the Merthyr riot of 1831 which was one of the most bloody in Welsh history of modern times. It was a complex affair in which political radicalism, food-prices, and workers' wages and conditions all had a part. But the central question was that raised by the colliers and furnace-men who had already been engaged in a number of strikes in resistance to cuts, for a regular wage, and an end of truck. These issues, compounded by others arising from an acute political and economic crisis, came to a head in the summer of 1831 and took shape in a vast movement of generalized protest in the course of which the workers disarmed the military sent to suppress them, destroyed the Memorial Court of Requests, and held the town for three days of fighting. As we noted in an earlier chapter, sixteen persons were killed by troops and twenty-six rioters were brought to trial at Glamorgan summer assizes. One man, Richard Lewis, was hanged and five were transported: four for life (after capital conviction) and one for seven years. One of the five, Lewis Lewis (nicknamed 'Lewsyn yr Heliwr', the Huntsman, or 'Lewys Shanco Lewis'), who had been saved from the gallows on the eve of execution, was a man of some note. He was born in the parish of Penderyn, Brecknockshire, in 1793, the son of a butcher, and was married with two boys and two girls at the time of the riots. He had held a number of jobs, including mining at Penydarren and Penderyn, and apparently enjoyed some influence in the town with persons in authority; for although he had been the most conspicuously violent of the riot's leaders, leading citizens spoke in his favour and helped to secure his reprieve. Among other leaders who sailed with Lewis Lewis to New South Wales on board the *John* were three miners: David Hughes, from Carmarthen, aged 35, married with a boy and four girls; David Thomas ('Dai Llaw Haearn' or Iron-hand), a 25-year-old Glamorgan man; and Thomas Vaughan, aged 21 and the youngest of the five, born at Dover and recently working (like

[11] HO 26/40; *Convicts Landed in the Colony of NSW*, 1836; Tas. Arch., CON 31/3, 10; 18/4, 10.

many others involved in the riots) at Crawshay's at Merthyr. The fifth man, John Phelps, a 45-year-old shoemaker from Carmarthen, had been given a fourteen-year sentence and sailed for Sydney on the *Heroine*, arriving a year later than his comrades, in September 1833.[12]

The other Welsh industrial movement of the 1830s was that of the 'Scotch Cattle', which had its base among the miners of Monmouth, the rival county to Carmarthen. It came to a head in the weeks before the spring assizes at Monmouth in March 1835, where three of the 'Cattle' were committed for trial and sentenced to death. One man, Edward Morgan, was hanged and two others—William Jenkins and John James ('Shoni Coal Tar')—were convicted of burglary at Dr. Rees's shop in Monmouth and transported for life; they sailed for Sydney on the *John Barry* in September 1835.[13]

So we come to the most riotous year of all, that of 1842: a year of political Chartism and industrial unrest, which led to the transportation of a far larger number of industrial protesters than even the Luddite riots of thirty years before. The 'industrial' riots of that year belong to a period that was dominated by Chartism and on which the campaign for the Charter left its mark as on everything else. Yet they have an identity of their own and, while there were times when the two movements ran in harness, they ran more often along parallel lines; so it seems more appropriate to include the industrial or near-industrial outbreaks of that year in this chapter rather than in the next. At the heart of the strike movements of 1842 lay the 'Plug-Plot' riots, which started at Stalybridge, near Ashton-under-Lyne, in late July, spread to Oldham and Manchester, and from there radiated over Lancashire, Yorkshire, Cheshire, the Potteries, Warwickshire, and South Wales and had offshoots reaching into Tyneside and the Lowlands of Scotland. The basic issue was wages at a time of acute depression; but as the movement gained momentum and was touched by local problems it added other issues to the list. At Manchester, the industrial question remained paramount: the 'turn-outs' closed down 130 cotton mills; but there was no pillaging except of bread, and remarkably little disorder. At Stockport, on the other hand, the workhouse was a major target and several hundred pounds of bread were looted. At Huddersfield an attempt was made to destroy the railways. In the pottery towns of Stafford-shire the pumps were stopped in the mines, the potters were called out, and every factory was closed down. But, after this, the leaders

---

[12] HO 27/41; Arch. NSW, 4/4017, 4136, 4142, 4144, 4164; and (above all) David Jones, *Before Rebecca*, pp. 133–60 (esp. pp. 142–55).

[13] HO 27/50; *Convicts Landed in . . . NSW*, 1835; Jones, pp. 86–113 (esp. p. 112).

(whether Chartist or trades-union) lost control and the close-down was followed by an orgy of rioting at Hanley, Fenton, Longton, Burslem, and Stoke-on-Trent in which police stations were raided for arms and prisoners released, poor rate books were seized and destroyed, and the houses and offices of magistrates, coal-owners, rate-collectors, and parsons 'pulled down' or set on fire; and, inevitably, as at Stockport and Preston, this was accompanied by looting and stealing of bread. This variety of activities was reflected in the charges made against the many hundreds brought for trial before the Special Commissions meeting at Lancaster, Chester, and Stafford in the first two weeks of October that year. At Lancaster, 119 persons were sent to prison and 13 transported for crimes as varied as 'putting out fires under boilers' (or plug-drawing), 'turning out workmen', and conspiracy, assault, unlawful assembly, riot, and seditious libel. At Chester, 11 were sentenced to transportation and at Stafford, where 274 persons were brought to trial and 146 sent to prison, 51 were transported: some for life, others for twenty-one, fifteen, ten, or seven years.[14] So, from these three assizes, there were 75 persons transported to Australia for a wide range of protest-crimes. They were all working men and most of them were young: their average age was only a little over twenty-six. They came from a variety of trades, but some were significantly more in evidence than others. There were 20 colliers, 14 potters, 11 weavers and spinners, 8 labourers of all sorts, 3 engineers, 2 bakers, and 2 carpenters; the remaining dozen were carters, tanners, stokers, shoemakers, grooms, and domestic servants. All but two of them sailed on one ship, the *John Renwick*, which arrived in Hobart in April 1843. The two exceptions—Richard Clay and Isaac Colclough, both colliers of Hanley—sailed on later ships, the one on *Equestrian* and the other on *Lord Auckland*, reaching Australia six months apart in May and November 1844.[15]

From the prisoners' statements on arrival in Hobart we learn far more of the actual crimes committed and the real nature of the riots than from the terse entries in the Criminal Register in London or the indents that came with the convicts on their ships. This is particularly true of the wild rioting at Hanley, Longton, and the other pottery towns. In view of the extensive destruction of property, it is not surprising that the charge most frequently entered in the case of the Stafford men should have been 'demolishing a house', with the occasional variation of 'larceny' or 'cutting and wounding' the

---

[14] HO 27/66–8; *Ann. Reg.*, lxxxiv (1842), 157–9, 161, 163.
[15] Tas. Arch., CON 33/38, 54, 61.

police; but it is only from the prisoners' accounts that we can place the crime within its wider context and discover what the riots were all about. Thomas Banks, for example, a young collier of Hanley, was charged with 'feloniously demolishing a house'; but we have no idea whose house, where it was, and how many persons were present until we read what he and other prisoners have to say. It appears that the house in question (and this is repeated in several statements) belonged to the Revd. Benjamin Vale of Longton, near Stoke-on-Trent, a magistrate who had aroused the particular fury of the local people. Banks tells us that he had broken into 'a box' there 'during a row'; and he adds (far more significantly): '500 were present. *The colliers were turned out because the wages were too low:* some got ½ a crown, some 3/- & some 3/6d.' Another prisoner charged with the same offence was Thomas Cotton, a 30-year-old labourer of Longton. He pleaded not guilty and gave himself a not altogether convincing alibi, but one that tells us more than we would otherwise have known about the riots: 'I was not present, having been at work until one o'clock, when I was driven out by the Mob.' Joseph Barrett, a 27-year-old shoemaker, who was convicted of larceny, also places his crime within a wider social context: '(I) was breaking into a pawnbroker's shop (Fenton's) and stealing a pick head. *4–5000 men were striking for wages.*' Edward Ellis, 23, a collier of Hanley, does the same thing when he tells us that he was demolishing another magistrate's, 'Squire Parker's, house at the Potteries, Staffs, *at the Riots for an increase of wages*', and John Hollis, 28, another collier, sentenced for 'stabbing with intent to do grievous bodily harm', explains that his victim was Benjamin Baynton (a special constable from Belston, as other prisoners tell us); and that he stabbed him with a knife '*at the riots for an increase of wages*'. Another policeman who got stabbed was called Hope, according to Samuel Crutchley, a 21-year-old potter of Stoke-on-Trent, who admitted he cut and wounded him 'with a knife during the riots'. So by piecing these testimonies together, we arrive at a fuller picture of the riots, both in general and in detail, and of the participants and the targets of attack.[16]

Other rioters' names appear in the report made by the *Annual Register* of the attack on Parson Vale's house at Longton. Those mentioned by name were Richard Wright, an 18-year-old collier from Orton; and Joseph Whiston (known as 'Joco'), a 22-year-old potter from Hanley, with a family of five, who was convicted of helping to demolish Squire Parker's house at Hanley, but seems

[16] HO 27/68; Tas. Arch., CON 33/68 (my italics).

(from the newspaper account) to have been actively involved at the Revd. Mr. Vale's as well. For the eyewitness of the scene at Vale's— George Bailey, a bricklayer—told the court that was judging the affair: 'I saw Wright put a bed upon the fire in front of the house. I had known him before. I also saw Joseph Whiston, who was known by the name of Joco. I saw him take a piano and put it on the fire. He said the Lord was at his side, and the flames would not hurt him.'[17] Another rioter whose name is worthy of mention is William Ellis, who was convicted (probably unjustly) of demolishing 'Parson Atkinson's house' at Hanley. Ellis was a Chartist of long standing, a close friend of Thomas Cooper of Leicester and a leading figure in the Potters' Union, with a reputation for militancy throughout the pottery towns; the *Annual Register* described him as being 'one of the most dangerous men in the Potteries'; and Frederick Harper, who gives a vivid picture of the riots in his *Joseph Capper*, calls him a firebrand ('if ever there was a firebrand it was Ellis').[18] Ellis was 33 at the time and lived at Burslem with his wife Emma and two sons and two daughters; his mother, Emma Ellis, lived near by. He was transported to Tasmania for twenty-one years and sailed on the *John Renwick* with most of the others.

As we have seen, there were some cases of larceny in the Potteries riots; and some of these may not have had any direct connection with the riots. One such case was that of Isaac Colclough, a 24-year-old collier from Hanley, but living with a wife and child at Burslem. He was sentenced for stealing money and admitted to 'rioting and stealing money and a silver tea spoon at the house of Mr Barwell, Burslem, the windows being broken & 1,000s assembled'. There was also Philip Hewson, a young millwright and machine joiner of Macclesfield, who confessed that he had stolen a pair of trousers from a Mr. Bellings of Macclesfield (why he was tried at Stafford and not Chester is not clear); and an older man, Thomas Owen, aged 43, a brickmaker born in Salisbury, who was also convicted of larceny and confessed that he had stolen tea and bread from a Mr. Platt at Shelton. But larceny—particularly of bread—was a far more common offence among the rioters sentenced in Lancashire and Cheshire, where there were towns like Stockport and Macclesfield in which the 'Plug-Plot' riots assumed the complexion of a food-riot rather than an industrial dispute. Among those sentenced at Lancaster were John and James Smith, father and son, the one an engineer and the other a stoker, both living at Macclesfield. They were con-

---

[17] *Ann. Reg.*, lxxxiv (1842), 158–9.
[18] Ibid., p. 163; F. Harper, *Joseph Capper* (London, 1962), p. 123.

victed of robbery and had (it appeared) demanded bread and cheese from a Mr. Traffert at Macclesfield during the riots (though John Smith, the father, said he had taken no part in the affair). They were both sentenced to transportation for ten years. In Cheshire, two men sentenced to transportation had been found guilty of stealing bread at the Union Workhouse at Stockport. James Derbyshire, a 22-year-old spinner of Compstall, near Stockport, who admitted stealing a pound of bread, was given a seven-year term; whereas Francis Warhurst, also 22, a farm labourer from Manchester, was transported for life for the same offence. But Warhurst had a longer criminal record: where Derbyshire had only one previous offence (apparently a minor one) that could count against him, he had already been in prison three times having spent six months for stealing a waistcoat, three for a pigeon, and fourteen days for an assault.[19]

Meanwhile, in Scotland, as an extension of the 'Plug-Plot' riots in the North of England, there had been a miners' strike in Ayr; and four miners were charged before the Court of Judiciary at Edinburgh in December 1842. The strike ('for wages', as a prisoner tells us) took place about mid-November and was, as usual, attended by riot; and the rioters (a witness reports) were armed with loaded firearms and knives, used to intimidate the 'blacklegs'; and a man named Davidson was killed. Two men were sentenced to transportation, one for seven years, the other for ten. The first, John Overin, a 20-year-old apprentice miner from Co. Down, was also charged with obstructing peace officers in the execution of their duty and with releasing prisoners. The other, William Gibson, was an Ayrshire man, aged 27, who had lost a finger on his right hand and was lame in one leg. They arrived in Tasmania on the *Mount Stewart Elphinstone* in June 1845 and were followed later in the year by two other miners also involved in a strike at Ayr, who had been sentenced by the same court at Edinburgh, but meeting six months after. So it may or may not have been the same miners' dispute as before. Certainly, the issue involved and the charges preferred were the same. Daniel McAulay, a 30-year-old Donegal man working at Ayr, described it as 'a strike for wages among the colliers', and continued his account: 'The men who came to do our work we assaulted and turned them off at the works. It was at Ayr; we struck for wages; we had 20d *per diem*.' His companion, Michael McMorrow, another Irishman by birth, confirmed that it was a 'strike for wages' and added: '800 of us struck from the works. One man was killed in the

[19] HO 27/66, 67, 68; Tas. Arch., CON 33/38.

row.' Both men were sentenced to transportation for ten years and sailed on the *Stratheden*, which arrived in Hobart, having first stopped at Port Philip on the Australian mainland, in December 1845.[20]

There was also a miners' strike in Yorkshire, leading to the conviction of two Sheffield miners by the York summer assizes in 1844. They came on separate ships; one on the *Sir Robert Peel*, the other on the *Hyderabad*. One of them, George Taylor, described the event as 'a strike over wages, prosecuted by the Government' and added that 'John Matthews, a policeman, was cut with a stick'.[21] The same year, Robert Brown, a miner from Newcastle upon Tyne, was transported for fifteen years at the Durham assizes for shooting at a certain John Walker—a policeman we must suppose, as he added that it was 'a strike business'. Brown, as became common in the mid 1840s, spent a preliminary two years in Norfolk Island before sailing on to Tasmania in May 1847.[22]

Finally, there were a small number of Irishmen transported for involvement in labour disputes in the 1830s and 1840s. Labour disputes in Ireland, as we have seen, were a comparatively unusual event at the time; and when they occurred it was generally in the North. But these all took place in Cork. The first one—towards the end of 1833—was evidently a bakers' strike as three bakers (including two brothers, Patrick and Timothy Manning) were convicted of 'combination and assault' at Cork City Lent sessions in 1834 and sentenced to transportation for seven years. A strike of wheelwrights and carpenters followed soon after and five wheelwrights were given the same term by the same court a few months later. Most were men of middling years—none of the wheelwrights was over 34. All seven came out together on the *Blenheim*, arriving in Hobart in November 1834.[23] The last incident involved a group of top-sawyers, who were convicted at Cork City in August 1842 of throwing vitriol in the course of a dispute; three of them were transported to Tasmania for life. Their crime, it appears from their own account, was to have thrown vitriol at Mr. John Wilson, a saw-mill keeper, 'for reducing the price of wages', and their victim lost the sight of an eye (if not the eye itself) in the action. Yet all three were described as 'well conducted' men, who had never been convicted before; and one of them, John Drew, a young man of 23, was employed as a school-

[20] SRO, JC 4/38, 40; Tas. Arch., CON 33/68, 73.
[21] Tas. Arch., CON 33/63, 86.
[22] Tas. Arch., CON 33/80.
[23] Arch. NSW, 4/4126.

master on the *Navarino* on which they sailed to Hobart with a life-sentence in September 1842.[24] Nor were the Irish top-sawyers the only ones to throw vitriol in the face of an unpopular employer. Four years earlier, an English top-sawyer, John Walmsley, aged 44, with a wife and eight children, was sentenced to fifteen years' transportation at Liverpool quarter sessions for 'combination'; but, according to the Criminal Register, it was for 'feloniously throwing vitriol over a person'.[25]

It was a far cry from the dignified procedures of George Loveless and his comrades at Tolpuddle; but, as we have said before, the men of Dorset were a rare phenomenon indeed in the stormy and violent years of a rapidly developing industrial revolution.

[24] Tas. Arch., CON 33/34.
[25] HO 27/55; *Convicts Landed in . . . NSW* (Sept. 1839).

5. Chartists

MOST of the Chartists, as we have seen, were transported to the Australian colonies as 'Plug-Plot' rioters in the general strike of 1842: the majority as the result of the destructive riots in the Potteries in August of that year. The two dozen that remain are the subject of the present chapter. All of them—with the exception of Richard Boothman, a Lancashire weaver (of whom more will be said later)— were sentenced for the part they played in the more directly 'political' events of 1839 and 1848.

The most bloody and dramatic of these events—though not in itself the most important—was the rising that took place at Newport, Monmouthshire, in November 1839. Previous to its outbreak there had been some months of drilling with pikes and muskets among the miners and weavers on both sides of the border with the neighbouring county of Montgomery. Three of the Montgomery men were arrested and charged with 'drilling the Mob in the use of firearms' in the summer of 1839. The oldest was Abraham Owen, a 45-year-old weaver, a widower with four sons; his companions were Humphreys Lewis, 29, a boot and shoemaker, married with one boy; and John Ingram, 36, single and described as a labourer and soldier. They were sentenced to seven years' transportation at the Montgomery assizes in July and were sent to Sydney on different ships in the following year: Owen and Lewis arriving by the *Woodbridge* on 27 February and Ingram on the *Maitland* on 14 July.[1] They were the only Chartists to be sent to New South Wales, but they have not been considered of sufficient importance to be mentioned in any of the numerous general histories of the Chartist movement.

Far more significant and the subject of frequent historical comment were the three leaders of the rising of 3–4 November, John Frost, Zephaniah Williams, and William Jones. The most eminent of the three, and a central figure in the whole history of Chartism, was John Frost, a prosperous woollen draper and former mayor of the town. He was born at Newport on 25 May 1789, the son of John and Sarah Frost, who kept the Royal Oak tavern in Mill Street, Newport, for close on forty years. He was brought up as

[1] HO 27/58; *Convicts Landed in the Colony of NSW*, 1840.

a strict Independent and sent to school at Bristol and, when sixteen, was apprenticed to a tailor at Cardiff, later working for some years as an assistant to a merchant tailor in London. On returning to Newport in 1811, he set up in business as a tailor and draper and, shortly after, married Mary Geach, a widow, by whom he had two sons and five daughters. He began to take an interest in politics around 1816, became a Radical in the Cobbett tradition, and advocated lower taxes and a programme of parliamentary reform that anticipated the later Six Points of the People's Charter. In 1822, as a champion of the burgesses of Newport, he came into conflict with Thomas Prothero, the Town Clerk, and spent six months' imprisonment for libel in Cold Baths Fields prison in London. At home he was not forgotten and when the Municipal Corporation Act was passed in 1835, Frost became a member of Newport's first town council, a justice of the peace and a harbour commissioner, and mayor a year later. Meanwhile, he had abandoned Cobbettite Radicalism for Chartism and was elected to represent the Monmouthshire working men at the first Chartist convention in London in February 1839. During the Convention's sittings, he was removed from the commission of the peace for using seditious language in the Chartist cause; and as he stumped the country in the spring and summer of that year he won great popularity and, as other leaders were arrested and convicted of sedition, Frost was among those who moved up to take their place; and it was when serving as chairman of the Convention (now meeting at Birmingham) that, on 14 September, he cast the fateful vote that dissolved the Convention, by now dangerously weakened by the arrest of its leaders and Parliament's curt rejection of the first national petition.

Frost, like other leaders not yet behind bars, went back to his home town to prepare for further action; and it was at Newport, which had been thoroughly aroused by the recent arrest of Henry Vincent, hero of the Monmouthshire miners, that he came together again with the two other leaders of the future rising, Zephaniah Williams and William Jones. Williams was born at Merthyr Tydfil around 1795, married and had a son and a daughter, and moved to Coalbrookvale, Blaina, in Monmouthshire, where he set up in business as publican of the Royal Oak Inn, an occupation that he combined with that of coal merchant and mineral surveyor. Brought up (like Frost) as a strict Nonconformist, he became an agnostic and by 1811 had won notoriety by his spirited polemics against the local clergy; and, a year later, he was charged with assaulting a constable, though he was later acquitted. Henry Vincent held him in high regard and described him as 'one of the most intelligent men it has ever been my good fortune to meet'; and it was probably due to Vincent that he became a Chartist in 1838 and turned his inn into a centre for Chartist activity and discussion. William Jones, the youngest of the three, was a watchmaker of Pontypool, aged 30 (Frost was 55, Williams 44) at the time of his arrest. He was the natural son of a tradesman at Bristol, became a strolling player after being apprenticed to a watchmaker, but returned to his trade in 1833 and rose from manager to owner of a watchmaking business at Pontypool (while, like Williams, running a tavern at the same time). Here he also joined the philanthropic society, became a leading figure among the local Chartists and gained great influence, as a flamboyant orator and advocate of physical force, among the industrial population.[2]

It was at Williams's beerhouse in early October that the first plans were made for a march on Newport. Frost and Williams, both inclined to be 'moral-force' men, urged caution; but Jones's spirited oratory in favour of direct action carried the day; and after considerable confusion (during which Frost appears to have been torn between his natural caution and his fear of being stamped a coward), the march was set for the night of 3–4 November. It had been agreed to march in three contingents, one from Blackwood under the leadership of Frost, a second from Nantyglo and Ebbw Vale under Williams, and a third from Pontypool under Jones, all three to meet for the final assault on Newport at Risca, a near-by village.

It proved to be a fiasco. Jones, who had returned to Pontypool for reinforcements, failed to keep his appointment; and the other contingents, having spent the night in soaking rain, marched on without him to be met by the fire of a unit of the 45th Foot at the Westgate Hotel. Having lost about twenty dead (accounts range between fourteen and twenty-four), the insurgents fled. There were numerous arrests made that evening: 125 according to some accounts, including Frost and Williams; while Jones, who had fled to the hills, was captured soon after.[3] Twenty-nine were committed for trial before the Monmouth assizes on 10 December, nearly all on charges of high treason—or, more precisely, of 'conspiring to levy war against the Queen'; and, of these, eight, including the three

[2] For Frost, see David Williams, *John Frost; a Study in Chartism* (Cardiff, 1939); *DNB*, xx (1889), 288–9; and *ADB*, i, 419–20. For Williams, see *ADB*, ii, 601–2; and for Jones, see Frank F. Rosenblatt, *The Chartist Movement* (revised edn., London, 1967), p. 195 n. 3; and D. Thompson, *The Early Chartists*, pp. 229–30.

[3] For the best account of the rising, see Williams, *John Frost*, pp. 195–239; see also Rosenblatt, pp. 191–207.

leaders, were sentenced to the grim penalty of being hung, drawn, and quartered. And it was not before seven weeks later, after a sustained campaign of public protest and legal manœuvres, that the sentence in the case of the three 'Welsh chieftains' was commuted to one of transportation for life. On 2 February they were taken to Chepstow from Monmouth jail and conveyed by steamer to Portsmouth; and from there they sailed on the *Mandarin* on the 24th to Tasmania, arriving in Hobart on 30 June.[4] A handful of other Chartist prisoners, sentenced to a life-term for 'demolishing a house by force' in the Birmingham riots of the summer of 1839, sailed with them on the same ship. They were Jeremiah Howell, 35, a Birmingham gunsmith; John Jones, 22, a wood turner from Welshpool, Montgomery; and Francis Roberts, 28, a blacksmith and shovelmaker from Sutton, near Birmingham. A further Birmingham prisoner, convicted of the same offence but (no doubt because he was only 16 years old) sentenced to a ten-year term, followed a few weeks later on the *Asia*. He was Thomas Aston, a gunsmith's labourer from Birmingham, who arrived in Hobart in August 1840.[5]

Richard Boothman was the young Lancashire weaver whom we referred to earlier as the odd man out among the Chartists sent to Australia between 1839 and 1848. He was not involved in sedition or conspiracy or in any specifically Chartist agitation; but he had (or so it was claimed) quite simply killed a policeman in a riot at Colne, a Lancashire cotton town, on 10 August 1840. Eighteen other convicts arrived in Tasmania and Western Australia, charged with cutting and wounding policemen, between 1841 and 1852—that is through the greater part of the Chartist period. 'Police-bashing' had, in fact, become a frequent occurrence in London and northern industrial towns; yet there is no good reason to connect these cases with Chartism, particularly as they occurred (like most cases of the kind) in years of Chartist lull rather than in the peak years 1842 and 1847-8.[6] In Boothman's case, too, the Chartist connection is not evident for all to see; but as the policeman—Joseph Halstead, who was killed with an iron bar—met his death in the course of a riot that was specifically directed against the police and not as the outcome of a drunken brawl, there is more than an even chance that political motives were involved. This seems all the more likely as

[4] HO 27/61; Tas. Arch., CON 33/1.
[5] HO 27/59; Tas. Arch., CON 33/2.
[6] Tas. Arch., CON 33/11–110 (*passim*) [seventeen cases]; Arch. WA, R.17 (one case). For 'police-bashing' as a form of workers' protest during these years, see R. D. Storch, 'The Plague of the Blue Locusts. Police Reform and Popular Resistance in Northern England 1840-57', *Internat. Review of Social History*, xx (1975), 61-90.

Boothman, though persistently claiming to have been the victim of mistaken identity, gave clear evidence of his hostility to the police in letters he sent to his father during his confinement in Lancaster Castle between October 1840 and June 1841. But, despite his protestations of innocence and the repeated representations made on his behalf by his father and other respectable citizens, Boothman was sentenced to death at the Lancaster assizes of March 1841. After his sentence had been commuted to a life-term in exile, he was transferred to the *Justitia* hulk at Woolwich in June; and here, it seems from the anguished tone of his last letter to his father in July, he became subject to apocalyptic visions. After some weeks on the *Justitia*, he was put aboard the *Barossa* which sailed for Tasmania on 16 August, arriving in Hobart on 13 January 1842. He was then barely 21 years old. We shall hear more of him in a later chapter.[7]

So we come to the last of the major phases of Chartism and the last batch of prisoners transported to Australia for Chartist activities. There were sixteen of them, divided fairly evenly between Englishmen and Scots, sentenced to seven or ten years' servitude as the result of the various Chartist riots and 'conspiracies' of 1848. The Scots were the last to arrive in Tasmania, but the first to be sentenced —one by the Aberdeen Court of Judiciary on 12 April and the rest by the Glasgow Judiciary Court on 5 and 6 May. The man sentenced at Aberdeen was Donald Davidson, a labourer, aged 33 (though in one record he appears as 53), born in Inverness, who was given a seven-year sentence for 'mobbing and rioting and culpable homicide'; though his own definition of the charge, as so often in such cases, was far more explicit: it was of 'assaulting a man who was killed at a riot at Stonehaven'. He was indicted with four others, who, though also found guilty, escaped with the relatively mild punishment of twelve to eighteen months in jail. Davidson sailed on *Nile II*, which arrived in Tasmania on 3 October 1850.[8]

The Glasgow prisoners were half a dozen working men, variously charged with 'mobbing and rioting', 'robbery and rioting', and 'riot and housebreaking' in Glasgow riots—presumably the food riots of 6 March 1848. The prisoners, on arrival in Tasmania, were as usual more explicit about their offence than their judges. One (Robert Main) explained that his offence took place at Irongate, where a gun

---

[7] HO 27/64; Lancs. RO, DDX 537/2-4, 9-10, 12-13; Tas. Arch., CON 14/12, 33/16. I am grateful to Mr. Storch for drawing my attention to the file of Boothman correspondence at Preston.

[8] SRO, JC 11/94; Tas. Arch., CON 33/97.

was stolen from a Mr. Musgrave; three others (James Campbell, John Lafferty, and Charles O'Bryan) stated that 'several houses' were plundered; while the other two (Peter Keenan and Thomas Walker) linked the rioting more directly with Chartism by stating that the housebreaking took place in a 'Chartist riot' (Keenan) and, even more explicitly (in the case of Walker): 'Chartist rioting; I was coming from work to my dinner at the time.' Walker, the youngest of the six, was a 23-year-old iron moulder from Bainsford, in Stirlingshire; Keenan, 25, was a farm labourer from Co. Monaghan; O'Bryan, 25, also an Irishman, was an ostler from Fermanagh; Campbell, 28, was a hammerer (or striker) from Glasgow; as were Robert Mair, a tin- and coppersmith, and John Lafferty, an ostler, both 45 years old. They sailed on different ships: Mair (like the Aberdonian, Davidson) on *Nile II*; Walker on the *William Jardine*, and Keenan on the *Rodney*, these three arriving in Hobart in October and November 1850. The remaining three arrived together on the *Lady Kennaway*, a few months later, on 28 May 1851. Some of the prisoners stopped at two or more English prisons on the journey southward to the hulks. Lafferty for one: his conduct, if his jailers may be trusted, appears to have been distinctly erratic, varying from 'good' at Millbank to 'indifferent' at Pentonville and 'idle and bad' at Portland.[9]

The nine Englishmen were all involved in the conspiratorial events that followed in London and the North after the collapse of the main Chartist movement, with the rejection of the third petition by Parliament, in April 1848. Four were young Chartists from the north of England, of whom the youngest was 20 and the oldest 34; they were all sentenced to a life-term at the Liverpool assizes in December. Their crime (or so it was said) was 'sedition', or (like the Newport rebels of 1839) 'compassing or devising to levy war against the Queen'. In one case—that of James Stott, a 24-year-old Oldham man—the charge of 'Chartism' is added to the rest. The only one of the four whose occupation is stated is Thomas Tassiker, a 34-year-old carder (native place not given); the others were, in addition to Stott, Joseph Constantine, aged 20, from Manchester; and Thomas Kenworthy, 29, from Ashton-under-Lyne, a place that was briefly held by insurgent Chartists in September of that year.[10]

The Londoners, all tried at the Central Criminal Court at the Old Bailey in September 1848, won greater renown as members of a

---

[9] SRO, JC 11/94, 12/91, 13/91; Tas. Arch., CON 33/97–9, 102.
[10] HO 27/85; Tas. Arch., CON 14/38; A. R. Schoyen, *The Chartist Challenge* (London, 1958), p. 175.

radical group during that final, 'conspiratorial' phase of Chartism that was dominated by Julian Harnay and Feargus O'Connor's former protégé and now bitter opponent, Ernest Jones. These were the Republicans who, while sentenced for 'sedition' and 'levying war', may well have deserved the more specific charge made against one of them—William Dowling—of 'compassing to depose the Queen', as they appear to have planned a *putsch* or armed uprising in the wake of the shattering of Chartist hopes at Kennington Common a few months before. It also appears that the rising—in both London and the manufacturing districts—was set for 15 September, but was betrayed to the police by an informer—one claiming to be the leader of a so-called 'Wat Tyler Brigade' in Greenwich— so that the conspirators were able to be seized by the police at their final conference at the Orange Tree public house in Bloomsbury. William Dowling, aged 25, was a portrait painter, a Roman Catholic and a Dubliner by origin. The youngest was Thomas Fay, also a Catholic from Dublin, described as a boot 'clover'. Two others were Englishmen of middling years: William Lacey, aged 39, a prosperous bootmaker from Keyworth, in Nottinghamshire, married with six children; and Joseph Ritchie, a 44-year-old Quaker and bricklayer from Newcastle-upon-Tyne. The leader was an older and more experienced man, who had been in politics since playing a part in a tailors' strike in 1834, was at one time auditor of O'Connor's National Land Company, an inveterate conspirator according to the more moderate Chartists, and certainly one of the most colourful figures in the later stages of the Chartist movement. This was William Cuffay (or Cuffey), a mulatto tailor, born in Chatham the son of a former West Indian slave, three times married but with no children, minute of stature (only 4 ft. 11 in. tall), and already 61 years old at the time of the 'Orange Tree conspiracy'. These five men and twenty others were tried at the Old Bailey on 18 September. The twenty were sent to prison for terms of two years or eighteen months, while Cuffay and his principal associates were sentenced to transportation for life. They and the four Northerners sailed together on the *Adelaide*, which dropped anchor in Hobart harbour on 29 November 1849.[11] Of Cuffay and his fellow conspirators, as of the Newport rebel-leaders, we shall also hear further in a later chapter of the book.

[11] HO 26/54 (Middlesex), 27/86 (Surrey); Tas. Arch., CON 14/36. For Cuffay, see also *Reynolds' Political Instructor*, 13 Apr. 1850, p. 177 (I am indebted for this reference to Dr. F. B. Smith of the Australian National University, Canberra); Schoyen, pp. 158, 175–7; D. Thompson, p. 9; and G. D. H. Cole, *Chartist Portraits* (London, 1965), pp. 260, 355.

6. Poachers, Cattle-Maimers, and Incendiaries

OF the *marginal* protesters by far the most numerous were the arsonists. In fact, during the whole period of transportation, about one in 160 of all the convicts sent to Australia was an arsonist, or, at least, had been judged to be so by the courts, amounting in all to just over a thousand, 653 Britons and 352 Irish. Arson, whether as crime or as protest, had a pattern all its own. In its temporal aspect, the peak years, in Ireland, were 1829 to 1832 and those immediately following the great Famine of the 1840s; in England, incendiary outbreaks were more widely spread over half a century and followed each other, at roughly ten-year intervals in 1822 (the first year to have a significant number of conflagrations), 1831–2, 1843–5, 1854–5, and 1863–6. Geographically, though rural incendiarism occurred in every region of the British Isles, it was significantly more prevalent in some regions than in others. In Ireland, the most incendiary counties before 1840 appear to have been Limerick, Longford, Roscommon, and Meath, with Tipperary trailing close behind; but in the post-Famine period, with the greater involvement of young servant girls, there was an appreciable shift to Cork, Tipperary, Clare, and Kildare. (In both periods the northern counties remained comparatively unscathed.) In England, the conflagrations of 1831–2 were mainly centred on the south-eastern counties of Kent, Surrey, and Sussex, with secondary centres of arson in Norfolk and Lincoln. In the 1840s there was a significant shift to the eastern counties; and, in 1844 alone, as many as eighty-five cases of arson were tried at the Norfolk and Suffolk assizes leading to the transportation of thirty-three persons to Australia. In the 1850s and 1860s the pattern changed again, spreading more widely over the country as a whole: of 361 arsonists sent to Western Australia, 33 came from Kent, 26 from Essex, 23 from Yorkshire, 20 from Oxford, and 16 from London. (In 1831–2, as the reader may remember from an earlier chapter, the hangman's noose was still in active use and only a handful of convicted arsonists had their sentences commuted and were sent to Hobart or Botany Bay.)[1]

[1] For the above, see records of individual convicts sent to Tasmania, New South

So much is fairly firmly established. But how many—and who—of the transported prisoners may reasonably be called protesters? It is the same question that we asked, in relation to all types of *marginal* protesters, at the beginning of the book. As I then suggested, unless the records give us a straight answer (as they seldom do), we shall only be able to resolve the problem by more indirect means, as by asking a number of questions, such as: who was the victim? who was his assailant, and how and where did he live and what, if any, was his previous criminal record? and (if the records will tell us) how and why did he commit the offence? It is not proposed, however, to place all the evidence before the reader; and in order to persuade him that, in making our selection, a rough-and-ready sort of justice has been done a few examples must suffice. The key questions, of course, are the intentions of the aggressor, which (if given) brings us close to a satisfactory answer, and the relationship between the assailant and his victim. As regards the first, a confession that a house or a barn was burned down to claim the insurance is clear enough evidence to close the debate. There are plenty of such cases: as with Peter McAllen, a watchmaker of County Kildare who, on arrival in Hobart in January 1846, told the authorities that 'it was insurance . . . it [his house] was insured at £3,000'; and Mary Christopherson, a widowed housemaid from near Carlisle, who, on arriving on the *Garland Grove* in January 1842, admitted that she had burned her own house down 'to defraud the Insurance Office'.[2] Some were less frankly outspoken, like Harris Rosenberg, a silversmith from Aberdeen, who, while admitting that he had set fire to a house, said it was all a mistake and that the one he had intended to burn was the jeweller's and furrier's shop next door![3] Or, again, like Thomas Elmer, a Bedfordshire farm labourer, who, after being convicted of setting fire to some stacks, claimed he had been 'persuaded to do it by a man for some beer'.[4] Others put themselves out of court by being hardened criminals or quasi-professionals at the job. Of the first there is the example of John Stewart, convicted of firing a barley rick at Suffolk quarter sessions in January 1839, who had already been in jail seven times on a variety of charges and added further to his criminal record after arrival in Tasmania;[5] and of the

Wales, and Western Australia; and David Jones, 'Thomas Campbell Foster and the Rural Labourer. Incendiarism in East Anglia in the 1840s', in *Social History* (Jan. 1976), pp. 5–43. These general trends are not exactly reflected in the transportation figures, as arson only became a common transportable offence after arsonists virtually ceased to be hanged in the course of the 1830s.

[2] Tas. Arch., CON 33/75; CON 15/2. [3] Tas. Arch., CON 33/36.
[4] Tas. Arch., CON 33/83. [5] Tas. Arch., CON 31/41.

second there was Abraham Farrer, a weaver from the neighbourhood of Leeds, who, when brought to justice for arson in Suffolk
in July 1844, was said to have lit fires at Nottingham and in other
northern and midland counties before.[6]

There were also those—frequent in Ireland—who claimed to have
committed their crime in order to be sent away to Australia, which,
they believed, would bring them better fortune; these, too, can hardly
be called protesters. One of these was Thomas Brown, a 50-year-old
widower of Abbotts Bromley, in Staffordshire, who said that he had
set fire to a stack of straw belonging to John Wilson at Ringley in
order 'to be sent away'. A more dramatic example is that of Jeremiah
Head, a young labourer of Great Saxham, in Suffolk, who, when
sentenced at Bury St. Edmunds in March 1845 for firing three barley
stacks, the property of Samuel Chivers, publicly thanked the superintendent of police who had arrested him with the words: 'I thank
you, Mr. English, and am very much obliged to you.'[7] And, early
in the book, we mentioned the three dozen and more young Irish
women who, in the wake of the Famine of 1845, had burned houses
and stacks in order to be sent out to join their husbands, brothers,
or lovers in Australia. One of these women, Catherine Smith, of
County Longford, whose husband had gone to Tasmania, appears
to have persuaded her son and daughter-in-law to help her in the
act.[8] There were many others, as we also noted before, who can
hardly be called protesters as they appear to have been totally
ignorant of the names of their accusers.[9]

It is, in fact, the relationship between victim and assailant that
so often provides the answer to our problem. In arson, where protest
was involved, that relationship was generally that of master and
servant or landlord and tenant. As an example of the second we may
cite the case of Peter McCloy, a 40-year-old labourer of Londonderry, who was given a life-sentence for attempting to burn down the
house and property occupied by Ambrose Hughes, in whose favour
(it appears from the prisoner's declaration) he had been evicted by
his landlord.[10] A master–servant relationship, however, was, in
England at least, by far the more common of the two. In such cases
arson, though often committed after that relationship had ceased,
was the rural equivalent of the strike in towns and manufacturing

---

[6] Tas. Arch., CON 33/86; D. Jones, p. 19.

[7] Jones, loc. cit.; Tas. Arch., CON 33/79.

[8] Tas. Arch., CON 40/10.

[9] See p. 5 above.

[10] *Convicts landed in the Colony of NSW, 1830–1842*, 1838. Petitions 1837
(O'Farrell).

districts. To take a few examples. There was Benjamin Hunt, 39, a Hampshire ploughman, married with seven children, who admitted on arrival in Hobart that he had set fire to a cottage belonging to Sir Joseph Pollard, adding 'in whose service [he] lived 20 years'.[11] There was also James Kidd, a Sheffield brushmaker, sentenced in March 1844, who confessed to burning a stack of barley at Pembroke, near Lincoln, belonging to a man who was once his master.[12] Similarly, William Simmonds, a 35-year-old Sussex labourer, fired a stack of wheat that belonged to William John Dyke of Lymington, who 'was my master about six months before I committed the offence'.[13] James Annetts, a 35-year-old Berkshire ploughman, who was given a life-sentence for firing a barn at Chilton, his native village, revealed a more pressing motive in admitting that he had been in the owner's service but 'discharged for neglect of work'. Sentenced with him was Joseph Blissett, a fellow ploughman of Chilton, convicted of inciting both Annetts and others to set fire to their masters' property.[14] A more doubtful case was that of George Barrett, a young ploughman from Icomb, in Gloucestershire, who was given a life-term at the Southampton assizes in July 1834 for burning down his master's cowhouse and stables. Barrett denied the charge: 'I never did it. I never had any ill-will, or cause for it, against my master.'[15]

Occasionally, a deeper personal hostility between worker and employer comes to light. Among several prisoners sentenced to transportation for arson at the Norwich assizes in 1844 was William Medlar from Burgh, Suffolk, a 40-year-old shoemaker, the father of five children, who admitted setting fire to a stack of corn belonging to his master, Robert Samuel Thorne. Medlar told the court that his employer had starved him and his wife and family and 'neither gave [him] work, nor suffered others to do so'. He was given a fifteen-year sentence, beginning with a two-year term at Norfolk Island. He sailed on the *David Malcolm*, arriving at Norfolk Island on 25 August 1845; and, having served the first part of his sentence, he went on to Tasmania in May 1847.[16]

At other times, it was the threat of arson, rather than arson itself, that was used to win concessions; on such occasions arson was used more as a bargaining weapon than as an act of revenge. This was a relatively common feature in the protracted struggle over rent and tithe in Ireland that followed the Napoleonic Wars. There was, for

[11] Tas. Arch., CON 33/86.　　　[12] Tas. Arch., CON 33/83.
[13] Tas. Arch., CON 33/20.　　　[14] Tas. Arch., CON 33/39.
[15] Tas. Arch., CON 31/5.　　　　[16] Jones, p. 30; Tas. Arch., CON 33/80.

example, the case of Michael Collins, a 36-year-old labourer of Ballingarry, Co. Limerick, the father of two boys and a girl, whose capital sentence for 'arson' was commuted to transportation for life at the Limerick assizes in March 1839. He admitted attacking Zechariah Ledger's house, demanding arms and threatening to fire the house if he failed to get them.[17] In England, the more common form of threat was to send an anonymous letter, threatening to burn down an employer's or landlord's or minister's house unless wages were raised, rents or tithes reduced, or obnoxious labour-saving machinery dismantled. This was a frequent occurrence in the English labourers' revolt in the summer and autumn of 1830 when close on a hundred cases of this kind were reported.[18] In the widespread incendiarism in the eastern counties in 1844–5, Samuel Stow, a 23-year-old Suffolk labourer, who had a past history of both arson and poaching, admitted he had sent a letter to William Bowbell threatening to burn his house down.[19] And, finally, there was an unusual case of an arsonist—a 'political' incendiary—who not only claimed to hold radical opinions but to have engaged in acts of arson other than the one of which he had been convicted. He was William Cooper, 34, a draper of Weldon, Northamptonshire, who was given a life-sentence for arson at the Northampton Lent assizes of 1844. He admitted setting fire to a cottage and two other farm buildings and said he was a Chartist. Previously, he had been convicted or trespass, assault, and damage to property (crimes suggestive of some degree of political involvement) and had, on another occasion, been bound over to keep the peace on a surety of £40; and, further, he added to his confession that one Thomas Hammerton, who sailed with him on the *Agincourt*, had been transported for an offence he had himself committed: 'burning a stack and other property of a farm belonging to the Earl of Winchester'.[20]

The killing and maiming, or 'houghing', of livestock was, as we have seen in an earlier chapter, a peculiarly Irish way of settling accounts with an unpopular landlord or farmer. Dr. A. J. Peacock has, it is true, made a strong case that this was a recognized form of protest in the English village as well—particularly in the eastern counties to which he has devoted an illuminating chapter.[21] But,

[17] *Convicts landed in . . . NSW*, 1840; Petitions 1839 (O'Farrell).
[18] Hobsbawm and Rudé, *Captain Swing*, pp. 304–5.
[19] Tas. Arch., CON 33/32; Jones, p. 17.
[20] Tas. Arch., CON 33/83.
[21] A. J. Peacock, 'Village Radicalism in East Anglia 1800–50', in ed. J. P. D. Dunbabin, *Rural Discontent in Nineteenth Century Britain*, pp. 27–61.

even here, it never reached anything approaching the scale that it did in certain counties of Ireland, notably the western counties of Clare, Galway, and Mayo, where it acquired a particularly savage fury in the post-Famine years of 1848 and 1849.[22] So it remains an essentially Irish phenomenon.

Yet the number of cattle-maimers transported to Australia was comparatively small, far smaller than the number transported for arson: I have counted thirty-one Englishmen and forty Irishmen. (Transportation is, of course, not an accurate reflection of the scale of the offence any more than it is of the scale of arson in England before the 1830s.) Yet small as the sample is, it is large enough to show us that cattle-maiming, like arson, could be of two kinds: an acquisitive kind (as a form of theft, whether for sale or for personal consumption) and a protesting kind, where a close-fisted employer or a rack-renting landlord was the target of attack. Again, we may apply the sort of tests we applied before with particular emphasis on the precise nature of the offence and the occupation of the victim or assailant. Among the Englishmen transported, for example, it is reasonable to suppose that James Bristow, a Guildford butcher, whom Surrey quarter sessions in January 1828 sentenced to seven years' transportation for killing sheep, had profit rather than protest in mind.[23] Similarly, when John Cowley, a Lincolnshire ploughman, killed a lamb belonging to Edward Pender of Louth 'with intent [in his own words] to steal the carcase', we may conclude that he either intended to sell it or to keep it for his own use.[24] The case is different where the prisoner appears to have quite deliberately killed or maimed a ram, a cow, or a horse without apparent intention of removing the carcass for consumption. Thomas Smith, a young ploughman from Weston, in Gloucestershire, who was given a ten-year sentence at Warwick assizes in August 1840 for killing two rams and wounding a cow, seems to be a case in point: he admitted the offence and added that he had wounded them 'in the breast'.[25] Others of the kind were Joshua Griggs, a 23-year-old Essex shepherd, who was given seven years at quarter sessions in January 1831 for 'maiming a sheep'; Henry Jackson, a 25-year-old groom, sentenced at the Wiltshire assizes in March 1833 for 'killing rams'; Edward Duffill, a ploughman of Bromsgrove, who was given a ten-year sentence at the Worcester assizes in July 1840 for 'maliciously killing cattle'; and Edward Ladkin, a 19-year-old stocking-weaver, who at Leicester Lent assizes in 1841, was given a similar sentence for

[22] See p. 35 above.   [23] Arch. NSW, 4/4013.
[24] Tas. Arch., CON 33/6.   [25] Ibid.

maiming (or, in his own words, 'hamstringing') four sheep.[26] From a rough-and-ready calculation, these English maimers of livestock are unevenly balanced between 'predators' and 'protesters' with the 'predators' taking a three-to-two lead.

In the case of the Irish, the scales are tipped conspicuously in favour of the protesters—among those transported to New South Wales and Tasmania, at least. The case is different with the eight sheep-killers who arrived together on the *Phoebe Dunbar* in August 1853, the only Irishmen to have committed such an offence to come to Western Australia. They all came from the traditional 'houghing' counties of the West: Galway, Mayo, and Clare. But their occupations betray them: five were tailors, two were matmakers, and one a shoemaker—hardly good material for practitioners of rural protest or 'social' crime![27] But these are exceptional cases, all the more so as, contrary to the usual experience of transported 'houghers' or maimers of cattle, all except one of them had had one or more previous convictions. So these must, presumably, be treated as urban offenders, maybe motivated by hunger (the Famine was not long since over) or maybe by profit, or a combination of the two. Elsewhere the evidence points the other way and, from the eastern colonies, there are comparatively few cases like that of Mary Hogan, 50, described as a maid-of-all-work from Clare, who was sentenced by a Clare court in 1835 for 'killing cattle with intent to steal'; and of Pierce Cantill (alias Grace), a 35-year-old Kilkenny ploughman, who, at the Lent assizes of 1844 at Kilkenny, was convicted of 'killing sheep' and himself admitted that he had killed '14 or 15 sheep . . . with intent'.[28] Here it is the 'malicious' or 'felonious' 'houghers' and 'killers' that are the more typical. To cite a few examples of men sent to the two convict colonies between 1818 and 1843. Francis Gallacher, a Mayo labourer, aged 22, was given a life-sentence at Mayo assizes in August 1817 for 'feloniously killing heifers'; he sailed on the *Minerva*, where he was described as 'very well behaved on board'.[29] In the summer of 1819, Timothy Corkerry, a young labourer of Co. Cork, was transported for life for 'killing sheep'; and in March 1824 Edward Kehoe, a Waterford plough-man, was given a seven-year sentence at Wexford for 'killing a cow or heifer'.[30] It might be a family affair, as in the case of the

---

[26] Arch. NSW, 4/4016, 4018; Tas. Arch., CON 33/10.
[27] Arch. WA, R.18 (*Phoebe Dunbar*).
[28] Arch. NSW, 4/7078; Tas. Arch., CON 33/58.
[29] Tas. Arch., CON 13/1.
[30] Arch. NSW, 4/4007, 4010.

brothers Michael and Martin Donoghue and their father, Patrick (aged 76), who were sentenced for life for 'houghing sheep' at the Lent assizes at Galway in 1832.[31] Others might be sentenced for 'killing a ram', like Patrick Cane of Co. Sligo in 1831; for 'killing a horse' (a common offence in Ireland), like the brothers Thomas, Philip, and Edward Cassidy of Fermanagh in March 1830; or for 'poisoning two cows', like John Fitzpatrick, a Fermanagh labourer, who was sentenced in March 1839.[32] A more ambiguous case dates from April 1847, when John Brien of Co. Kilkenny, aged 30, was given a seven-year sentence for 'larceny' or—according to his own version of the affair—for 'killing a sheep and hoarding firearms'. Brien left his wife, Anastasia, and their three children at his native parish and arrived in Hobart on the *Pestonjee Bomanjee* on 2 January 1849.[33]

Poaching—like smuggling and assaults on revenue officers—presents a somewhat different problem. It has in common with arson and cattle-maiming, it is true, that it tended to be more prevalent in some English counties and in some parts of England than in others (for Ireland played no part): as we saw in an earlier chapter, between 1830 and the early 1850s at least, indictments for poaching were conspicuously more frequent in Yorkshire, Lancashire, Stafford, Suffolk, and Norfolk than elsewhere.[34] The convict records suggest a similar pattern: of more than 200 poachers arriving in Australia between 1825 and 1852, nearly a half came from half a dozen counties fairly evenly distributed between east and north, between Essex–Norfolk–Sussex on the one hand and Lancashire–Yorkshire–Stafford on the other. But, unlike cattle-maiming and arson, poaching was continual rather than sporadic and never appeared within the context of a mass movement, whether as curtain-raiser or accompaniment, like cattle-maiming in Ireland in the 1790s and 1840s and arson in the English 'Swing' counties in the early 1830s. In what sense, then, may poaching be treated as protest rather than as a form of sport or self-help? Earlier, it has been suggested that it should perhaps be seen as such when serving, or appearing to serve, as a challenge to the landowner's claim to reserve the right to hunt and fish to himself and to refuse it to others—in much the same way as the enclosure rioter challenged the right of the large farmer or village squire to fence off land that used to belong to the poorer villagers or to be held in common. It has also been argued— and this is a different point—that poaching, while not intimately

[31] Arch. NSW, 4/4017.   [32] Arch. NSW, 4/4016, 7076.
[33] Tas. Arch., CON 33/92.   [34] See p. 19 above.

linked with a movement of rural protest (as in the 1820s), may be seen as an indicator of a mounting 'groundswell of village opinion' in the years leading up to more explosive events.[35] These then are grounds (though somewhat tenuous ones) for including poaching, alongside arson and cattle-maiming, as a form of *marginal* protest in which some attempt must be made to separate the sheep from the goats. But how do we set about it in this case? How do we, among the 226 poachers transported to Australia, distinguish the protester from the 'social' offender (in E. P. Thompson's sense), the professional, the sportsman, or simple predator that we discussed at the beginning of this book?

To make our selection, we must begin, as before, by looking at the prisoner's occupation, his criminal record (imperfect in this case, as two in every three poachers went to New South Wales) and, for the minority that went to Tasmania, his 'confession' or statement. But, this time, the statement will not prove nearly as useful as it has before; for, while it may tell us something of the circumstances attending the offence, it will tell us nothing about any sense of grievance that he may have felt or any intention he may have had to restore a long-lost right. So, having, by means of such information as we have available, deducted a score of professionals and a further couple of dozen 'doubtful' occupations and dubious prison records, we are left with some 180 cases of whom, for lack of further evidence, there is no way of knowing whether they should be counted among the protesters or not.

Among these 'possibles' there was Thomas Taylor, a farm labourer of Measham, Leicestershire, 28, married with no children, who was given a fourteen-year sentence at Leicester Lent assizes in 1842. His only previous conviction, for which he served six months in jail, was for the similar and comparatively 'respectable' crime of stealing fowls. He sailed on the *Waterloo* (of which more will be said in a later chapter) and explained to the authorities on arrival in Hobart that he had been poaching with four others and had released a man whom the gamekeeper had taken into custody.[36] He was one of the comparatively few who was sent to Tasmania and, therefore, one of the few whose impressions were recorded. From the rest— those who went to Sydney—let us select a few cases at random: such as George Oakes, a farm labourer, aged 24, sentenced at Chester in April 1826 for poaching and shooting a gamekeeper; and Joseph Brett, a 19-year-old ploughman, convicted at Leicester quarter

---

[35] *Captain Swing*, p. 79.
[36] Tas. Arch., CON 33/30.

sessions in January 1830 of shooting pheasants, for which, like Oakes, he was transported to Sydney for seven years.[37] And, finally, into exile in Victoria in 1846 went Thomas Crush, a Chelmsford tailor, and James Lonbron, a Dorchester shoemaker (perhaps unlikely professions for protesters?), both convicted of 'night poaching', one given a seven-year term and the other ten;[38] while to Western Australia went the last poacher but one to sail on a convict transport: James Ross, convicted of 'night poaching' at the Aylesbury assizes, who arrived on the *Belgravia* at Fremantle in July 1866.[39]

[37] Arch. NSW, 4/4011; *Convicts landed in . . . NSW,* 1830.
[38] PRO Victoria, *Victoria, Shipping List for Immigrants,* vols. 2–3 (Feb. 1842–July 1848).
[39] Arch. WA, R.14. The last poacher of all to land in Australia was William Sykes, who was given a commuted life-sentence at Leeds in December 1865 after being involved in a poaching affair in which a gamekeeper was killed. He is the principal character in Alexandra Hasluck's sympathetic study, *Unwilling Emigrants. A Study of the Convict Period in Western Australia* (Melbourne, 1959). But for the kind of reason stated above, I have not counted him among the likely protesters.

PART FOUR

AUSTRALIAN EXILE

1. The Voyage

IN the eighty years of transportation, some 750 convict ships sailed from England and Ireland to the convict settlements of Australia; on about one in five of these, protesters sailed along with other offenders. On some ships they formed a majority, or else a substantial minority, and so were able to leave their mark, as a group, upon the whole ship; on most, however, particularly among the more 'marginal' of the social protesters, they formed small, relatively isolated, groups; but, in such cases of course, the degree of their isolation or cohesion depended on the degree to which the crime for which they were being transported had given them a sense of identity as a group.

The *Surprise*, the first of the transports to carry protesters, arrived in Sydney in October 1795, bringing four of the six Scottish Jacobins —Muir, Palmer, Skirving, and Margarot; but, though a small group, they were (despite their misunderstandings) a fairly compact one, all the more as they travelled on a small ship, carrying ninety-three convicts in all in addition to a few stores and provisions. The most compact—and largest—groups to sail were the English machine-breakers of 1830. All but a couple of dozen of them arrived in three ships: 224 who came to Hobart on the *Eliza* in May 1831 and 133 who came to Sydney on the *Eleanor* in June were the only prisoners on board; and the *Proteus*, which followed the *Eliza* to Hobart in August, carried ninety-eight machine-breakers and only four others. The 325 Irish rebels of 1798 arrived at Sydney Cove on half a dozen ships, but nearly all came on four: the *Anne* with 102, the *Minerva* with 73, and *Friendship II* and *Atlas* II with about sixty men apiece; and on the *Anne* and the *Friendship* the rebels outnumbered all other prisoners by two to one.[1] The forty-two Luddites of 1812–17 came on five ships, three-quarters of them evenly divided between the *Fortune* and the *Earl Spencer*, which arrived in Sydney in June and October 1813; and seventeen of the twenty-six Bristol rioters sailed together to Tasmania on the *Katherine Stewart Forbes* in 1832. On the other hand, the Pentrich rebels, the Yorkshire

---

[1] These figures are disputable: see my article 'Early Irish Rebels in Australia', *Hist. Stud.*, xvi (Apr. 1974), 17–35.

radical weavers and the Young Irelanders of 1848 were split up into smaller groups; and the Cato Street conspirators, while sailing together on one ship, formed a small island in a sea of larcenists and other common-law offenders. Larger units appeared again with the Canadian rebels, Chartists and Fenians of the 1840s and 1860s. Seventy-eight Upper Canadians and fifty-eight Lower Canadians, accounting for all but a dozen of them all, sailed together on the *Buffalo* in September 1839, reaching Hobart on 12 February 1840 and Sydney a fortnight later. Seventy-two of the seventy-five Chartists convicted after the 'Plug-Plot' riots of 1842 sailed together on the *John Renwick*, arriving in Hobart with eighty-eight other prisoners in April 1843; and the sixty-two Fenians came together on the *Hougomont* to Western Australia in January 1868. By contrast, the great majority of the marginal protesters—the arsonists, poachers, and cattle-maimers—sailed in small groups thinly spread over a large number of ships. Yet, among the arsonists, there were exceptions: several English ships brought thirty or more at a time to Norfolk Island or Tasmania in the late 1840s and early 1850s and to Western Australia soon after; and among the last ships to sail to Hobart in 1850–2 were half a dozen that between them had nearly 160 Irish women incendiaries on board.

Over the eighty-year transportation period, the ships changed considerably in size, tonnage, and armament, timber gave way to iron with the 1860s, and where the *Anne* took 240 days (admittedly after some mishaps) to complete her course in 1800 and the *William Metcalfe* (which brought George Loveless to Tasmania) took 104 days in 1834, the *Hougomont* took a mere 89 days to cross the ocean to Western Australia in 1867. (An earlier ship, the iron-built *Corona*, the quickest of them all, took only 67 days to cover the same distance the year before.) But this depended, of course, not only on a more advanced technology, but the state of the weather, on ports of arrival and departure, and the route taken by the ships. Most English ships sailed from Portsmouth and Spithead; but others—including Irish Fenians and three of the four 'Canadian' ships—sailed from London, Falmouth, Torbay, the Downs, or from the Thames at Sheerness; while Irish ships sailed nearly all from Cork—or, more properly, from the bay at Cobh—until 1837 and switched to Dublin between 1838 and 1852. (Only one Irish ship—the *Phoebe Dunbar*, with eight west-country cattle-maimers on board—was among the thirty-seven ships sailing to Western Australia between 1850 and 1868.) The route taken might be the most direct one—across the Atlantic and around the Horn; or it might be via the Cape, with stops at Gibraltar, Madeira or Bermuda; or, especially in the earlier days, it might be via Rio, entailing the longest voyage of the three.[2]

Before sailing, the convicts were taken from prison to the hulks at the port of departure, mustered, sent on board the transports, washed and shaved (if men), and issued with their ration of clothing and food for the day. With inevitable minor alterations over such a long span of time, the male prisoners were issued with the regulation dress of jackets and waistcoats of blue cloth or kersey, duck trousers, check or coarse linen shirts, yarn stockings, and woollen caps. In winter, woollen shirts and undergarments, too, would have been more suitable; but the naval authorities at first chose economy, pleading hygiene as their excuse; but warmer clothing was added in the 1830s, bringing in flannel underclothes and raven duck overalls. Generally speaking, the women's clothing was more inadequate still: up to the late 1820s at least, they wore on departure such clothes as they brought with them, though, before landing in Australia, they were given a brown serge jacket and petticoat, a couple of linen shifts, a linen cap, a kerchief, a pair of worsted stockings, and a pair of shoes. In the 1830s, ladies' committees were formed, inspired by Elizabeth Fry; and gift-parcels began to be given to each woman prisoner before she sailed. By the early 1840s, they were further supplied with white jackets and checked aprons for use in the tropics.[3]

Food was considered adequate—by the authorities at least—and was generally thought to be of better quality than that served to the army or navy. 'The rations are good and abundant', wrote a ship's surgeon of the convict-ships of the 1820s, 'three-quarters of a pound of biscuit being the daily ration of bread, while each day the convict sits down to dinner of either beef, pork or plum-pudding, having pea-soup four times a week, and a pot of gruel every morning, with sugar or butter in it. Vinegar is issued to the messes weekly, and as soon as the ship has been three weeks at sea, each man is served with an ounce of lime-juice and the same of sugar daily, to guard against scurvy . . .'[4] It sounded less appetizing when described by William Gates, one of the *Buffalo*'s American passengers: a daily ration (he wrote) of 'one-half pound of bread, one-pound of meat— pork and beef alternatively—a pint of skilly in the morning, a pint

---

[2] For details of ships, their cargoes and voyages, see Charles Bateson, *The Convict Ships 1788–1868*, pp. 287–341 (Appendix).
[3] Bateson, pp. 56–7.
[4] Cit. Bateson, p. 58.

of cocoa or tea at night, a pint of water, and a small quantity of duff [flour pudding]'.[5]

The prisoners' quarters lay between-decks; after improvements made in 1817, they usually consisted of two rows of sleeping-berths, one above the other, each 6 feet square and made to hold four convicts, so that each man had 18 inches of space to sleep in: 'Double bunks with a little bedding', wrote Gates, and 'tubs for the reception of filth' as 'the sum total of our conveniences'; while Léon Ducharme, one of the French-Canadians on board, added that the ceilings were no more than four and a half feet high and that 141 men were packed in a space of about 25 feet square.[6] On an earlier 'Canadian' ship, the *Marquis of Hastings*, which brought nine of the Short Hills prisoners to Hobart, Benjamin Wait, another diarist, describes his first encounter with his sleeping quarters in more passionate terms:

> When the whole number, including twenty-three state prisoners and eleven felons, had been searched and sent below together . . . a scene of confusion and tumult commenced which beggars description . . . The shouts and curses of the felons, fighting for pre-eminence, mingled with the clanking of chains, aided by the frigid chilliness of the atmosphere and the damp fetid smell arising from the bilge water created peculiar sensations of gloom and dread and forebodings.[7]

He had cause: the prisoners' quarters, on the *Buffalo* and elsewhere, were dark and gloomy and the ventilation was universally bad; and never so bad as when a ship was becalmed in the tropics or when, in stormy weather, the hatches were battened down and prisoners, instead of taking their daily exercise on deck, were compelled to endure the foul atmosphere of the hold for hours, and even days, on end. John Boyle O'Reilly, the Fenian poet, who sailed nearly thirty years later on the *Hougomont*, described the sufferings of men becalmed in the tropics in his novel *Moondyne*. Then, he writes:

the sufferings of the imprisoned wretches in the steaming and crowded hold was piteous to see. They were so packed that free movement was impossible. The best thing to do was to sit each on his or her berth, and suffer in patience. The air was stifling and oppressive. There was no draught through the barred hatches. The deck above them was blazing hot . . . There was only one word

[5] From William Gates's *Recollections of Life in Van Diemen's Land* (New York, 1850); cit. E. C. Guillet, *The Lives of the Patriots*, p. 198.

[6] Ibid.; Léon (Léandre) Ducharme, *Journal of an Exile in Australia* (Eng. edn., Sydney, 1944), pp. 15, 17.

[7] Benjamin Wait, *Van Diemen's Land, written during Four Years' Imprisonment* (Buffalo, 1843); cit. Guillet, p. 203.

spoken or thought—one yearning idea in every mind—water, cool water to slake the parching thirst.[8]

While exercising, a welcome part of the daily routine, the convicts were given a change of air up on deck, but handcuffed together and secured by leg-irons. 'Ironing', as this was called, was next to flogging the most common punishment for men. Women prisoners were also on occasion flogged; but more commonly their heads were shaved, or they were placed in a scolder's bridle or in the coal-hole, or made to suffer the ignominy of parading the deck in a tub. But, of all punishments, flogging was the most brutal, the most dreaded and resented. On some early ships, before the authorities stepped in to restrain the ardour of over-zealous or sadistic captains, floggings could be so savage as to kill men or maim them for life. Perhaps the worst recorded example is that of the *Britannia* (which brought a large number of Defenders of Ireland to Sydney in 1796-7), on which a combination of short rations and physical brutality killed off one in every seventeen prisoners embarked.[9] Things were not much better on the *Hercules* and *Atlas I*, which brought some of the Irish rebels to Sydney a few years later: on these ships floggings and overcrowded conditions combined to reduce the number of arrivals by forty-four in the first case and sixty-five in the second.[10]

Disease was another mortal enemy. The over-all death-rate was one for every sixty-eight men and eighty-four women carried. But, as with flogging, there was a considerable improvement through the years: 'for men, from one in nine before 1800, to one in twenty-four between 1801 and 1815 and one in 113 thereafter, and, for women, from one in thirty to one in sixty-seven and ninety-four respectively'.[11] So much for the average; but long after the statistics began to show a steep downward trend, individual cases of heavy mortality persisted. A notable example was the *Katherine Stewart Forbes*—bringing most of the Bristol rioters to Hobart—which lost thirteen men from cholera in 1832.[12] The *Hashemy* lost sixteen men from sickness and disease in 1849 and the *Phoebe Dunbar*, the only Irish ship to carry prisoners to Western Australia, arrived ten men short in 1853.

[8] J. B. O'Reilly, *Moondyne* (Melbourne, 1880), p. 186.
[9] Bateson, pp. 143-4.
[10] Rudé, in *Historical Studies*, p. 17.
[11] A. G. L. Shaw, *Convicts and the Colonies*, p. 116.
[12] The same year, the *Asia*, bound for Sydney with sixty-six Irish land-'warriors' on board, lost eleven men, including six rebels (Bateson, p. 333).

But, though disease was by far the greater scourge, boredom was the more constant companion, striking all—men and women, young and old—alike. The tedium that most prisoners experienced is well captured—though perhaps involuntarily—by the monotony of Léon Ducharme's day-to-day recital of the *Buffalo*'s long passage to Australia: sailing out of Quebec harbour on 28 September and only weighing anchor in Sydney, her final port of call, close on five months later.[13] Under such conditions, prisoners were glad to be set to tasks, even to such a normally uncongenial task as picking oakum. Some, the more favoured ones, picked out for good conduct or superior intelligence, might even be allowed to assist in navigation or be selected to teach their less lettered companions to read and write. It was a function performed by many a protester on a long series of ships: among others by Robert Mason, the Hampshire machine-breaker, on the *Eleanor* and by Lewis Lewis, the Merthyr riot captain, a year later on the *John*.[14]

The long and tedious voyage might also be enlivened by disaster. This could take the form of bad weather, shipwreck, or mutiny. One ship that suffered a particularly stormy and uncomfortable passage was the *Tottenham*, on which most of the convicted Pentrich rebels came to Sydney in 1818. From the start she was buffeted by heavy gales, had to return to port for repairs, and ten of her convicts, weakened by seasickness and disease, died before her arrival in port. Even worse disasters befell the *Amphitrite* in 1833, the *Neva* and *George III* in 1835, and the *Waterloo* (with two of our 'selected' poachers, Thomas Taylor and Edward Capstack on board) in 1842. The *Hive* was badly mauled but limped into port for the loss of no lives; but 106 women from the *Amphitrite* and 138 from the *Neva* were drowned. The *George III* struck a rock in the D'Entrecasteaux Channel, a few miles out of Hobart, and lost 127 men; while the biggest shipwreck of all was that of the *Waterloo*, which was battered to pulp by a hurricane off the Cape, drowning 143 convicts and forty-three others and leaving the seventy-two convict survivors (including our two poachers) to sail on to Hobart on the *Cape Packet* after a voyage of 176 days.[15]

For the officers, if not for the convicts and crew, mutiny—or the rumour of mutiny—was an even greater, and certainly a more continuous, hazard. There were mutinies, both among convicts, on the *Anne* and the *Hercules*, in 1801. The outbreak on the *Hercules*,

[13] Ducharme, pp. 15–31.
[14] Arch. NSW, 4/4513, 4/4144.
[15] Shaw, p. 116; Bateson, pp. 190–1, 232–7, 260–7; Tas. Arch., CON 33/30.

occurring off Cape Verdes in late December, was quickly and brutally put down. The mutiny on the *Anne*, involving Irish rebels, was a political affair, in which thirty prisoners seized weapons from the ship's armoury, attacked officers and guards and took hostages among the officers, before they were overcome. One of the leaders, Christopher Grogan, received a flogging of 250 lashes; and another, Marcus Sheehy, a United Irishman from Limerick, was executed on board by a firing squad, the first and only convict to suffer such a fate. More serious still was the outbreak on the *Chapman*, also bringing Irish political prisoners to Australia, in March–April 1817. A month out from port, an informer disclosed a plot to seize the ship and take her to America. All convicts were clapped in irons and extreme precautions were taken to ensure the safe custody of arms. But a false rumour of a planned convict rising was started two days later; and in the ensuing panic the captain ordered fire to be opened, without discrimination, on the prisoners in the hold. Three or more were killed and twenty-two wounded. Further rumours provoked further panics and further bloodshed; and the ship arrived in port, some weeks later, after fourteen convicts and two sailors had been shot dead and two further prisoners had died from dysentery. A court of inquiry referred the matter for trial in London at the Old Bailey, where half a dozen officers and soldiers were acquitted of excessive brutality a year and a half later.[16]

In January 1820 a plot was conceived by a number of convicts to seize the *Castle Forbes*, recently arrived from Ireland, as she lay at anchor at Hobart and take her out to sea; but the inevitable informer reported the plan, and it came to nothing. Informers were also prone—and this should not surprise us—to invent conspiracies where they did not exist, as apparently happened in the case of the *Ocean* and *Isabella* in 1823, the *Mangles* in 1824, and the *Royal Charlotte* in 1825.[17] And on the *Buffalo*, two of the Americans, Stephen Wright and Daniel Heustis, refer to a mutiny that they believe was plotted among the political prisoners to seize the ship and take her to New York—a plot, wrote Wright, that was betrayed to the captain by one of the Patriot prisoners (presumably John Tyrrell, whom Ducharme, in relating the incident, presents as *inventing* rather than betraying the plot).[18] The same theme of a thwarted conspiracy to seize the ship appears in O'Reilly's semi-fictional account of the *Hougomont*'s last voyage.[19] More authentic was the mutiny attempted by some of the seamen of the *Isabella*

[16] Bateson, pp. 158–62, 184–8.   [17] Bateson, pp. 192–3, 199–201.
[18] Cit. Guillet, pp. 198–9; Ducharme, pp. 18–19.   [19] *Moondyne*, pp. 174–5.

in a later voyage, when she was carrying 224 English convicts—
including a handful of machine-breakers of 1830—to Sydney. Ten
weeks out from Plymouth, a sailor refused to obey orders and was
clapped in irons; several of the crew mutinied, and the ship arrived
in Sydney Cove with fourteen men in chains. The convicts, despite
early rumours to the contrary, were not involved: in fact, some
helped the officers, the ship's carpenter, the boatswain, and the
remaining seamen to bring the vessel into port.[20]

Yet there were occasions—and not only in the earliest days—
when protesters and other convicts joined (or appeared to join) in
attempts to seize a vessel and sail her to another port. There was
the case of the *Katherine Stewart Forbes* in the course of the same
ill-fated voyage on which she suffered a severe attack of cholera on
her way to Tasmania. Ten days after her departure from Plymouth,
as Lt.-Col. Arthur reported to London in July 1832, there had been
'a general spirit of insubordination' among the prisoners followed
by an attempted mutiny which, however, had been 'foiled by the
judicious conduct of the Surgeon Superintendent'.[21] Among the
ringleaders, it emerged after the ship had anchored in Hobart, was
one of the Bristol rioters of November 1831, Charles Williams, a
young Bristol carpenter, who had been given a life-sentence for
'riotously demolishing a house' and was now given a further three-
year sentence in the penal hell of Macquarie Harbour for 'having
on April 4th, 5th and 6th aboard the Kath^e Stewart Forbes conspired
to take that vessel' and 'induced others to join in the same'.[22]
A second occasion came ten years later, when the *Isabella Watson*
was carrying 197 Irish convicts from Dublin to Hobart between May
and August 1842. Among the prisoners were eight protesters,
Ribbonmen and others convicted of robbery of arms or administering unlawful oaths, five of whom were suspected of planning a
mutiny and put in irons for the rest of the voyage; while two others
—Peter Smith and Patrick O'Hara—were later commended for
informing the surgeon of what was afoot. Among the suspects were
two brothers, Hugh and Francis Gafney, both labourers of Co.
Cavan, who placed the blame squarely on the shoulders of a man
from a very different background from their own: Richard Jones,
a Dublin clerk and Ribbonman, who figured in an earlier chapter.
According to Francis Gafney's account of the incident, given after

[20] Bateson, p. 198; Hobsbawm and Rudé, *Captain Swing*, p. 267.
[21] Arthur to R. W. Hay, 20 July 1832, Tas. Arch., GO *Despatches* (Outward),
vol. 11, pp. 82–5.
[22] Tas. Arch., CON 31/46.

the ship's arrival in Hobart: 'Some time in May last Peter Smith and my brother told me that Richard Jones was going to speak to me about taking the ship. They advised me to shun him. I did so.' In this case, if we may believe Francis Gafney's story, virtue was clearly not its own reward; for both he and his brother were kept in irons, with Jones and two others, until the vessel arrived in port. Whatever the truth of it, the 'conspiracy' obviously came to nothing and the ship almost achieved a record by completing her voyage from Dublin in 93 days.[23]

And, finally, whatever the boredom and excitement, brutality and tribulations, there was the sudden, unexpected, relief of seeing land and sailing between the gently rising wooded slopes of the Derwent to Hobart or below the towering Heads leading into Sydney Cove. Ducharme, who experienced both as for him Hobart dock was only a stepping-stone to Sydney, gave a new lilt to his account as he gazed with mixed feelings of relief, awe, and trepidation at the strange land and brooded on the uncertain future that lay before him, while the *Buffalo*, with the French-Canadians still on board, plunged through heavy seas between the Heads.

Towards ten o'clock [he concluded this section of his *Journal*] the weather cleared, and once again we caught sight of land. The coastline still appeared to us very precipitous, and, the sea breaking upon it, the water rose up more than fifty feet into the air. About noon we caught sight of a lighthouse on a point dominating the shore; at the same time a pilot came on board, and we successfully entered Port Jackson and came to anchor at Sydney Cove. So we arrived all safe and sound at our place of exile after a voyage of five months. It is astonishing to observe that so long and dangerous a voyage can be made without accident, even though we had experienced bad weather that might have placed us in great danger . . .

Although we knew that our situation would not be very pleasant, we nevertheless experienced much pleasure at the thought that we had at last reached our destination. One must pass five long months at sea to understand how sweet it is to set foot on shore and to be free from the constraint of the ship.[24]

[23] Tas. Arch., CON 33/26.
[24] Ducharme, p. 30.

2. The Convict System

THE convict system was designed to meet three needs: to remove what were believed to be dangerous criminals from England's (and Ireland's) prisons which were overcrowded or said to be so; to regenerate men who were deemed to be in particular need of moral regeneration; and to provide labour for the colonial government and settlers. Contemporaries and historians have differed in their order of priorities,[1] but few have followed Governor Arthur of Tasmania in attaching prime importance to the second of the three. However, this problem of origins and why transportation to Australia began at all need not concern us here. Our concern is rather with what role the convicts were made to play when they got there and how they played it. And here the answer is a fairly simple one: whatever the original intention, once the convicts arrived in the colony they were cast for an economic role and if they became reformed in the process so much the better; and even so stern a moralist as Colonel Arthur conceded—in his evidence before the Molesworth Committee in 1837—that the convict could be likened to a slave, a man 'deprived of liberty, exposed to all the caprice of the family to whose service he may happen to be assigned, and subject to the most summary laws'.[2]

As the use of labour lay at the core of penal transportation, it is natural that every time the system was changed careful consideration should be given to how that labour could be best employed; and, conversely, it is evident that once there ceased to be a regular demand for servile labour—or when such a demand was overridden by others of a political nature—the system, having outlived its purpose, broke down or was abolished by the Government at home. With this in mind, it is appropriate to divide the transportation period into two main parts, with a break around 1838–40: the period when convicts were assigned on arrival for work with free settlers or government (the 'assignment' period) and that in which they served a preliminary 'probationary' term in a penal settlement on public works before being allowed to work, as relatively free men,

[1] For a discussion of these views, see Geoffrey Blainey, *The Tyranny of Distance* (Melbourne, 1966), pp. 18–33. See also Shaw, pp. 38–57; and C. M. H. Clarke, *A History of Australia*, 4 vols. (Melbourne, 1962–78), i, 59–72.

[2] *Eng. Hist. Docs.*, vol. xii (1833–74), ed. A. Aspinall, p. 515.

for the settlers or government departments (the 'probation' period). So, in theory, there were two main periods separated by the 'great divide' of the Molesworth Report (published in 1838). But, in practice, there were not two but four or five. There was the initial period up to about 1817, particularly in New South Wales, during which, although assignment had been agreed to in principle, there were rarely enough jobs to employ the rapidly rising number of convicts. There followed the assignment period proper, which lasted in both colonies between 1818 and 1839 but probably worked better in Tasmania than it did in New South Wales. Soon after this, New South Wales ceased to take on new convicts and the probation system worked—often nominally rather than actually—in Tasmania alone until it also closed its doors to further transportation in 1853. Meanwhile, Port Phillip, Victoria, had (between 1845 and 1849) become a place of 'exile' for men who had already served their prison-term in England; and Western Australia, both when it served as a kind of subsidiary to Tasmania in the early 1850s and when, after 1853, it remained as the only penal colony in the field, had (as we shall see) a system all its own.

And now, to see how these systems worked, let us take a number of examples from the 3,600 protesters on our cards. In the earliest period in New South Wales the governor, though guided by general directives from home, had a good deal of discretion in disposing of his convicts as he chose. In practice this meant that, such being the superfluity of labour, assignment was allowed to go by the board. The Scottish Jacobins, the earliest of our protesters, were given a special status as political prisoners (a status refused to the Cato Street conspirators a generation later) and were allowed to work and earn a living on their own account: Thomas Muir, for example, went to live, soon after his arrival, on a small farm across the harbour from Sydney Cove.[3] A few years later, there is no sign of the early Irish rebels—arriving on the *Anne*, *Friendship*, *Minerva*, and other vessels—being assigned for work with private employers (in fact, we hear little further of them until the Muster of 1806); but we do know that a great number of them were employed by government at Parramatta, a few miles out of Sydney, from September 1800 onwards. It was here that a succession of 'insurrections' and 'conspiracies' were hatched (or said to have been so) among the Irish labourers, culminating in the Castle Hill Rebellion of 1804.[4] Michael

---

[3] *ADB*, ii, 266.
[4] For details and bibliography, see G. Rudé, 'Early Irish Rebels in Australia', *Hist. Studies*, xvi, 25-6.

Dwyer and the other four State prisoners arriving with him on the *Tellicherry* were, like the Scottish Jacobins, a special case. A deal had been struck with the British Government before they sailed; so, on their arrival, Governor King accorded them the status of free settlers and made each man a free gift of a hundred acres of land;[5] but at least two of their fellow prisoners, and possible fellow rebels, Darby Murray and Daniel Kelly, were refused the concession and assigned to work for private employers at Parramatta.[6]

When this began to become a regular practice is hard to determine; and, once more, there are no assignment lists for the Luddites arriving in Sydney in 1812 and 1813; but, in Tasmania, George Green, a Nottingham frame-breaker who was one of the earliest protesters to be sent there, was, a few months after arrival, assigned for service with A. W. H. Humphrey (no address given) and continued to work for him until he gained his freedom six years later.[7] In Sydney, too, the system appears to have become well established by the end of 1817; for we find two of the later Luddites—John Clarke and James Watson, stocking-weavers sentenced for assaulting a watchman at Loughborough—assigned to work at Windsor after arriving on *Ocean II* in January 1818.[8] Soon after, the next great batch of Irish protesters, sentenced under the Insurrection Acts of 1814 and 1822 (but mainly the latter), were beginning to arrive in large numbers in New South Wales. One of the largest groups came on the *Mangles* in November 1822, forty-three of them from Co. Limerick alone. Most of these and most of those arriving in the Irish ships that followed were assigned for agricultural service at Airds, Bringelly, Evan, Minto, Windsor, and Parramatta, all lying in the wealthy Cumberland Plain within a few hours' travel from Sydney.[9]

By the time the 'Swing' rioters arrived in Australia in the early 1830s, the assignment system was in its heyday, particularly in Tasmania under the conscientious and ever-industrious Colonel Arthur. In New South Wales the areas of settlement had been extended further inland[10] and the machine-breakers (whose assign-

[5] Arch. NSW, 4/4004; T. J. Kiernan, *Irish Exiles in Australia* (Dublin, 1954), pp. 29–30.

[6] ML, Muster Roll, 1806.

[7] Tas. Arch., CON 31/13.

[8] Arch. NSW, 4/3497, pp. 307–8. Some of the Pentrich rebels, too, also arriving in 1818, were sent to work on arrival, or soon after, at Parramatta (see p. 192 below).

[9] Arch. NSW, 4/430-2.

[10] See T. M. Perry, *Australia's First Frontier. The Spread of Settlement in New South Wales 1788-1829* (Melbourne, 1963).

ment lists are quite complete) were assigned for service not only at Sydney or in the Cumberland Plain; but several went to Bathurst, towards the colony's western limits, north-west to the Hunter River Valley, and north as far as Newcastle and Port Stephens, a hundred miles and more along the coast from Sydney.[11] In Tasmania, when the *Eliza* arrived in June 1831, Arthur reported to London that of the 224 men she carried thirty had been retained for service as craftsmen with government departments at Hobart, twenty-eight had been sent north to work for the Van Diemen's Land Company at Circular Head and others of their numerous establishments, while the rest had been widely distributed among farmers and other private employers in different parts of the island. (All but two of the *Proteus* men, landed soon after, were assigned to private employment.)[12] The economic uses of transportation (and its limits) are neatly brought out in the story of how prisoners were selected for work with the Van Diemen's Land Company. The Directors were well placed to steal a march on their rivals, as two of them were Members of Parliament for disaffected counties and one, Joseph Cripps, was also Chairman of the Gloucester quarter sessions that sentenced twenty-four villagers to transportation. Their aim was to get fifty men or more (including these twenty-four), farmworkers and craftsmen, put aboard the *Eliza*, the first ship to sail, and have them landed if possible at Launceston, which lay conveniently close to their estates; in return they would send out at their own expense three free servants for every five convicts they acquired. But the plan miscarried, largely owing to the scruples of Colonel Arthur, who, as we have seen, did not believe that penal transportation should have as its main purpose to cater to the economic interests of the wealthier settlers. So the Company's Directors had obstacles put in their path and had to be satisfied with only half the number they had asked for; and only ten of these were from their original list of fifty.[13]

Soon after, the assignment system came under heavy fire and complaints against its operation were heard by the Molesworth Select Committee when it met in 1837. By now, the number of assigned convicts in Tasmania was nearly 6,500 and in New South Wales a little over 20,000. One complaint (doubtless influenced by such cases as the one just cited) was that, as the demand for convict labour now greatly exceeded the supply, there was a serious danger

[11] Arch. NSW, 4/4016 (assignments); HO 10/32-6 (Muster Rolls, Dec. 1837).
[12] Tas. Arch., GO 33/8, pp. 431-3.
[13] G. Rudé, '"Captain Swing" and Van Diemen's Land', *Tas. Hist. Assoc.* xii (Oct. 1964), 16-17, 23.

of abuses in its distribution, especially of craftsmen, domestic servants, and experienced country labourers who had a valuable commodity to offer. Moreover, among further abuses was cited the tendency of employers, fearful of losing such labour as they had, to defeat the ends of justice by either not reporting their convict labourers for misdemeanours or by settling for a flogging rather than a spell in a chain-gang or a prison term. So for these and other reasons the Molesworth Committee recommended (and the Government agreed) that, as assignment made for inequality in both labour and punishment, it should be replaced by another system that made for neither.[14] 'The certainty of a given quantity of punishment' must replace the 'uncertain coercion which is the consequence of assignment', as the Under-Secretary at the Colonial Office told Arthur in March 1837.[15] The outcome was probation, a brand-new creation intended to cure all ills. From now on, prisoners on arrival would be divided into three classes, depending on character and record, and sent to work at one of a score of Probation stations scattered along the Tasmanian coast. (New South Wales had by now become virtually closed to convict traffic.) After serving a two-to-four-year period, tailored according to the original sentence, they would emerge with a pass and be allowed to seek service for wages with government or private employers.

Among the first prisoners to come under the new system were John Frost, Zephaniah Williams, and William Jones, the Newport rebels of 1839. They arrived on the *Mandarin* with 207 other convicts on 30 June 1840. Three days later, Sir John Franklin, who had succeeded Arthur, reported the ship's arrival to Lord John Russell in London and wrote that the prisoners would be 'placed in a probationary gang on the Roads' with the exception of the three leaders whom he had thought it best 'to forward direct from the vessel to the Tasman Peninsula'.[16] So they were separated from their fellow Chartists, John Jones, Jeremiah Howell, and Francis Roberts, who were sent for a two-year probationary period, the first to Brown River, the second to Bridgewater, and the third to the New Wharf at Hobart before being sent on to Port Arthur for misconduct a year later.[17] But probation was still at a tentative, experimental stage. It was more securely established by the time the next, and largest, batch of Chartists—the north-country rioters of 1842—arrived on

---

[14] *Eng. Hist. Docs.*, xii, 541.
[15] Cit. Shaw, p. 268.
[16] Tas. Arch., GO *Despatches* (*Outward*), xxx, 593–7.
[17] Tas. Arch., CON 33/1.

the *John Renwick* on 10 April 1843. Their term of probation appears to have gone strictly according to plan. Joseph Talks, a young miner from Macclesfield, who had been given a seven-year sentence for stealing bread from the Stockport workhouse, did two years' probationary labour at the coal mines on the Tasman Peninsula and was discharged with a record of good conduct on 10 April 1845. Thomas Banks, who had received a ten-year sentence for rioting at Handley, spent thirty months in labour gangs at Rocky Hills and Maria Island; while Edward Walshe, a 15-year-old boy from Blackburn, spent three years at Impression Bay, and Robert Clish, a 'lifer' from Walshaw, Staffordshire, was sent to the coal mines for four years and had two further months added for 'disobedience and neglect of work'.[18] But even now there were exceptions. Isaac Colclough, another Handley rioter, spent seven months of his seven-year term at Millbank prison and arrived in the colony a year and a half later than the rest. Owing to this spell of prison in England he was issued with a 1st-class pass by order of the Secretary of State and allowed to forgo his period of probation.[19]

By the mid 1840s exceptions to the probation system had become almost as common as the rule. There were, for example, the two Irishmen from Ayr, who had taken part in a miners' strike over wages. They arrived at Hobart on the *Stratheden* in December 1845, but having first spent their two years' probation at Port Phillip, in Victoria on the way.[20] (Many more—including large numbers of English arsonists—spent the years of probation at Norfolk Island as a stepping stone to Tasmania.)[21] More commonly, however, Port Philip had by this time come to be used as a place of 'exile' for men who had committed what still rated as transportable crimes and spent a term of prison in England before rounding off their sentence in Victoria with 'conditional' pardons and working as assigned servants for local employers. The system only lasted from 1845 to 1849, during which years eleven ships brought 1,162 'exiles' to Victorial ports, Geelong and Port Philip. Among them were seven arsonists, three sheep-killers (no protesters among them), and one solitary rioter. One of the arsonists, Joseph Clough, was a 20-year-old collier and sometime matmaker, who had received a fifteen-year sentence at Stafford in July 1844 and arrived at Port Phillip with 298 other 'exiles' on 9 November 1846. Of these, 196 came from Pentonville, seventy from Parkhurst, thirty-two from Millbank, and one from the *Institution* at Woolwich. Clough himself spent some

[18] Tas. Arch., CON 33/38.   [19] Tas. Arch., CON 33/61.
[20] Tas. Arch., CON 33/73.   [21] Tas. Arch., CON 33/76, 79–80, 83, 86–8.

months in Millbank before being moved to Pentonville. Like others, he arrived with a 'warrant Pardon' that had been issued as they boarded the ship at London. Before we lose sight of him, we learn that, in the colony, he went to work for a Miss Ham for £20 a year.[22]

By the time Western Australia was opened up as a penal colony (the first convict ship arrived there in June 1850), probation, like assignment before it, was in total disarray. At first, there were only English (or Scottish) prisoners—the first and the only fully Irish ship arrived in 1853—and they (like the Victorian 'exiles') spent a term in a British jail before coming to Australia. But how long that term should be and why one man should stay longer in England after sentence than another there seems no way of knowing. Joseph Clayton, for example, an arsonist with a fifteen-year sentence, was kept in jail in Chester for two years three months before sailing on the *Hashemy* in July 1850;[23] whereas Robert Dixon, also a fifteen-year arsonist, spent only eighteen months in jail before he left on the next ship to Clayton's, the *Mermaid*, in February 1851. Similarly, in 1856, of two fifteen-year arsonists sailing together on the *William Hammond*, one (George Bray) had been in prison for five years and the other (William Reed) for eighteen months; and so we could go on.[24] But, a year later, as Western Australia was entering upon its second stage as a penal settlement, probation was revived and tightened up (in theory if not in practice) and a time-scale was devised to relate the period of probation strictly to the term of servitude prescribed. Each prisoner, regardless of the length of his sentence, was now to spend nine months in 'separate confinement'— an invention of well-meaning but misguided reformers!—before serving a probationary period (whether at home or in the colony was not made clear), starting with twelve months for a man with a three-year term, eighteen months for a four-year term, rising by stages to five years for fifteen years and above, while 'lifers' (becoming comparatively rare by this time)[25] were 'to be separately reported

---

[22] PRO Victoria, *Shipping Lists of Immigrants*, vols. 2–3.

[23] Arch. WA, R.17.

[24] Arch. WA, A.128, R.19. Of course, there were cases (though comparatively rare) where the operation went strictly according to plan: as that of two other arsonists of 1856—ten-year men this time—who, though one (James Kemp) was convicted in Scotland (Stirling) and the other (Lawrence Day) in England (Norwich), spent almost identical terms in prison before sailing together on the *William Hammond* and receiving their 'ticket of leave' on the same day: 29 Mar. 1856 (ibid.).

[25] One reason was that the British Government had agreed not to send its worst criminals to Western Australia. Cherry Gertzel, 'The Convict System in Western Australia, 1850–70' (B.A. hons. thesis, Univ. of Western Australia, 1949), p. 4.

on'.[26] And this appears to have worked according to plan in some cases but not in others: we find, for example, that Edward Finch, a young labourer given a twenty-year sentence for arson at Bedford in March 1857, sailed with the *Edwin Fox* in June 1858 after spending fifteen months in Chatham prison, and receiving his 'ticket of leave' (thereby ending his period of probation) in November 1861.[27]

It was a modified form of this system that was due to apply to the Fenians when they arrived on the *Hougomont* in January 1868; the main difference being that in their case the whole period of probation would be spent in the colony after a brief wait in prison before they sailed. In theory, this should have applied to all; and for each of the prisoners a time-table had been drawn up as to when he might expect the probation period to end and his freedom to work where and how he pleased to begin. But, in practice, about half the prisoners —all but a handful of those convicted of 'treason felony'—were given 'free pardons' in May 1869, a mere sixteen months after the vessel's arrival. A small number sentenced for high treason—Edward Kelly, of Cork, and Patrick Doran, of Dublin—were not included on this list; nor were the far larger number of 'mutineers', who accounted for one-third to one-half of all the prisoners. Most of these had to serve their allotted time of probation, deductions being made for meritorious behaviour. Some, however, had the good fortune to escape the net. One of these fortunates was John Boyle O'Reilly, the Fenian poet, who absconded on 17 February 1869, 'supposed (it was officially reported) to have left the colony in an American whaler'.[28]

So far in this chapter we have been mainly concerned with the use to which convict labour was put during the period of penal servitude. In theory, this continued for the whole length of the sentence; but, in practice, even from the earliest days of settlement in New South Wales, it was agreed (though it took some time for the intention to be given formal definition) that a man should be able, through hard work or meritorious conduct, or as an incentive to reformation, to secure some degree of remission of his term of servitude. So, already in the 1790s, a 'pass' system was devised which would secure the prisoner his freedom from compulsory labour subject to periodic reports to the police and the obligation to reside in a place of abode

[26] Gertzel, Appendices, Table 2.
[27] Arch. WA, A.128, R.1.
[28] Arch. WA, R.16, V.10. For O'Reilly, see also Martin G. Carroll, 'Behind the Lighthouse' (unpub. Ph.D. dissertation, Univ. of Iowa, 1954).

prescribed by the authorities; this 'pass' was later to be known as a 'ticket of leave'. A more sweeping concession was for a prisoner to be pardoned before his sentence expired. Some early governors, like Governor King, were comparatively generous with such concessions and among the 'emancipists' listed on the Muster rolls of 1806 are the names of William Redfern, the naval mutineer, and of several Irish rebels of 1798: they include Henry Alcock, a former captain in the Wexford militia who arrived on the *Minerva* and whose life-sentence was converted to a seven-year term for good conduct in the colony; also, among the 'lifers', Joseph ('General') Holt, of Wicklow, who was emancipated by King in 1802, and Bryan O'Connor, a doctor from Cork, who was allowed to go free and practise his profession in August 1801. But later governors proved less indulgent; and we find men who, before 1806, had been 'emancipated' by King being granted 'conditional' pardons by his successors. (One such case was that of Jeremiah Cavanagh, of *Friendship II*, who, though an emancipist in 1806, was petitioning for his pardon to be made absolute four years later.)[29]

So, by this time, there were normally three stages in a convict's progression to freedom. It began with a ticket of leave and ended with a certificate of freedom, passing through the intermediate stage of a 'conditional pardon', which allowed him to work and live where he pleased providing he did not leave the colony. An 'absolute pardon' was something else, granted by the Secretary of State on comparatively rare occasions, yet granted more readily to a protester—particularly a 'political' protester—than to anyone else. It was a privilege accorded, in the early days as we have seen, to the Scottish Jacobins and several of the United Irish under Governor King; and it was used again to free, after varying periods of servitude, the Scottish rebels and Yorkshire weavers of 1820, the machine-breakers of 1830, the Tolpuddle Martyrs of 1834, the Newport rebels of 1839 (though not the Chartists of 1842 and 1848), as well as the more 'treasonable' among the Fenians of 1868. A special case was that of the six men of Tolpuddle who, after massive demonstrations in London, were not only freed from captivity but had their return passages paid by government as well.[30]

As the system of partial freedom became more formalized and ceased to be exercised at the governor's whim, a prisoner might, on arrival, have some reasonably accurate notion of when to expect a ticket of leave and a conditional pardon; both, of course, were

[29] Rudé, 'Early Irish Rebels', pp. 23-4; *ADB*, i, 368-71 (Redfern).
[30] *ADB*, i, 419-20.

strictly related to the length of his sentence. But other, imponderable factors entered into the calculation, high on the list being his record of conduct in the colony at the time when the decisions were made. There were other imponderables as well, as we may see from an example taken from the middle years of settlement in New South Wales. John Clarke and James Watson, whom we have mentioned above, arrived together on *Ocean II* in January 1818 after being sentenced to transportation for life for 'ludding' at Loughborough the year before. Clarke received his ticket of leave from the Sydney bench in January 1832, almost fourteen years from the date of his arrival. Watson received his certificate from the Evan magistrates in June 1830, when it was counted in his favour that he had 'apprehended three runaways'; and he went on to receive his conditional pardon in February 1839 whereas Clarke had to wait until 1847.[31] It is, in fact, only with the 'warming-up' of transportation to Western Australia in the late 1850s, that, as in the case of probation, a formal time-scale was devised for these intermediate steps towards freedom. It was then prescribed (this again was intended for British convicts only) that a three-year man should wait nine months from arrival for his ticket of leave and two years six months *from the date of his sentence* for a conditional pardon; that a four-year man should wait one year for the first and three years three months for the second; and so on up to the fifteen- or twenty-year man ('lifers' again were excluded), who should receive his ticket four years three months after arrival and his conditional pardon ten years after conviction.[32] This is roughly how it worked out in the case of English and Scottish convicts of the 1860s (and of those arriving on the solitary Irish ship before 1868), allowing as usual for such remissions and additions as might be made for good or bad conduct. And, again with modifications, this was broadly how it worked out for those Fenians who were not included in the general pardon of 1869. To cite two examples. John Shine, a Dubliner who had been given a ten-year sentence for mutinous conduct in August 1866 and served his full sentence in the colony, was given his ticket of leave, only a few weeks off schedule, on 12 September 1871; while John Lynch, convicted of the same offence by the same court but given a five-year sentence, received a ticket of leave in June 1869 and a conditional pardon in December 1870. So these went as near as could be expected according to plan.

---

[31] Arch. NSW, 30/947, 32/397 (tickets of leave); 39/290, 47/16 (conditional pardons).
[32] Gertzel, loc. cit.

But there were times when the plan, in spite of all the efforts of authority, went awry; as in the case of Robert Cranston and five others, all Dubliners who had been given a life-sentence by court martial for mutinous conduct and desertion. The 'mutinous conduct' of which Cranston was convicted was to have endeavoured 'to induce 1153 Pt Forby of the 61 Reg't to join an illegal society called the FENIAN BROTHERHOOD'. He was a model prisoner: recommended for outstandingly good conduct by the ship's surgeon on the voyage, made a constable in December 1872, and given consecutive remissions of gang labour for good conduct amounting to eighteen months in all. Yet his term of probation—as a 'lifer'—had still another eleven years to go; and his ticket of leave was not due until May 1879. So he and his five companions, like John Boyle O'Reilly before them, decided to jump the gun and absconded on an American whaler in April 1876.[33]

Another feature of the convict system was the severe—and often savage—punishment of offenders against the penal code. The supreme penalty, which applied to free settlers as well as to convicts, was to be hanged. Execution was generally reserved for armed robbery or murder or for stabbing a policeman; but, in the early years at least, it might be imposed for political crimes as well. Among the first arrivals to be hanged, for example, were nine Irishmen who had taken part in the Castle Hill rebellion of 1804, including their leader, Philip Cunningham, a Tipperary man who had come out on the *Anne* as a rebel of '98. Among others later sentenced to execution by the Supreme Court at Sydney or Hobart, but for strictly non-political crimes, were several Irish land-and-tithe protesters and English arsonists of the 1830s and 1840s. Next to hanging, the most dreaded sentence was to be further transported to one or other of the penal settlements that were set up from the earliest days to deal with hardened offenders. They included Port Macquarie, Moreton Bay, and Norfolk Island in the case of New South Wales, and Macquarie Harbour and Port Arthur in Tasmania; with Cockatoo Island in the first colony and Maria Island in the second playing a minor, and less awe-inspiring, role. Norfolk Island was opened as an occasional place of exile for serious offenders in the very earliest days. Among its inmates at the time were several Irish rebels suspected or convicted of inciting further disorders after their arrival in Sydney. They included the Revd. James Harold, a Catholic priest from Kildare, who spent seven years there as the result of alleged complicity in the first of the three 'conspiracies' at Parra-

[33] Arch. WA, R.16, V.10. See further on p. 233 below.

matta; and, a few years later, Michael Dwyer and one of his companions from the *Tellicherry* were sent there by Governor Bligh.[34] It was closed down as a penal settlement soon after but was revived in 1825 (the year that Moreton Bay began its brief career) and, as Port Macquarie closed down and Moreton Bay was phasing out, reached its peak, with 1,400 prisoners, in 1838.[35] (Among them was Joseph Arney, a Hampshire wheelwright and machine-breaker of 1830, who had been given an eight-year sentence for cattle-stealing.)[36] When Sydney closed its doors to further convicts, Tasmania took the Island over and, in the 1840s, used it mainly as a probation centre for men serving long sentences (life or fifteen-year terms) and who were on their way to Hobart.

In Tasmania, the most sinister of the settlements was Macquarie Harbour, founded by Governor Sorell in 1822 on the rugged, and almost inaccessible, west coast of the island. It came to enjoy a reputation almost as evil as that of Norfolk Island itself; it was the scene of some of the earlier chapters of Marcus Clarke's grisly novel, *For the Term of his Natural Life*; and Arthur, who inherited it, found it little to his taste and closed it down soon after he was ready to open his own creation, Port Arthur, in 1834. The new settlement became a thriving concern: where Macquarie Harbour had never held more than 300 prisoners, Port Arthur held 1,172 (eight per cent of Tasmania's male convicts) in 1835; and, of course, a far higher percentage of convicts came there at one time or another in the course of their penal careers. The protesters (as we shall argue in a later chapter) were less likely to do so than others; and of the 326 machine-breakers who came to Hobart in 1831 and 1832, only seven appear to have been sent there, mainly for house-breaking and other relatively serious crimes.[37] Among other protesters to be sent there at this time was Richard Vines, a groom and one of the most turbulent of the Bristol rioters of 1831, who, having absconded from a chain-gang from Bridgewater, was sent to Port Arthur for two years' hard labour in November 1836. Two of the Warwickshire Chartists of 1839 also served time at Port Arthur: Jeremiah Howell, a Birmingham gunsmith, was sent there for 'gross insubordination' in November 1841; and John Jones, a wood-turner from Welshpool, followed him with a fifteen-month sentence for larceny in August 1855. But Jones, unlike most protesters, had a remarkable record of crime;

[34] Rudé, 'Early Irish Rebels', pp. 25-6.
[35] Shaw, pp. 203-12.
[36] Rudé, '"Captain Swing" in New South Wales', *Hist. Stud.* vii (Apr. 1965), 472.
[37] Tas. Arch., CON 31/2-47 (conduct registers).

and he had already been sentenced to four years with hard labour at Norfolk Island (a rare combination) for larceny in January 1850.[38]

As a less costly substitute for the penal settlement there was the chain-gang: 'hard labour in Chains in settled Districts' in Arthur's phrase. In New South Wales, where the first chain-gangs had been introduced by Darling in 1826, they were used for road-building; in Tasmania they served a wider purpose, including the construction of wharves and bridges. Arthur, who thought highly of them, kept them going even after Port Arthur was working at full steam: in 1835, when Port Arthur had over 1,100 inmates, there were over 800 working in gangs.[39] Many more were working out of chains, including four of the machine-breakers who helped to build the bridge at Ross in the summer of 1835; and there was also Stephen Gaisford, another Bristol rioter, who, in August 1839, was sentenced to fourteen days' hard labour 'out of chains' for 'tippling at a public house'.[40] Gaisford, who had a moderate record of misconduct in the colony, also spent four months in the House of Correction at Longford for larceny (he was 67 years old by this time) and, for minor offences, he had two spells—one of seven days, the other of fourteen —on the treadmill. The treadmill, like solitary confinement, being put on bread and water, and fines up to 40s., was reserved for minor misdemeanours like drunkenness, breaches of the peace, staying out at night, minor cases of insolence, or staying away from church. Yet the treadmill could be a harrowing experience: there was the case of Laban Stone, a Wiltshire machine-breaker sent to New South Wales, who, after twenty-nine days on the treadmill, found his weight had fallen—but surprisingly only from 160 pounds to 155.[41]

The most savage instrument of physical punishment was, apart from the hangman's noose, the whip or 'cat-o'-nine-tails', usually administered by a brawny prison officer to a man securely bound to the 'Triangle'. Floggings, from the earliest days until the end of assignment, were frequent and vicious—at first for every imaginable misdemeanour and later, most typically, for absconding, refusal to work, disorderly conduct, or disobedience or insolence to one's employer. An early Irish rebel who was almost flogged to death before being sent to Norfolk Island for several years was Patrick Galvin, a 20-year-old prisoner from *Friendship II*. The Island soon developed an unsavoury reputation for the freedom with which the

---

[38] Tas. Arch., CON 31/22, 33/1.
[39] Shaw, pp. 212–14.
[40] Rudé, '"Captain Swing" in Van Diemen's Land', p. 17; CON 31/16.
[41] Arch. NSW, 4/4569 (House of Correction Register, 1837).

whip was used: one particular notorious commandant, named Morisset, was reported to have ordered one flogging per man per year; even at the hell-hole of Macquarie Harbour in the 1820s, the average (possibly more accurately computed) was only a flogging for every two men per year. By the 1830s, as flogging became a public scandal provoking searching questions at home, records were more carefully kept; and it could now be shown that about one in four convicts in New South Wales were flogged each year between 1833 and 1836 (with a sharp fall in 1837). In Tasmania (excluding penal settlements), the average was considerably lower: about one in six each year between 1832 and 1834 (with sharp and progressive falls in 1835 to 1837); and, even at Port Arthur, the yearly proportion of convicts being flogged was no higher than it was in New South Wales. The number of lashes given had also, of course, to be taken into account: at Port Arthur, in 1833 (the peak year) the average was fifty per flogging; in New South Wales it was forty-six in 1835; and, in Tasmania (excluding penal settlements), it was thirty-seven in 1833.[42] So Tasmania, under Arthur (who disapproved of flogging as lacking reformatory virtues), was relatively sparing in its administration; yet it was frequent enough as we can tell from the records of punishment of the machine-breakers of 1830; and these were men who (as we shall see in a later chapter) committed comparatively few crimes during their years in Tasmania. (In the case of those transported to Sydney I have found only three cases of flogging between 1831 and 1835: two for absconding and one for receiving stolen goods; but these records are certainly incomplete.)[43] Altogether, there were 50 cases of flogging between 1831 and 1836; 15 involving Wiltshire men, 8 for Essex, 7 for Buckingham, 6 for Hants, 5 for Sussex, 3 for Gloucester, 2 each for Norfolk and Berks., and one each for Huntingdon and Kent. The most frequent victims were David Hawkins, a Berkshire ploughman, who was given 50 lashes for insolence and disobedience on one occasion and 50 for an assault and 25 for drunkenness on others; John Hart, an Essex labourer, who, on two occasions, was given 50 lashes for neglect of duty and drunkenness and, on others, 25 lashes for neglect of work and for being out at night; Isaac Miller, a Wiltshire ploughman, who received 35 lashes for being drunk and abusive; 25 for disobedience, and 50 for stealing wine; and (most frequent recipient of all) Thomas Read, a Kentish ploughman, who was flogged six times with 35 lashes for stealing food, 25 for idleness and disobedience, and 30 on two

[42] Shaw, p. 202.
[43] Arch. NSW, 4/1123.1 ('Machine-breakers').

occasions and 20 on a third for neglect of work in a chain-gang.[44] Richard Vines, the Bristol rioter whom we have already noted as an unruly subject, also received 50 lashes (in August 1833) for neglect of work, fighting, and disobedience of orders; and, while at Port Arthur in January 1837, he was given what was by then the unusually severe punishment of 75 'stripes' for leaving his work for a day at Coal Point.[45]

Soon after, flogging virtually ceased with the discredited assignment system, which (as we have seen) was held responsible for many of its grosser excesses; so it was sparingly used to punish even the most turbulent of the Irish land-protesters or English and Irish arsonists, let alone the Chartists of 1839 and 1842; and if space would permit (which, fortunately for the reader, it will not) it might be instructive to contrast the remarkably muted forms of punishment— mainly fines or bread and water—meted out to the law-breakers from the *Hougomont*—and there were some hardened offenders among them—with those administered to their forebears committing similar crimes in the period of assignment.[46]

Intended as one further incentive to good conduct was the grant of a free passage to the colony to a prisoner's wife and children. We have seen that special favours were granted to some of the Irish State prisoners of 1798 and 1803, allowing them to bring their families with them on the ship. But these were early, halcyon days when special arrangements could be entered into; and as the treatment of prisoners became normalized under Governors King and Macquarie, a system had to be devised to meet this problem as so many others; and this now emerged in Macquarie's time and provided for the concession to be made to prisoners who, after a year or two of transportation, were considered to have proved their worth. By the 1830s, the scheme applied to an average of two hundred cases a year in New South Wales alone; this meant, as only about one in four male convicts were married at the time of their conviction, that nearly one-sixth of the married prisoners had their families brought out to them at the government's expense.[47] But, of course, it depended not only on the government's offer but on the prisoner's readiness to take it up. Some men appear to have been

---

[44] Tas. Arch., CON 31/2 etc., 53/4328.   [45] Tas. Arch., 31/44.

[46] I have found one case of flogging among the earlier convicts sent to Western Australia. He was James Snell, convicted of house-breaking in England in 1850 and twice transported in the colony, the first time (in 1859) for arson when he received a seven-year sentence and 100 lashes (Arch. WA, R.12). For crimes and punishments of *Hougomont* men, see Arch. WA, V.10.

[47] Shaw, p. 229.

reluctant to make the application: of the large number of married men among the machine-breakers of 1830 (in their case, over one in two) we have found only six who did so in Tasmania and three in New South Wales.[48] An interesting case, also dating from the 1830s, was that of George Loveless, the Tolpuddle Martyr, who at first refused to have his wife and three children sent out to him while still a prisoner in Tasmania, then, having changed his mind, refused his own free passage back to England until he received an assurance that his wife was not already on her way.[49] But Loveless, as we shall see further, had a mind of his own.

Far more frequently—as most male convicts were bachelors— men sought permission to marry in the colony. Of the labourers of 1830 there are about eighty such cases recorded in the marriage registers in Tasmania and a dozen more in New South Wales. Generally, after an inquiry had been made at home to ensure that the prisoner was free from other ties, the request was granted. Among those who passed the test and married in Tasmania were Thomas Goodman, who had been sentenced for firing stacks at Battle; Peter Withers, one of the Wiltshire men who had been 'left for execution' and only escaped with a last-minute reprieve; and John Boyles, the Hampshire farmer who had been transported for 'conspiring to raise wages'; and, in New South Wales, there was Robert Mason, the radical Hampshire smallholder, who married Lydia Mills, a ticket of leave convict woman, at Paterson in November 1841.[50] Of the Irish female arsonists who came to Tasmania between 1842 and 1853, only eight per cent (half of them widows) had been married before; but a great many—nearly seven in ten— married in the colony, several of them having a child first and marrying the father later.[51] It was inevitable, though, in spite of the preliminary inquiries made at home, that many of these men and women committed bigamy in the process. Among the machine-breakers there was one such case at least, though it took some time to be discovered. David Bartlett, a Wiltshire labourer, described on his arrival in Tasmania as being married with one child, married Agnes Skewes at St. George's, Sorell, on 31 January 1842; and, seventeen years later, in January 1859, was convicted of bigamy and sentenced to a year's hard labour at Port Arthur.[52]

[48] Hobsbawm and Rudé, *Captain Swing*, pp. 247, 271.
[49] Tas. Arch., CON 18/22, 23/2.
[50] Hobsbawm and Rudé, p. 271.
[51] Arch. Tas., CON 40/2, 4, 10; 41/5, 8, 12, 16, 19, 20, 22, 24, 26, 28, 30, 33, 35, 36.
[52] Hobsbawm and Rudé, p. 272; Arch. Tas., CON 31/4.

3. New South Wales

In October 1794, when four of the six Scottish Jacobins arrived in Sydney, the settlement was less than six years old and was still largely confined within the 800 square miles of the wealthy Cumberland Plain. Yet further expansion had already begun; and, only a few months before the prisoners' arrival, a new settlement had been founded at Hawkesbury on the alluvial soils along the Hunter River.[1] However, the 'beautiful and fertile island of New South Wales' (as its earliest chronicler calls it) was far from self-supporting; and it is not surprising that the arrival of each ship bringing stores and provisions from England or Norfolk Island should be eagerly— if not despairingly—awaited, as, even in September 1796, there were still only 5,400 acres under cultivation to feed a population of nearly 4,000.[2]

The new arrivals were, as we have seen, given special privileges as political prisoners and allowed to settle in small farms and houses within easy reach of Sydney Cove: Thomas Muir (as we saw) in a farmhouse across the Harbour; William Skirving on a 100-acre farm at Petersham; while Joseph Gerrald, who arrived a year later on the *Sovereign*, was allowed to buy a small house and garden at Farm Cove. Both he and Skirving died in March 1796, within a year or two of their arrival. Gerrald who was suffering from acute tuberculosis even before he sailed from England, lived for a year as an invalid; he died at Thomas Palmer's house and was buried, at his own wish, in his garden at Farm Cove, where his tombstone bore the inscription: 'He died a martyr to the liberties of his country in the 36th year of his age.'[3] Skirving survived him only by two weeks, dying of dysentery, aggravated (it was said) by acute depression caused by his separation from his wife and two boys and his disappointment at not making a success of his farm.[4]

The three survivors followed separate paths. Muir escaped from the colony on an American ship, the *Otter*, in February 1796; and, after hair-raising adventures, including four months in a jail in

[1] Parry, *Australia's First Frontier*, pp. 20–1.
[2] G. Barrington, *The History of New South Wales* (London, 1810), pp. 169–70.
[3] *ADB*, i, 438.
[4] *ADB*, ii, 449–50; Barrington, p. 539.

Havana and several more as a prisoner of the Spaniards in a hospital at Cádiz, he was rescued by the French and brought to Paris as an honoured guest of the Directory in December 1797. He settled at Chantilly, near Paris, and died there in January 1799.[5] Thomas Palmer stayed on for some years in the colony and, after his farm proved a failure, went into a profitable partnership with John Boston and James Ellis, former shipmates from the *Surprise*, and built ships for the Norfolk Island trade; he also became interested in natural history and exploration and took a sympathetic interest—unusual at that time—in the aboriginal population. His sentence expired in 1800; and, soon after, with his two partners, he bought an old Spanish craft and sailed for England; but the boat became marooned and declared unseaworthy at Guam; and Palmer, weakened by the voyage, died there, aged 53, in June 1803. His remains were later recovered by an American captain who brought them to Boston for re-burial.[6] Margarot, the last of the five, was the only one to keep up his 'conspiratorial' activities after his arrival in Sydney. His mysterious intrigues with Governor King on the one hand and the United Irish on the other led to the suspicion that he was a double agent. Yet, when it came to the point, he appears to have thrown in his lot with the Irish; for, being strongly suspected of helping to plan the Castle Hill rising in 1804, his papers were seized and he was transported to Norfolk Island and Van Diemen's Land in turn; he ended up at Newcastle, back in New South Wales, in early 1806. Little is known about him during the next four years; but he returned to England in 1810 and died in London on 11 November 1815.[7]

But one further, lesser known, Scottish Jacobin remains to be considered. He was George Mealmaker, the Dundee handloom-weaver we spoke of in an earlier chapter, who arrived in Sydney on the *Royal Admiral* in November 1800. King, who was anxious to establish a weaving industry, made Mealmaker supervisor of weaving at the Female Factory at Parramatta. He soon put four looms to work; and for the next four years the enterprise was a great success and he was rewarded with a conditional pardon. But the factory was severely damaged by fire in March 1807; and when Bligh, King's successor, showed little interest in its restoration, Mealmaker took to drink and died, destitute, from alcoholic suffocation. He was buried at St. John's Church, Parramatta.[8]

The next protesters to arrive in the colony were the fifteen men who had been sentenced by military courts to transportation for

[5] *ADB*, ii, 266-7.   [6] *ADB*, ii, 312-13.
[7] *ADB*, ii, 206-7.   [8] *ADB*, ii, 218.

their part in the mutinies at the Nore and Spithead. Some were sentenced in 1797, others in 1798 or 1799 and some for life and others for seven years; but they all sailed on twin-ships, the *Minorca* and the *Canada*, which docked in Sydney on the same day in December 1801. The majority were Irish—including John Burns, Patrick Devoy, Terence Dunn, James Hailey, John Hoare, Thomas McCann, Christopher Mahane, John Murphy, and Peter McGuire; but some were not and most notably William Redfern, an Englishman who was probably a Canadian by birth. About most of them we know nothing after their arrival in the colony; but three are listed in the census of 1828, taken nearly thirty years after they arrived. From this we learn that John Hoare was by now 50 years old and free, living with a wife, Elizabeth, and three boys and four girls and farming 90 acres at Airds. Peter McGuire (also free) was now 60 and working as a labourer for John Town at North Richmond. Patrick Devoy had fallen on harder times and was serving a life-sentence at Moreton Bay to which he had been sent for committing an unspecified crime.[9]

The only one to win fame in the colony was William Redfern who had started life with certain advantages over the rest. He was already a qualified surgeon before becoming involved, and playing a conspicuous role, in the mutiny at the Nore: he was said to have advised his men on H.M.S. *Standard* 'to be more united among themselves'. Owing to his medical skill he was drafted to Norfolk Island as assistant surgeon, soon after his arrival, in May 1802. King gave him a conditional pardon in June 1803 and he returned to Sydney five years later with an established reputation. He was given a post as surgeon at the dilapidated hospital at Dawes Point; and when Governor Macquarie had a new building put in its place, Redfern (though nominally serving under D'Arcy Wentworth) was effectively put in charge. As an emancipist, Redfern encountered frigid disapproval from some; but he developed a highly successful practice and was at one time family doctor to both the Macarthurs and the Macquaries. In 1819, he left medicine for the Bench, to which he was appointed by Macquarie; but he was removed from it a year later by Bathurst, who disapproved of 'nominations of Convicts to the Magistracy'. However, he continued to amass wealth, gave his name to a Sydney suburb, and when he died in Edinburgh in July 1833, having gone there with his son in 1828, he left an estate of 23,190 acres in New South Wales, including 6,296 acres at Airds and 11,362 at Bathurst.[10]

[9] Arch. NSW, 4/3999, 4004.
[10] *ADB*, ii, 368–71.

Hard on the heels of the naval mutineers and the last of the Scottish Jacobins came the far larger number of Irish rebels of 1798 and 1803, the largest group of protesters to arrive in New South Wales. Nearly all of them—whether seven-year men or 'lifers'— were to spend the rest of their days in Australia; little more than a handful are known for certain to have returned to Ireland after emancipation. Many petitioned to be allowed to go home (there were several such petitions in 1810), but few appear to have been successful. Among those who were there were three Catholic priests who had travelled out on separate ships: on the *Minerva*, the *Friendship*, and the *Anne*. The first of the three to leave was the Revd. Peter O'Neil, of Co. Cork, who was pardoned in 1802 and allowed to return to Ireland in 1803, having spent the larger part of his two years in the colony on Norfolk Island. He was followed by James Dixon, of Wexford, who, in April 1803, had been the first Catholic priest to celebrate mass in the colony and went back home in 1808. The third, and oldest of the three (he was past 50 on arrival), was James Harold, of Kildare, who (as mentioned in our last chapter) was banished to Norfolk Island, and later to Tasmania, for believed complicity in the first of the three 'conspiracies' at Parramatta. He returned to Sydney in 1808, was pardoned, and left the colony on board the *Concord* in June 1810, spending three years in America on his way home. He died in 1830 and was buried in Dublin. All three priests lived to a ripe old age, O'Neil dying at seventy-nine, Dixon at eighty-two, and Harold at eighty-five.[11]

Others who returned were William Orr, a watchmaker from Co. Antrim, and Joseph Holt, the Wicklow farmer and rebel general of whose exploits we have already spoken at some length. Orr was one of those unfortunates who had been put on a convict ship and sent to Australia by mistake. In his case, the ship—the *Friendship*—had already sailed when the order for his release arrived at the dock. The amends for this bureaucratic error eventually took the form of a curt note sent to Governor King from Dublin Castle in May 1805; it ran: 'Orr may have leave to return.' But whether he actually returned to Ireland or not at this time remains in doubt; one authority, at least, has it that he stayed on in Australia 'for many years'; then went to India, where he made a fortune, before returning to Ireland to settle near Ballymena, in Co. Antrim.[12] Holt, as we have seen before, was one of the few leaders of the rebellion to be

[11] *ADB*, ii, 301–2 (O'Neil); i, 309 (Dixon); i, 512–13 (Harold).
[12] SPO Dublin, Prisoners' Petitions, no. 1140 (28 Jan. 1805); R. R. Madden, *Antrim and Down in '98* (Glasgow, n.d.), pp. 53–6.

sent to New South Wales. As such, he was an obvious target of suspicion for those in authority, and he was arrested three times for suspected complicity in plans for an Irish rising at Sydney; and, the third time, after the Castle Hill affair, he was sent to Norfolk Island for a year. In the 1806 Muster he appears as an emancipist with a holding of 110 acres; and, from a memorial he wrote four years later, we learn that he had by then extended his holding by a further 100 acres of grazing land, with 30 cattle and 410 sheep. Nevertheless, having secured his pardon, he sold his properties for over £1,800 and, leaving his daughter and two sons behind, returned with his wife to Ireland in 1814. He became a publican and property-owner near Dublin and died at Dún Laoghaire, aged 70, in May 1826.[13]

Of the notables remaining in the colony, Michael Dwyer and his four companions all appear in the 1806 muster as settlers with grants of 100 acres each near Liverpool, at Cabramatta Creek. But, like Holt, as we have seen, they were suspected of sedition and, in the summer of 1807, were sent to separate penal settlements, some (including Dwyer) to Norfolk Island, others (including Martin Burke) to Port Dalrymple and the Derwent Settlement in Tasmania. But when Bligh was deposed following the 'Rum' Rebellion in January 1808, his successor, Paterson, allowed them to return once more as free settlers to Sydney. Their grants were confirmed but, soon after, their fortunes began to diverge. In 1820, Burke was a constable at Bringelly, lying south of the Nepean River, his holding now reduced to 50 acres; but, in 1828, he reappears as a tenant farming 200 acres at Pittwater, to the east of Sydney. Arthur Devlin and Michael Dwyer apparently fell on harder times. In 1822, Devlin was living, it seems as a lodger, at Sydney; while Dwyer, although he died as Chief Constable at Parramatta in 1825, had been forced two years before to sell his lands to pay his debts.[14]

The great majority appear—from the petitions and memorials, the muster and census rolls—to have spent comparatively peaceful and uneventful lives. The tradesmen and craftsmen among them generally settled in Sydney, though many, as new communities grew and opportunities beckoned, moved outwards to Camden, Liverpool, Newcastle, or Windsor; or, if they acquired land, to developing

---

[13] ML, Mutch Index; *ADB*, i, 550. Another prisoner who may have returned was William Alcock, the Wexford Militia captain of whom we spoke before. He had his sentence reduced to seven years and King made him Assistant Engineer. He then requested to return to Ireland, which may have been granted as we hear no more of him after the Muster of 1806. See SPO Dublin, Prisoners' Petitions, no. 861 (8 Mar. 1804).

[14] ML, Mutch Index (Musters, 1806, 1822); Census of NSW, 1828.

country districts at Appin, Evan, Wilberforce, Hawkesbury, or the
Hunter River. Among such migrants was William Lett, a shoemaker
from Co. Wexford, who had arrived on *Atlas II* and, having worked
for government at Parramatta and Castle Hill in 1806, had set up
shop in Kent Street, Sydney, by 1822 and held ten acres of land along
the South Creek at Evan in 1828. Many others, both labourers and
craftsmen, were, like Lett, sent to work at Parramatta and Castle
Hill; while others, also assigned to the Parramatta district, worked
for substantial notables like the Macarthurs, D'Arcy Wentworth, or
the Revd. Samuel Marsden. Others again, the farmworkers or
farmers, appear to have migrated to country districts, as ticket
of leave men or emancipists, even before the Muster of 1806, and
then moved on as new land and opportunities offered. A few, the
less fortunate—such as Stephen Dodd and John Hickey of the *Anne*
and Roger Maguire of *Friendship II*—ended their days in mental
asylums at Castle Hill, Parramatta, and Liverpool. One, at least,
met with a violent death: Anthony Curran, of the *Friendship*, who
was murdered in 1823.[15]

Many prisoners—I have counted over fifty, but there must have
been many more—received grants of land from successive governors
from 1806 on and, in some cases, as time went by were able to enlarge
their holdings by lease or purchase. These initial grants might range
between 30 and 135 acres. Among the recipients were Joseph Holt,
Andrew Burne, John Reddington, Edward Redmond (or Mc-
Redmond), and the Revd. Henry Fulton, a Protestant parson born
in England, all of the *Minerva*; the brothers Michael and Moses
Brennan, Hugh Crabtree, and William Hawkins of the *Anne*; and
John Brennan, James Meehan, Philip Hogan (a Defender of Ireland), and David McCallum (who already held 206 acres in 1806)
of the *Friendship*; and several others from *Atlas I* and *Atlas II*. Some
of these remained smallholders or returned to Sydney, or even (if
their fortunes declined) went to work for others. Others, the more
fortunate, acquired more land and became substantial owners or
tenants. Such were James Byrne and Thomas Burke of the *Anne*, of
whom the first increased his 40-acre holding to one of 200 acres
between 1820 and 1828 and the second from 100 acres to 306. Even
more impressive was the rising prosperity of Michael Bryan, of
Atlas I, who, starting with a 40-acre grant from Macquarie, held
540 acres (mostly pasture) at Seven Hills, near Evan, in 1828.
Another substantial landholder at Seven Hills was John Good, of

---

[15] For this and much that follows, see Rudé, 'Early Irish Rebels in Australia',
Hist. Stud., xvi (Apr. 1974), 23–35.

Atlas II, who was farming 415 acres that year. More spectacular still was the rise to fortune of the Revd. Henry Fulton, the Protestant parson who, having played an active ministerial role in the Anglican Church and served on the bench at Hawkesbury, appears in the 1828 census as farming 900 acres at Evan and Mitchells Plains.[16] Another *Minerva*-rebel who made good was John Lacey, an iron-founder from Dublin, who had been given a 100-acre grant in 1809 and, when living in one of his two houses at Parramatta in 1828, held 1,080 acres in four holdings distributed between Parramatta, Cow-pastures, Windsor, and Bargo. And, finally, at the top of this economic pyramid of those who survived to be recorded in the census of 1828 (I have counted eighty-one), were William Davis, of the *Friendship*, who held 1,700 acres, with 700 cattle and 200 sheep in the county of Argyle and was a highly esteemed benefactor of the Catholic Church in Sydney;[17] and James Browne, a former Pro-testant weaver, of the *Minerva*, who owned 1,920 acres of pasture, with 200 cattle and 700 sheep in the neighbourhood of Richmond.

There are four others who made their mark in the colony; but as their stories are told in some detail in the *Australian Dictionary of Biography*, they will be repeated only briefly here. One was James Meehan, who, on arrival on the *Friendship*, was assigned for service with Charles Grimes, the acting surveyor-general. This gave him a good start to a highly successful career. After a fact-finding mission to Tasmania and service as acting surveyor of lands (at a salary of £182. 10s.), he became deputy-surveyor of lands to Macquarie in 1812 and played a large part in fixing the boundaries of land-grants and mapping Sydney and several of the new townships of the now rapidly expanding colony. He also became a landowner, eventually holding 1,140 acres at Ingleburn to which he retired with a govern-ment pension of £100 in 1823. He died there in April 1826.[18]

There were two that made their fortunes in Tasmania. Richard Dry, the former Protestant woollen-draper of Dublin, was sent to Port Dalrymple in 1807, became a storekeeper and received a pardon and, in 1817, entered the public service as a commissariat clerk. But the post was not confirmed; so he resigned his office and, in com-pensation, built up a large fortune in land. By 1827, he owned some 12,000 acres mainly around Westbury in the northern half of the island. He also became a respected citizen of Launceston, becoming

---

[16] For more on Fulton, see *ADB*, i, 421-2.

[17] See also James Waldersee, *Catholic Society in New South Wales 1788-1860* (Sydney, 1974), pp. 254-5.

[18] *ADB*, ii, 220.

successively assistant secretary of the local British and Foreign Bible Society (1823), and a founder of the Cornwall Bank (1828) and of the Tamar Steam Navigation Company (1837). He died near Launceston in 1843.[19] Denis McCarty, a former Wexford farmer, was sent to Tasmania in August 1803; he became a constable at New Norfolk in 1808 with a small 5-acre farm and was pardoned in 1810. His farm prospered and he became a shipowner involved in profitable business ventures at Sydney and along the Tasmanian coast. But he also made enemies and engaged in lawsuits; and Lieutenant-Governor Sorell described him as 'one of the most turbulent and insubordinate Men in the Settlement'. In 1818 he undertook to build a road from Hobart to New Norfolk (with bridges thrown in) in return for 2,000 acres of land. Two years later, he was drowned in the Tamar (possibly as the result of foul play); and the *Hobart Town Gazette* wrote of him that 'he had been many years in the settlement, was *of a speculative turn*, had been the owner of three vessels [and] had acquired considerable land and other property'.[20]

And, finally, the most remarkable case was that of Edward McRedmond who, from being an illiterate labourer in King's County who came to Australia at the age of thirty-two, had by middle age become a wealthy landowner and a highly respected citizen of Sydney. He started as a small dealer in the city around 1803 and, in 1809 (the year of his pardon), acquired a wine and spirit licence as well as a grant of 135 acres of land. In 1815, in partnership with Patrick Cullen, he leased the profitable tolls between Sydney and Parramatta. A year later, he became one of the original shareholders of the Bank of New South Wales and, a few years after, he figured with William Davis among the principal benefactors of the Catholic Church in Sydney.[21] He extended his holdings in land and real estate in various parts of the colony; and when he died in 1840, he left his widow and children farms at Bathurst, Bingham, Annandale, and on the Hawkesbury River, as well as houses at Windsor and Liverpool and three others at Sydney.[22]

There are no such success-stories to relate about the Luddites, most of whom arrived on the *Fortune* and *Earl Spencer* in 1813. They were humble men to begin with and appear to have remained so.

---

[19] *ADB*, i, 328–9.
[20] *ADB*, ii, 159 (my italics).
[21] Among these benefactors Dr. Waldersee cites for special commendation John Dempsey of Co. Wicklow (*Atlas II*, Oct. 1802). *Catholic Society in NSW*, p. 255.
[22] *ADB*, ii, 371.

We know little of their careers in the colony excepting what appears in the census of 1828, which lists eighteen of them, fairly evenly divided between the two ships. By now all of these, whether sentenced to seven or fourteen years, had obtained their 'freedom from servitude', which means that no one among them had committed any major crime during his first fifteen years in the colony. From the *Earl Spencer*—the second ship to arrive—there was Thomas Etchells (alias Brunt), former hatter and rioter at Joseph Clay's corn-mill near Chester and now married, aged 50, and running his own hatter's business in George Street, Sydney; and working for him we find another Luddite, Samuel Lees, presumably an old acquaintance as he had also been a hatter at home and had become involved in the same riot as Etchells. Some, whatever their original trade, had by now become labourers: such as William Greenhaugh, former weaver and rioter at Alice Barry's at Tintwistle (Derbyshire), now 64 and working for William Blackwell at Evan; John Heywood (here written as 'Hayward'), former cotton spinner and machine-breaker at Sidebotham's factory, now working for James McAllister at Richmond; and Edward Redfern, a labourer at the time he was convicted of destroying meal and flour in the Huddersfield Canal Company's granary at Staley and now a labourer at Liverpool. Another, James Tomlinson (no earlier profession given), who had been sentenced for extorting 7s. from John Parker, Esq., was now a servant to William Kempton of Clarence Street, Sydney. Others, like George Spray, a Nottingham hosier, one-time stocking-frame breaker, had been able to return to their craft: he is listed in the census as a weaver at Wallis Plains, by the Hunter River, with a small herd of a dozen cattle of his own. William Thomson, a Cheshire weaver—also sentenced for extorting money from John Parker— now appears as a tinman (presumably self-employed) trading, like Etchells, in George Street, Sydney. In George Street there was also Thomas Whittaker, one-time joiner and oath-giver and described in a Home Office report as 'a man of superior ability and education', who was now teaching mathematics at Richard Cooper's private academy.[23]

From the earlier ship, the *Fortune*, there was James Crossland, a Derbyshire shoemaker, convicted of rioting at Thomily's cotton manufactory at Tintwistle, who was now working at his old trade at Parramatta. Another who was back at his old trade was Christopher Metcalf, a tailor from York, who now had his own tailoring shop at Liverpool. Two others that came (or appear to have come) to

[23] Arch. NSW, 4/4004; ML, Census 1828; HO 27/8, 42/123 (Whittaker).

Parramatta were John Hope, one-time weaver, sentenced for 'riot and robbery', and now a servant to a certain John Moore; and James Brierley, a Lancashire weaver sentenced for unlawful oaths, who appears to have died there and left an orphan child, Thomas, aged 5 years 6 months; for in the census the child is listed as 'an orphan at Rob't Foulchier's Parramatta'. A few went to work on the land: like John Fisher, former bleacher and oath-taker, who appears as stockman to James Underwood at Mount Pleasant, Sutton Forest (Argyle); and Joseph Greenhaugh, another oath-taker and one-time weaver, now working as overseer for Edward Cox at Evan.

Another case of two men who appear to have come together again in the colony after knowing each other at home was that of Samuel Radcliffe and Henry Thwaite (or Thwaites), both Lancashire weavers and both convicted at Lancaster, in May 1812, of administering unlawful oaths. In the census of 1828 we find Samuel Radcliffe working as a weaver for Henry Thwaite, who must have become a man of at least moderate substance as the census records him as being a miller 'with 4 horses and 40 hornéd cattle'.[24]

Also from the *Fortune* was Thomas Holden, the young master weaver from Bolton, whose correspondence with his wife and parents we have spoken of before. From the first letter written from Sydney, only two weeks after arrival, his parents learnt that he had already found work and 'a pleasant home' (they refer to this in their reply written nine months later). In a letter of 30 June 1815 (also written at Sydney), he describes conditions of life and work in Australia:

Things in this Country is very dear. Mens hats is too pounds too shillings and stockings ten shillings per pair and shoos sixteen shilling per pair, sugar 3 shillings per pound and Butter 7 shilling . . . and although the prices is so high we are verry glad to get at any price so I must inform you of my wages. I have twenty pounds per year in currency money it will be More than 12 pounds in English coin.

And he added for good measure that 'the natifs of this contry they are Blacks and they go naked just as they came into the world and they live on nuts of trees'.[25] Much of the correspondence, however, deals with such practical matters as the steps that are being taken at home and should be taken by himself in the colony to secure his emancipation. On 17 March, he asks his wife to sell his clothes and his looms to help pay his passage home. Two months later, he sends the good news that his freedom has been promised for 'first Monday

[24] Arch. NSW, 4/4004; ML, Census 1828; HO 27/8.
[25] LRO, DDX 140/7/14–18.

in next December'; but he adds a sad postscript that his savings had been stolen.[26] Yet the money must have been found and the pardon granted; and we must assume that he sailed back to England, for at this point the correspondence ends.

There followed, in the next half-dozen years, the agricultural rioters of 1816, the Pentrich rebels, the Cato Street conspirators, and the Scottish weavers and miners of Glasgow and Bonnymuir. In each case our knowledge is comparatively sketchy—most of all in the case of the Isle of Ely rioters of 1816. Of seven that arrived on the *Sir William Bensley* in March 1817, four—Jefferson, Jessop, Rutter, and Newell—received their tickets of leave some time in 1825; but only Newell appears in the census of 1828. James Newell was 21 years old when brought to trial before the Special Sessions at Ely; he was then said to be a labourer earning 8s. a week.[27] Some time after his arrival, he was sent to Liverpool where he received his ticket of leave in June 1825. In the census he is described as a Roman Catholic, aged 32, working as a labourer on the Liverpool Road, Lower Minto. He was still working within the jurisdiction of the Liverpool magistrates when his ticket of leave was renewed in March 1833; and it was from Liverpool that his death was reported on 26 February 1834.[28]

We know more about the fourteen Pentrich rebels who arrived in the colony on the *Isabella* and *Tottenham* in September–October 1818. Soon after the *Isabella*'s arrival, a note records that 190 of its 227 convicts had been assigned for work at Parramatta, Liverpool, or Windsor.[29] This appears to have included the four Pentrich men on board; and it was to one of these three places (though mostly to Parramatta) that the ten who arrived on the *Tottenham* appear to have been sent a month later. Some, the census tells us, were still at Parramatta in 1828: Joseph Turner for one and Samuel Hunt for another. More had moved on to Sydney; among them John Onion the Elder, who was now working as a labourer at Thomas Evans's in Elizabeth Street; Edward Turner, now a stonemason in Kent Street; Thomas Bettison, one-time miner, who was lodging at William Rigby's in Sussex Street; and German Buxton, now a brewer and living with his wife and three children in Campbell Street. John MacKesswick may, too, have been in Sydney as he had

[26] Ibid., fols. 20–21a. Holden also gives news of two fellow Luddites from Bolton, John Fisher and James Knowles (fol. 21a).

[27] A. J. Peacock, *Bread or Blood*, p. 40.

[28] Arch. NSW, 4/4005, pp. 284–5, 4/4060–2 (tickets of leave); ML, Census 1828.

[29] Arch. NSW, 4/3499, pp. 57–9.

been given his ticket of leave there and allowed to remain there eighteen months before. Others moved further inland: John Hill, a former stocking-maker, now a stonemason for W. T. Jamison at Cabramatta; George Brassington, one-time miner and later foreman at Sydney, and now working as a labourer for James Bowman at Patrick's Plains; and Thomas Bacon, now 74 and living as an invalid at the government establishment at Rooty Hill. The fourteen-year men—in principle at least—received their 'freedom by servitude' in 1832 (Thomas Bettison, for example, received his on 30 January of that year); while the 'lifers'—or, rather, the survivors among them—were pardoned on 1 January 1835. Some, however, did not live that long. Josiah Godber, once a labourer of Ripley, Derbyshire, died on 19 November 1822, aged 60, and was buried at St. Philip's, Sydney; Thomas Bacon, by now 77, died on 3 July 1831 in the parish of Macquarie; while his younger brother John died before him early in 1829 at the age of 64; it was then recorded by the police at Parramatta that his ticket of leave (first issued by the Evan bench in June 1827) had been torn up after its owner had been 'reported Dead'.

In a number of cases we can put together a few more details. John Hill, whom we found working at Cabramatta in early 1828, received his ticket of leave from the Liverpool magistrates in late December of that year; and, in January 1835, received his absolute pardon with other 'lifers' at the age of 46. George Weightman, a labourer and sawyer from Pentrich, is not listed in the census (unless it is he who is listed as 'George Weighma, a Pensioner in the Benevolent Asylum'), but already in December 1822—far earlier than anyone else—he was given a ticket of leave as a reward for volunteering to go up north to work at Port Macquarie. By May 1827 he was back in Sydney, and it was here that the permission was given to settle at Illawarra; and when he was pardoned with other 'lifers' in January 1835, it was ordered that 'the Pardon [to] be sent to Illawarra'.

Of the numerous Turners of South Wingfield that were implicated in the Pentrich affair, we have seen that one—William—was hanged and that two others came to Sydney: Edward, William's youngest brother, with the *Isabella*; and Joseph (known as 'Manchester' Turner from his place of birth) with the *Tottenham*. Edward Turner was working at Parramatta by 1821; and, in December of that year, he was married at St. John's, Parramatta, to Ann Cawson, a 17-year-old Sydney girl, before two witnesses, John Hann and Hannah Booth. Soon after, he moved to Sydney where he received his ticket of leave in September 1827; and we find him, a year later, living at Kent Street, Sydney, with his wife Ann and four young children (two boys and two girls) of whom the youngest was 1 and the eldest 6. As a reward for good conduct he was given an early conditional pardon in April 1833; and, of course, he was finally pardoned with the rest in January 1835. Joseph's career was not far different. On arrival, he was assigned (like so many others) for work with settlers at Parramatta. He was still at Parramatta when given his ticket of leave in June 1827; and he was a clerk there at the Female Factory when the census was taken in 1828. The following year, he was married at St. John's Church to Ellen Hatton (or Frazer), aged 26, a female convict, also by the Revd. Samuel Marsden. Like Edward, he was given an early conditional pardon by order of Governor Darling, in June 1831; and he, too, was among those pardoned in January 1835.

The only one of them to leave the colony (though not Australia) was Samuel Hunt, who was 25 years old when he arrived on the *Isabella*. He, too, was probably assigned for work at Parramatta for, in August 1819, he was married there at the same church as the two Turners, to Elizabeth Civill, 26, a free woman born in the colony; and, like Joseph Turner, he received his ticket of leave in June 1827 when he was stationed at Bringelly. But he was back at Parramatta within the year for the census records him as working there as a hedger and living with his wife and four children aged 1 to 6. From this point his life becomes more eventful. After being pardoned, he appears to have moved at some time to the newly founded colony of South Australia; for it is recorded that it was here that, in November 1841, he received a life-sentence for sheep-stealing and sailed on the Brig *Emma* for a destination not disclosed.[30]

The five Cato Street conspirators, who had been convicted of plotting to blow up the British Cabinet, arrived together on the *Guildford* in September 1820; theirs was an unusual type of arrival as they were dropped off at Sydney by a ship that was bound, as were the rest of the convicts she carried, for Hobart. Beyond that, they were afforded no special privileges and were sent up north to work in a jail gang at Newcastle. Three of them moved off, in the next years, to Bathurst, where John Harrison, a former baker, and John Shaw Strange, once a Birmingham bootmaker, both appear in the census as constables; and James Wilson was back at his former trade as a tailor working for a Mr. McLeod. Two are not listed: Richard

[30] Arch. NSW, 4/4006 (indents), 3493 (distribution lists), 4060-2 (tickets of leave), 4488, pp. 4-5 (absolute pardons, 1832-43), 4549 (death register, 1829-79), 4511 (applications to marry, 1825-51); ML, Mutch Index of Births, Deaths, and Marriages, 1815-1915.

Bradburn, a carpenter born in Dublin who, while at Liverpool, received a ticket of leave as a reward for helping to bring in bush-rangers up at Port Macquarie; and Charles Cooper, another one-time bootmaker, who was also given a ticket of leave at Liverpool (in 1833), but had it cancelled (presumably for some misdemeanour) in 1837 and was given another only in 1841. In two cases, we can follow their careers a little further. John Harrison went on from being a constable to resume his former baker's trade at Bathurst, where he also received his ticket of leave in August 1829. John Strange, the youngest of the five, appears to have spent four years in Sydney before coming to Bathurst; for it was at Sydney that we hear of him living with a certain Elizabeth Hanks in 1824 and that he received his ticket of leave in November 1825, it would seem in response to a petition he wrote claiming to have brought four bush-rangers to justice. Moving to Bathurst in 1827, he rose to become Chief Constable of the town; and it was here, too, that he was con-ditionally pardoned in May 1837 and fully pardoned—the only one of the five to be so—in 1842.[31]

The Scottish rebels arrived on the *Speke*, a few months after the 'conspirators', on 20 May 1821.[32] Once more, failing assignment and distribution lists, our main source of information about their early years in the colony has to be the invaluable census returns of 1828, on which most of their names appear. By this time ten were working at Sydney. Thomas Pike, a Glasgow weaver, had been pardoned in December 1827 and was now working for Frank Gerardy, a miller. Thomas McCullough and James Clelland, both of Glasgow, were living or working in Clarence Street: McCullough as a labourer with his wife Sarah and three children (two of them born in Scotland), and Clelland as a locksmith—his former trade—lodging in Alexander Johnson's house. Thomas McFarlane and James Wright were in Sussex Street: the first labouring for Thomas Hasker, the second lodging at Mary Green's. John Macmillan, a blacksmith of Camelon, was working at his old trade in Cumberland Street. Allan Murchie, another blacksmith from Glasgow, is now described as a dealer or tailor, living in York Street with a wife Elizabeth and three small children (all born in the colony).[33] Among others who had

---

[31] Arch. NSW, 4/4007, 4060, 4488, 1817, 7172; and see George Parsons, 'The Cato Street Conspirators in New South Wales', *Labour History* (Canberra), May 1965, pp. 3-9.

[32] Arch. NSW, 4/4007.

[33] For Murchie's request for Elizabeth (then his fiancée) to be allowed to join him, see letter from his father, William Murchie, to Sir William Rae, Lord Advocate of Scotland, on 2 Sept. 1820, SRO, RH.2/4, vol. 135, fol. 279.

married since coming to Sydney was William Clarkson, a shoemaker, now working at his old trade in Phillip Street; while John Barr, a weaver from Condorrat, was employed by a woollen manufacturer in Pitt Street and Andrew Hart, a cabinetmaker, was back at his old craft in Macquarie Street. Three others had settled outside the city: Benjamin Muir as a constable at Parramatta; David Thompson as a shepherd to Captain Barlow at Gundaroo, Goulburn Plains; and William Smith, former weaver now 'manufacturer' at Parramatta, where he lived with his wife Lavinia, who had followed him from Scotland on the *Jupiter* in 1823, bringing with her their two daughters, Ann (now 12) and Mary (8), to whom had by now been added a third, Elizabeth (aged 2).

Some had received tickets of leave at Sydney or Parramatta between 1825 and 1827; several of the fourteen-year men had been pardoned in 1827 and most of the 'lifers' would be so in 1832. But this is dull stuff of which we will spare the reader the dreary details. It is perhaps of some interest, however, to add a further note directly concerning two prisoners, James Clelland and Andrew Dawson, but having some relevance for the prisoners as a whole. These men were the subject of a letter sent to the Colonial Secretary by Captain Irvine of Elderslee in April 1822, requesting that they be assigned to him as blacksmiths on three grounds: first, on account of their superior skill and the high cost of free labour of this kind; second (and this, in particular, has a wider relevance), because '*they who are in the number of political convicts are men of industrious habits and fair moral character, and it is expected they will set a good example to others*'; and third, because 'they want to settle with their families away from the city'; and, he added, Dawson had already applied for his wife and family to be sent out and Clelland was likely to follow his example.[34] The upshot was that Dawson went to Sydney to work as a blacksmith for a year for William Dumaresq—until June 1828, when, at Dumaresq's suggestion, he went to Newcastle as Principal Overseer of Gangs. Three years later, when the Newcastle establishment was due to close down, he applied for a post with government as a blacksmith and wrote to his former employer for a reference.[35] And, at that point, we lose sight of him as of so many others.

Meanwhile, the next large contingent of Irish protesters—those sentenced under the Insurrection Acts—had begun to arrive. There were about 570 of them and they came to Sydney on thirty-two ships spread over a dozen years. They were mainly seven-year men, con-

[34] Arch. NSW, 4/1760, p. 135 (letter of 22 Apr. 1822) (my italics).
[35] Arch. NSW, 4/2167 (letter of 7 July 1831).

victed of such crimes as breaking the curfew, concealing arms or (simply) 'sedition'; unlike the '98 men, there were no notables among them; and as they were nearly all country labourers or small tenants, very few settled in Sydney and the great majority went out to, and remained in, country districts at Appin, Windsor, Liverpool, Bathurst, Goulburn, Cabramatta, and the like; and this is where we shall find them in the census returns of 1828. (A dozen, however, were sent to Moreton Bay, for a variety of more or less serious offences, between 1827 and 1832.) So, in this case, let us not look for too much variety where it does not exist and merely take a representative sample of a score of cases, selected year by year and drawing substantially, once more, on the census of 1828:

Edmond Moore, Kerry labourer (*Canada*, 1815), was in 1828 a landholder at Wilberforce, holding 34 acres, with a wife and three children.

Antony Boylan, Antrim soldier and servant (*Surrey I*, 1816), assigned to Windsor on arrival. In June 1827 sent to Moreton Bay for three years for assaulting an overseer. Ticket of leave at Bathurst in 1836. Died there in 1842.

James Slaney, Waterford labourer (*Guildford*, 1816), assigned to Parramatta. In 1828, labourer to John Atkinson at Wilberforce, with a son Edward, aged 6. Died in Windsor hospital on 22 February 1847.

John Stapleton, Tipperary labourer (*Guildford*, 1816). In 1828, sawyer to Simeon Lord at Botany Bay.

William Brien, Tipperary labourer (*Guildford*, 1818), In 1828, labourer to John Blaxland at Newington.

Michael Cronin, house painter from Limerick (*Tyne*, 1819). In 1828, painter to Thomas Jones, Phillip Street, Sydney. In 1831, sent to Moreton Bay for seven years for theft and died there in hospital, November 1832.

John Donnelly, of Kerry (*Dorothy*, 1820). Killed by natives near Bathurst, May 1824.

Patrick Goulding, Roscommon labourer (*Dorothy*, 1820), assigned to government at Emu Plains. In 1828, farmer at Evan with 4 acres, living with wife Mary, a former convict.

Patrick Leadon, of Londonderry (*Almorah*, 1820). At Airds in 1829 at Appin in 1830 and Illawarra in 1831. In October 1835, killed by a dray.

Bryan Coyle, of Co. Dublin (*Prince Regent II*, 1821). In 1828, labourer to John Macarthur at Camden. In 1831, sentenced at Sydney to seven years at Moreton Bay for house robbery. Returned to Sydney in 1838.

Denis Murphy, Tipperary ploughman (*Mangles*, 1822), assigned to Parramatta. Still there in 1828 as storekeeper to the Revd. Samuel Marsden.

John Collins, Tipperary ploughman (*Brampton*, 1823). In 1828, shepherd to Mr. Macarthur at Arthursleigh, Sutton Forest.

Brothers Stephen and William Fitzgerald, ploughmen of Co. Clare (*Medina*, 1823). Farming together at Brisbane in 1828: 100 acres, 60 cattle.

Eugene Sweeney, Limerick ploughman (*Castle Forbes*, 1824). Sentenced at

Argyle in January 1828 to three years at Moreton Bay for harbouring bush-rangers. Back in Sydney in 1831; ticket of leave in 1837.

James Cassidy, schoolmaster of Co. Cavan and 'Ribbonman' (the first of his kind to arrive) (*Ann and Amelia*, 1825), assigned to Evan. In 1828, a master at R.C. school and clerk to chapel at Parramatta. In 1830, at Sydney, sent to Moreton Bay for three years for defrauding the customs.

Daniel Neville, Limerick blacksmith (*Boyne*, 1826). In 1828, labourer to William Byrne, general dealer at Airds. Moved to Bathurst in 1834; certificate of freedom in 1840.

Patrick Houlehan, coachman and butler of Co. Cork (*Sir Godfrey Webster*, 1826), assigned to the Revd. S. Marsden at Parramatta (then holding 5,140 acres with 1,200 sheep); and still working for him as a servant in 1828.[36]

The last of the 'insurgents' arrived on the *Cambridge* in September 1827; they were immediately followed by the next great batch of Irish protesters: those transported for their part in the land-and-tithe war of the 1820s and 1830s. There were just over 600 of them, arriving in fifty-two ships and spread over the years 1827–40. The crimes for which they were sentenced were seizing firearms, armed assault, compelling to quit, unlawful oaths, Ribbonism and White-boyism, the latter mainly centred on the west and with major outbreaks in the early and late 1830s. (Over thirty Whiteboys, all from Galway, arrived on a single ship, the *Eliza*, in 1832.) Like the 'insurgents' before them, they were generally farmworkers and smallholders who were sent to work on farms and estates in all the settled areas—some to Parramatta and Camden; many more beyond the Nepean and Hunter Rivers to Brisbane in the north, down to Illawarra in the south, to Bathurst in the west, and south-west to Goulburn, Argyle, and Yass. Once more, let us take a few examples; but remembering that once the census of 1828 is past our information will be far more meagre:

James Shee, farm labourer, of Sligo, came out on *Eliza II* in November 1827; in early 1828, he was labouring for Dr. George Rutherford at Luskentyre near the Hunter River.

Thomas Singleton, a ploughman of Co. Cork (*Borodino*, 1828), assigned to J. P. Wilmot at Sydney; and in 1828 (he is the last of our sample to appear in the census), he was working in a road gang in Dogtrap Road, Parramatta.

James Saunders, groom of Co. Longford (*Guildford*, 1829), assigned to John Lamb at Sydney, and sentenced at Campbelltown in 1835 to spend three years at Moreton Bay for larceny.

Martin McCormick, of Kilkenny (*Forth*, 1830), assigned to Alexander McLeay at Sydney; died at the Watch House, Hyde Park Barracks, on 31 December 1835.

James Gevern, miller's labourer of Roscommon (*Asia*, 1831), assigned to

[36] Arch. NSW, 4/4005-12 (indents), 4060-2 (tickets of leave), 4432-49 (condit. pardons), 4549 (death register); 2/8259-79 (location); ML, Census 1828.

Richard Longford at Sydney; and was murdered by Brian Vyne, a fellow convict, at the residence of Solicitor-General Plunkett at Waterview, on the Parramatta River on 26 December 1833.
Two other men from the *Asia*—Thomas Corry and Edmond Scallon, both oath-takers from Co. Clare, died in the General Hospital at Sydney a few days after arrival, and three others—Patrick Flaherty, Patrick Geady, and James Neylan (also oath-takers from Co. Clare)—died at sea in September and November 1831.
John Kelly, Whiteboy from Co. Galway (*Eliza*, 1832), received his ticket of leave and went to Bathurst in June 1841. He had his 'ticket' taken away in January 1849 'being unable to support himself', and died at Bathurst five months later.
Thomas Humphries, a farm servant of Queen's Co. (*Roslin Castle*, 1833), was one of the few real criminals among them. He spent some months at Cockatoo Island and Nobby's Island in 1845; and, in January 1847, he was convicted of house-breaking at Parramatta, sentenced to three years in irons and went to Norfolk Island.
John Cantwell, farm servant of Kilkenny (*Java*, 1833), held ticket of leave at Sydney in 1841; moved to Cook's River to work for David Hannan in 1842; back to Sydney the same year to work for Mr. Kilsey; and to Campbelltown in 1843 and to Camden in 1846, where conditionally pardoned a few months later.
James Cantwell, coalminer of Kilkenny (*James Laing*, 1834), acquired his ticket of leave at Port Stephens in 1845, moved to Maitland in 1847 and was conditionally pardoned in October 1849.
Daniel Fox, farm servant of Co. Tyrone (*Forth*, 1835), went to work at the Female Factory at Parramatta and died there in hospital in November 1837.[37]

Nearly all the English machine-breakers of 1830 who came to Sydney arrived on the *Eleanor* in June 1831; only a dozen others followed on five further ships in the course of the next two years. The story of the *Eleanor* men—where they went to live, for whom they worked and how they secured their pardons—has been told in some detail before. We then found that remarkably little is known about them once they were free; and it was assumed (for lack of more certain knowledge) that the great majority, having won their freedom, stayed on in the colony as farmers, tradesmen, craftsmen, stockmen, and labourers of every kind; and none appears to have won fame or notoriety, not even the two brothers, James and Robert Mason, who had made their mark, even before the riots began, in the Radical movement in Hampshire.[38]
Yet a few cases may be worth noting, either because they have not

[37] Arch. NSW, 4/4012-19, 7076-8 (indents); 4/4063-180 (tickets of leave), 4449-60 (condit. pardons); 2/8242, 8257-64, 8276 (location).
[38] Rudé, '"Captain Swing" in New South Wales', *Hist. Stud.*, Apr. 1965, pp. 467-80; and Hobsbawm and Rudé, *Captain Swing*, pp. 276, 279.

been noted before or because they are worth looking at again. One concerns Charles Fay, a Hampshire tanner, who had been transported for his part in the riot at Andover. Like many others—as we noted in our previous chapter—Fay sought leave to marry once he had become established in the colony; the lady was Jane Burrows, a 23-year-old spinster of Lane Cove. The request was refused as Fay's indent revealed that he already had a wife, Harriet, at home. He claimed, however, that Harriet had died since his departure from England; and to prove it he produced a letter that his mother-in-law, Mary Arlott, had sent him some years before, a moving document that revealed that his small son believed that his father had 'gone to fight the Blacks' and that his wife, having heard no news of her husband, thought he was dead and died of a broken heart. As Fay had earned himself a good reputation, the Colonial Secretary, briefed by the Revd. Charles Dickinson, minister at Parramatta, decided to accept his story and withdrew his objection; so, after some months of delay, Fay was allowed to marry again.[39]

Two other documents concern two prisoners who came out on the *Surrey* and the *Captain Cook*, many months after the *Eleanor*, and, in consequence, were omitted from Lord John Russell's pardon of October 1836. One of them, Jacob Wiltshire, a Hampshire farm labourer, voiced his complaint to the Colonial Secretary in a letter written from Wellington on 23 September 1838 and couched in the following terms:

To D. Thompson, Secretary, Sydney.

Mr. Thompson, Sir, pardon me for taking the Liberty of a Drass you but mi torobles calls me to do so. I rived by the ship Captain Cook in the Year 1833 Santanse Life for Riating & Meshan Braking. I saw the newspaper with menn that was triad with me the have goot ther Liberty. I have been in no troble since mi arivale. I hope you will be so kind as to in form me if theires anthing aganst me mi name is Jacob Wilsher and it so far up the contry I have no ways of guting Down to make in qury I have sined Sarvent to Mr. Thos BEATTS of Paramatta and is at Molongl/y?/ in the Districk of Willington . . .

Your humble sarvent &&
Jacob Wiltsher.[40]

The other document is even more remarkable. Its presumed author was Thomas Cook, the young attorney's clerk who (as we saw in an earlier chapter) was given a fourteen-year sentence at Shrewsbury for sending a threatening letter to an auctioneer. After his arrival in Sydney, the account continues, he was sent to work in the office

---

[39] Arch. NSW, 4/2443.5.
[40] Arch. NSW, 4/1123.1. Wiltshire's plea was heard and he was pardoned soon after.

of the Superintendent of Convicts, where he fell foul of two of his superiors and was given a two-year sentence to work in a road party in the Blue Mountains a hundred miles from Sydney. He was later sent on to Mount Victoria, and from there to Bathurst in December 1833 with the task of aiding settlers to bring in the harvest. While at Bathurst, he found work as a clerk in the Police Office and in the office of the Surveyor of Roads, became involved in another quarrel and was sentenced to a further twelve-month term. This brought him to Port Macquarie, where he suffered from dysentery and escaped with forged papers. He was caught and brought to Maitland, where he was convicted of forgery (it was now 1836) and sentenced to spend the rest of his days on Norfolk Island. He remained there until October 1841, becoming Principal Overseer of Convicts; and then, under the more benevolent regime of Alexander Maconochie, he was allowed to return to Sydney, from which he absconded a short while after. Maconochie, who appears to have held him in some esteem, left a note suggesting he might have found his way to France.[41]

Four of the five Merthyr rioters of 1831 came, as 'lifers', with the *John* a year after *Eleanor* docked in Sydney Cove; a fifth, John Phelps, with a fourteen-year sentence, followed on the *Heroine* fifteen months later. Thomas Vaughan had an uneventful career in the colony, receiving his ticket of leave at Goulburn in August 1840 and a conditional pardon in 1848. David Hughes was given a ticket of leave at Campbelltown, also in August 1840; but it was cancelled for 'immoral conduct' in January 1846; yet it made little difference as he was pardoned two months later. David Thomas was convicted of a more serious crime: having received his ticket of leave at Newcastle in July 1842, he was convicted of rape by the Supreme Court at Maitland in September 1848 and sentenced to spend seven years working on the roads 'and other public works of the Colony'. Lewis Lewis, the rioters' principal leader, whose earlier career we traced in a previous chapter, appears to have had a good record, receiving his ticket of leave at Port Macquarie in June 1840; and his conditional pardon, applied for in September 1846, was due to reach him when he died suddenly at Kempsey near the Leay River, in September 1848.[42]

Other small groups to arrive in Sydney in the 1830s were four Chartists of 1839 (of whom there is little to record) and five of the

---

[41] *The Exile's Lamentations; or Biographical Sketch of Thomas Cook*; see also ML, A.1711 (microfilm).

[42] Arch. NSW, 4/4136, 4142–4, 4164 (tickets of leave).

six 'men of Dorset' sentenced on the spurious charge of 'administering unlawful oaths' at the village of Tolpuddle in the late winter of
1834. These five were James Loveless, George Loveless's younger
brother; John Standfield, the Lovelesses' nephew, and his father
Thomas; James Brine, who was married to Thomas's daughter
Elizabeth; and James Hammett, the only one of the group not
related to any of the others. On arrival in Sydney, Hammett was
separated from his comrades and sent to work deep in the interior
of the colony. The four others were assigned for work with farmers
on the Hunter River; and James Brine was to relate on his return to
England that the master to whom he was sent thought he was one
of the Dorset machine-breakers of 1830 (some of whom had worked
in that district) and received him with the challenging greeting: 'You
are one of the Dorchester machine-breakers; but you are caught at
last.'[43] We have seen that these men—including George Loveless,
who had been sent to Tasmania—had the unique distinction of
having their fares paid home by the British Government after their
pardon had been proclaimed. It took time for the pardon, announced
by Lord John Russell in March 1836, to reach them in New South
Wales; and it was not until 11 September 1837 that James Loveless,
Brine, and the two Standfields sailed from Sydney on the *John Barry*,
which reached Plymouth in March 1838. James Hammett, buried in
the interior, took even longer to reach; and he only arrived in
England in September 1839.[44]

The last group of protesters to be sent to New South Wales were
the fifty-eight Lower Canadians from the rebellion of 1838. They
arrived, as we have seen, on the *Buffalo*, having dropped their
American fellow rebels at Hobart on the way. These French-
Canadians, for all their feeling of alienation in a foreign land, had
at least the advantage of forming a tightly knit group, bound
together by a common culture, language, and religion, and—though
this would assume a greater importance later—to have two articulate
chroniclers to recount their sufferings and plead their cause. On
arrival, they were visited on board by John Bede Polding, the
Catholic bishop, and Father Brady, a fellow priest. This gesture
of denominational solidarity (Ducharme relates) afforded them
pleasure and consolation; and he added (was it sardonically?) after
a further visit:

We were all most gratified and affected to see these respectable gentlemen

[43] *A Narrative of the Sufferings of James Loveless, James Brine, Thomas and John Standfield . . . displaying the Horrors of Transportation* (London, 1881), p. 11.
[44] *ADB*, ii, 132–3 (George Loveless).

extend their zeal for religion and their charity so far, and particularly to see the Bishop come and crawl about for three days in succession in the depths of a ship's hold, so as to bring us back to Jesus Christ, and to console us in our tribulations.[45]

The initial formalities took rather longer in their case than with others; and it was two weeks before they were taken by boat to their probationary station at Longbottom, on the Parramatta River; and here Prieur noted the 'terror and hatred' they appeared to inspire and the 'prejudices and ill-will' that awaited them.[46] However, this wariness on the part of the authorities was soon dissipated and, after a month, the guards were withdrawn and the prisoners were allowed to appoint their own overseers under an English superintendent. During their stay at Longbottom, where they were put to work in a stone-yard, they lost two of their comrades: Gabriel Chèvrefils and Louis Dumouchelle, victims (Ducharme supposed) of dysentery. Probation was over after little more than eighteen months; and they were broken up as a group and assigned for service at low wages— it was a period of depression—with various employers in and about Sydney. Ducharme became a clerk and salesman to a furniture manufacturer and Prieur worked first for a confectioner's and later as a gardener for a Sydney merchant. But they chafed at the separation and, when tickets of leave were issued in February 1842, several of them—including Ducharme and Prieur—set up a saw-milling business together at Balmain on the Parramatta River; but when a bush-fire put an end to that enterprise, they became involved in a succession of others. But, in November 1843, free pardons began to be issued and the French-Canadians, who were eager to return home at the earliest opportunity, turned their attention to scraping together such savings as they could to pay for the homeward journey.

Ducharme and thirty-seven others sailed together on the *Achilles*, bound for London, in July 1844. Prieur, who was helping a French businessman to wind up his affairs in Sydney, left with him on the *Saint-Georges* in February 1846; and fifteen others, at first unable to pay their passage-money, also sailed on later ships. Two stayed behind in Australia: Benjamin Mott, the solitary American in the group, had gone in February 1844 to join his compatriots in Tasmania; and Joseph Marceau, a widower, who had remarried in the colony, stayed on to farm at Dapto, in New South Wales, and died there in 1883. The remaining fifty-four, aided by generous support from North America, travelled on from London to Quebec and

[45] Ducharme, *Journal*, pp. 71–2.
[46] F.-X. Prieur, *Notes of a Convict of 1838* (Sydney, 1949), p. 83.

Montreal. Most went back to their old occupations as lawyers, merchants, or farmers at Montreal or in the Eastern Townships, in some cases with compensation paid to them for damage done to their properties; in the few cases we know of these ranged from Prévot's £125 (or was it his widow's?) to the £526 recovered by Joseph Dumouchelle. Some—a mere handful—met with fame or fortune. Prieur became a prosperous merchant and a pillar of the new establishment; and, doubtless with his Australian experience to recommend him, rose to become Superintendent of all prisons in Canada. Ducharme moved from Châteauguay to Montreal where he married and bought a small business. Both he and Prieur died at an advanced age: Prieur, at 76, in 1891, and Ducharme, at 80, in 1897; and they both lie buried in the cemetery of the Côte des Neiges at Montreal at the foot of the commemorative Monument des Patriotes, which bears the names of all but five of the fifty-four who returned from exile.[47]

[47] *Convicts Landed in . . . NSW*, 1840; Ducharme, *Journal* and Prieur, *Notes*, *passim*; A. Fauteux, *Patriotes de 1837–1838*, pp. 85–387. The five missing names are those of Jacques Goyette and Charles Roy (*dit* Lapensée the Elder), both *cultivateurs* of St. Clément; Étienne Langlois, of L'Acadie; René Pinsonnault, of St. Edouard; and Jean-Marie Thibert, of Châteauguay. Their exclusion, French-Canadian colleagues tell me, is due to their having fallen out with the Church.

4. Van Diemen's Land

VAN DIEMEN'S LAND—as Tasmania was called during the transportation period—was, like Port Phillip, occupied by the British in 1803. There were two good reasons for this: one was to prevent the French from taking it over first; and the other was to relieve the growing pressure of Sydney's expanding convict population. In the next few years, as we have seen, the early Tasmanian settlements— Port Dalrymple, along the northern coast, and Hobart, on the River Derwent in the south—were already being used as temporary stations for convicts from New South Wales: Denis McCarty went there in 1803 and Maurice Margarot, Richard Dry, and Martin Burke in 1807 and 1808. But it was not until 1812 that Tasmania entered the lists as an alternative to New South Wales as a long-term depository for convicts sent directly from English or Irish ports. In October of that year the *Indefatigable* arrived in Hobart, bringing 199 convicts from Britain, including half a dozen Luddites convicted of frame-breaking at Nottingham. One of these was George Green, the young hosiery-worker who has been briefly mentioned before. He was one of those who did far better for himself in the colony than he could possibly have hoped to do at home. He worked for the same employer—a Mr. Humphrey—until his sentence expired in 1819. In the late 1820s he owned 200 acres of land (100 by grant of Colonel Arthur and 100 by purchase) and was renting a further 1,450 acres at Kilby's Corner, near Bothwell, thirty-five miles north of Hobart. In March 1831, an additional grant of 300 acres was made to him and, at this time, his stock was said to include seven head of cattle, six horses, and 2,500 sheep.[1]

The next ship to come—*Minerva I* in June 1818—had the distinction of being the first ship to bring Irish prisoners to Hobart. This was followed by another contingent of 136 Irish on the *Castle Forbes* in March 1820; after which, for reasons that have often been discussed but never satisfactorily explained, no further ships brought Irish prisoners from Ireland to Hobart until Sydney refused to receive further convict transports at the end of 1840.[2] *Minerva I*— if we omit half a dozen Ulstermen transported for 'burglary and

---

[1] Tas. Arch., CSO 1/272/6565 (memorial of George Green); CON 31/13.
[2] Bateson, *The Convict Ships*, pp. 306, 326; Shaw, pp. 183, 364.

robbery of provisions'—had ten protesters on board: most of them men convicted of administering unlawful oaths, or of robbery of arms, some of whom had been sentenced for fourteen years, others for life. On the whole they had a good record in the colony, particularly the 'lifers'. One of these, Francis Cunningham, was given a free pardon (still a rare privilege) in October 1836, eighteen years after arrival; a second, Denis Carring (or Carrin), received one in December 1837; and a third, Thomas Stafford, in July 1840. Cunningham, a labourer from Co. Longford, who had been given a life-sentence for treason, was warmly commended by Colonel Arthur himself: in requesting a conditional pardon for him in August 1830, Arthur justified this 'indulgence' on the grounds of his 'having been upward of 12 yr in the Col. *without an offence*, having held a T of L 10 years; having a *wife & family* whom he has supported in a creditable manner; & being strongly recommended by J. Gordon Esquire, Police Magistrate of the district in which he resides'.[3]

Of the twelve weavers and shoemakers convicted of high treason at York in 1820, eleven arrived on the *Lady Ridley* in June 1821 and one—Michael Downing, a soldier—on the *Phoenix* in the following year. On arrival, owing to the nature of their offence, they were ordered to be 'kept apart'; but it was noted that the conduct of those sailing on the *Lady Ridley* had been, in nearly every case, 'exemplary'. Then, in most cases, we know nothing further for the next five years; except that Joseph Firth, Joseph Chapiel, William Comstive, and Benjamin Rogers were assigned to 'public works' and Charles Stanfield to work for a private employer, and that, in carrying out their duties, Firth distinguished himself as a 'good overseer' and Comstive as a drunkard, while Stanfield received fifty lashes for absconding from his master's house and Rogers and Chapiel received fifty lashes each for harbouring stolen goods.[4]

In December 1826, however, the *Lady Ridley* prisoners combined to address a joint petition to the Colonial Office through Lieut.-Governor Arthur, pleading that they had been 'the dupes of artful and designing men, who acted upon [their] distress and ignorance' and begging for a pardon, as had already been granted to ten of their fellow culprits who had been tried with them at York. In forwarding the petition, Arthur took the unusual step of marking out for special consideration four 'deserving characters who have had no offences in the colony': Joseph Firth, John Burkinshaw, William Rice, and

[3] Tas. Arch., CON 13/1; GO *Despatches* (*Outward*), viii, 744 (Arthur's italics).
[4] Tas. Arch., CON 31/6, 34, 38; CSO 1/9108.

Richard Addy.[5] The plea was only partially successful as Peel observed 'that it was somewhat extraordinary for the Governor of a colony to press upon the consideration of the Government at home the claims of persons transported for High Treason'. This decision (in Arthur's words) put him 'in a situation of much embarrassment'; but he refused to accept defeat and returned to the fray in forwarding a further petition from Rice—this time addressed to William Huskisson—in June 1828. He insisted that a distinction should be made 'between convicts of different characters and classes' whether convicted of high treason or not; and, to support his case, he enclosed a letter from Chief Justice Pedder, for whom Rice had been working as a constable for the past four years and who described him as 'as upright and good a member of society in every way as I have ever met with here or elsewhere'.[6]

But the Colonial Office had its own priorities and the upshot was that Michael Downing (who had come on the *Phoenix* and was not mentioned in these dispatches) received a free pardon in January 1826, Joseph Firth in September 1827, John Lindley (another *Lady Ridley* prisoner) in May 1828, John Peacock in June 1835, William Rice in 1836, John Burkinshaw in July 1839, and Charles Stanfield in September 1840. Some were less fortunate. Joseph Chapiel died on his employer's (F. Allen's) property at the Bushy River on 17 July 1832. Benjamin Rogers became a constable at Launceston in February 1825; but, though he held the post at least until 1834, he was often in trouble and frequently fined or reprimanded for neglect of duty and had to content himself with a conditional pardon (granted in February 1833); while William Comstive, the public works overseer, continued on his drunken career (there were fourteen charges against him in all) and even as late as 1834 was still in possession of no more than a ticket of leave.[7]

The next large consignment of protesters—the largest of all to come to Tasmania—were the rest of the machine-breakers of 1830, of whom all but a handful arrived on the *Eliza* in May and the *Proteus* in August 1831. We have seen in an earlier chapter that, on arrival in Hobart, the great majority were assigned for service with private employers in every habitable part of the island, while a minority (sixty in all) were retained for service with government or sent to work for the Van Diemen's Land Company in the northern half of the island. After this, except in the case of the few who fell

[5] Tas. Arch., GO *Despatches (Outward)*, i, 1154–64.
[6] Ibid., iv, 30–5, 37.
[7] Tas. Arch., 31/1, 6, 9, 13, 27, 34, 38.

consistently foul of their employers, the records tell us little about them in the course of the next few years. But we catch fleeting glimpses of some of them as postal messengers, constables, watchmen, and overseers (these are the selected few); as servants at the Female Orphan School or at Giblin's private school at New Town; working for merchants and drapers at Launceston or for auctioneers at Hobart; employed by parsons, doctors, and Army officers; or serving their time in road-parties, building the bridge at Ross, or in a chain-gang. Most, however, worked on farms and agricultural estates—for Thomas Reiby at 'Entally' on the South Esk River, for the Archers and Bryants near Launceston, for Deprose in Epping Forest, for Youl near Campbelltown, de Gillern and Desailly at Richmond, Hobler at Launceston, and for Roderick O'Connor (Feargus's eccentric half-brother), on one of his numerous properties, near Oatlands.[8]

As at Sydney, most of the machine-breakers received their free pardons between 1836 and 1838. But how many chose or were able to return to their homes in England? To go home was a costly business, as free passages were not provided. Arthur told the Molesworth Committee in 1837 that 'very few indeed [and he was talking of convicts 'of the better sort', such as he believed the machine-breakers to be] seek to return to England'; and, on an earlier occasion, he reported to the Colonial Office that, of 102 men to whom he had issued pardons between 1826 and 1833, only eight had left for England and four for Sydney. On the other hand, the Hammonds quote W. H. Hudson's remark in *A Shepherd's Life* that, in the case of the machine-breakers, 'very few, not more than one in five or six, ever returned'. This may be so but it is probably an overstatement, for we have found records of only two such cases out of over 480 men and women who were transported to the two colonies for this offence. One was William Francis, a Wiltshire ploughman who sailed (or was due to sail) to England with his employer, Major Thomas Livingstone, the Solicitor-General of New South Wales, on the *Duchess of Northumberland* in February 1837. The other was John Tongs, a blacksmith from Tinsbury, in Hampshire, who returned to England from Tasmania shortly after his pardon in 1836. But he did not remain there long and, in January 1843, he reappeared in Hobart as a free migrant with his wife, a daughter, and three sons.

[8] For this and much that follows, see G. Rudé, '"Captain Swing" and Van Diemen's Land', *Tas. Hist. Res. Assoc. Papers & Proceedings*, xii (1964), 14–21; also Hobsbawm and Rudé, *Captain Swing*, pp. 269–79.

Several moved to other parts of Australia and, from there they may have gone further afield. Two of the Sydney men accompanied their masters to Tasmania while still serving their sentence: John Shergold, a Wiltshire labourer, sailed to Port Dalrymple at the end of 1832; and Solomon Allen, a Berkshire ploughman, followed him to Hobart a few weeks later. Charles Bennett, a servant of the Van Diemen's Land Company, found work at Western Port, in present-day Victoria, after his pardon in February 1836; and two other Tasmanians—Thomas Fisher, of Buckinghamshire, and Thomas Hardy, of Hampshire—almost certainly made for the mainland after absconding from their chain-gangs. Many more were tempted to seek their fortune in Victoria during the Gold Rush of the early fifties; and we have found the names of twenty *Proteus* and *Eliza* men among over 50,000 who sailed from George Town, the port of Launceston, to Melbourne and adjacent ports between June 1848 and November 1854. (There must have been many more that sailed from other ports, but there are no other detailed shipping lists to guide us.)

However, it seems likely that the great majority of the prisoners, having won their freedom, stayed on in the colony and, like the Irish of 1798, lived out their lives as farmers, tradesmen, craftsmen, stockmen, and labourers of every sort. Yet we know comparatively little about them. A handful—perhaps three or four—are recorded as having bought small lots of government land during their first twenty years of freedom. Some twenty-five to thirty are listed in the census of 1842 and 1851 as lease-holders or owners of shops, pubs, farms, houses, and cottages in different parts of the island. Of these we seem to know more about the publicans than any others. John Eyres, a Wiltshire ploughman, became licensee of the Cape of Good Hope Inn at Black Marsh, Oatlands, in October 1842 and appears to have passed it on to an old shipmate and fellow Wiltshire man, William North, who still held it six years later. John Boyes, the Hampshire farmer, was the publican of the Hog's Head Inn in Melville Street, Hobart, from October 1839 to May 1853.[9] Another Hampshire man, Isaac Isles, took over the Canterbury Inn, Hollow Tree Bottom, Colebrook, in October 1836. He moved to Richmond, within the same district; and, in 1842, he was living at Tee Tree Bush near by with a wife and four young sons. By 1851, his children had become eight—seven sons and a daughter—and he was living at Brandy Bottom, Colebrook; and he was still there in 1865, when he owned 100 acres valued at £25 per annum. He, at least, was not broken by

[9] *Hobart Town Advertiser*, 3 May 1853.

his experiences, for he died on his property in September 1897 at the age of 95.[10]

Among others who acquired property and fortune were William North and Robert Blake, who came from the same Hampshire village, sailed out on the same ship, married sisters in Tasmania, and at one time shared a farm at Bothwell. Robert Blake, the elder of the two, was a 26-year-old shoemaker who had been sentenced to seven years' transportation by the Special Commission at Salisbury. Like William North, he was living at Bothwell in April 1834, having been assigned there for service two years before. In September 1835 he received permission to marry Mary Bowden, elder sister of North's future wife Sarah. Like North again, he was pardoned in February 1836, though his record may not have been so clean; he was charged, at least, in August 1831, with having issued a counterfeit dollar; yet there is no record of a conviction. In 1840 (as appears from a local residents' petition), he was living at Bothwell with his wife and four children; and, soon after, was sharing a farm with his brothers-in-law, William North and John Bowden, in the same district. By January 1848 he was living in his own brick house at Bothwell; at this time he had four sons and four daughters and is described as a farmer and Wesleyan Methodist; a fifth son was born in April 1850. He acquired further property; for, according to the local evaluation rolls, besides occupying his own house and property of thirty acres (assessed in 1861 at an annual value of £30), he owned at least three other houses at Bothwell in 1858 and seven (with a gross value of £108) in 1861. Robert Blake was still living at Bothwell in 1867, when a local Directory describes him as a 'landholder'; but his death was not recorded in the Bothwell district. His wife Mary had died of consumption in 1861. Two of his sons, William and Isaac, became brewers and carriers—the former at Bothwell, the latter first at Bothwell and later at Hobart. Isaac's Hobart brewery, the Jolly Hatters in Melville Street, purchased in 1885, was bought by a mammoth rival, the Cascade Brewery Company, as recently as 1922.[11]

Another machine-breaker (though not of this contingent) who achieved substance and respectability was Thomas Burbury, the young cattle-doctor who received a life-sentence for the part he

[10] Tas. Arch., Census 1851; *Hobart Town Gazette*, 25 May 1852, 28 March 1865 (valuation rolls); Hobart *Mercury*, 5 Sept. 1896.
[11] For William North's case history, see *Captain Swing*, pp. 277–8. For both case studies I am much indebted to Mr. G. T. Stilwell, Keeper of the Special Records, Hobart.

played in burning down Beck's steam factory at Coventry in 1831. He became district constable at Oatlands, in the Tasmanian midlands, and as the result of his excellent record and his skill in tracking down sheepstealers and bushrangers, was rewarded with a free pardon in 1839. He prospered and acquired a butchery, a dwelling-house and land about Oatlands, where he became successively clerk of the race-course and district poundkeeper, before being elected to the newly formed municipal council in January 1862. He died at Oatlands in July 1870, a prosperous and respected member of the community; and his obituary notice in the local press was able, as in the case of many others, to throw a discreet veil over his convict past.[12] Among these 'others', and the last of the would-be (if not of the actual) machine-breakers, was Gifford White, a Huntingdon-shire ploughman, who achieved a certain immortality by featuring in Thomas Hood's 'The Lay of the Labourer'. White was transported in 1844 for sending a letter to two farmers of Buntisham threatening to destroy the machinery they had just installed. He arrived in Hobart, via the Cape and Norfolk Island, on the *Hyderabad* in February 1845. He received a ticket of leave in 1854 and a conditional pardon two years later. He then travelled all over the island and bought land in the backwoods on the banks of the Shannon River. He died there in 1895 at the age of 76 and was described as 'a substantial landed proprietor' and a man of 'unblemished reputation'.[13]

Somewhat different was the reputation earned for themselves by the eighteen young Bristol rioters who came on the *Katherine Stewart Forbes* and the *England* in July 1832. They achieved a remarkable record of colonial offences, with an average of just under ten per head.[14] Charles Williams, the young carpenter who spent three years at Macquarie Harbour for incitement to mutiny, went on to commit ten further offences before being recommended for a conditional pardon in February 1842. (He received it only three years later.) But he was by no means the worst. That distinction must be held by Patrick Kearney, a 25-year-old linen draper from Co. Armagh, who, as a sign of his devoutness, had a crucifix and the letters INRI tattooed on his right arm. Appointed constable at Hobart soon after arrival, he was suspended for drunkenness and, on a second charge of unlawfully impounding cattle, was dismissed from the force. He

---

[12] Tas. Arch., CON 31/5, 18/21; *ADB*, i, 178-9.
[13] Allport Collection, Hobart.
[14] Compare with Dr. Robson's figure of an average of six colonial offences per head committed by male prisoners sent to Tasmania up to 1840 (*The Convict Settlers of Australia*, p. 101).

went on to commit another twenty-one offences in the course of the next nine years, receiving thirty-six lashes on one occasion and fifty lashes on another and spending various spells in the stocks and six months' hard labour at Jerusalem. His conditional pardon was granted in July 1848, sixteen years after his arrival in the colony. Yet he was not the last to receive one. George Andrews, a groom, and James Snook, a brickmaker, who also had a long string of colonial crimes to their names, had to wait for theirs until 1850.[15]

In sharp contrast to the colonial careers of the Bristol rioters was that of George Loveless, the only one of the six men of Tolpuddle to be sent to Tasmania. On arrival in Hobart in September 1834, he was exempted, by express orders from Colonel Arthur, from all forms of penal observance and sent to work as a shepherd and stock-keeper on the domain farm at New Town and, later, for Major de Gillern at Glen Ayr, near Richmond. It was here that he learned the news that he and his five companions had been offered a free pardon and a free passage to England. Having made certain that his wife had not already left home to join him, he accepted the Government's offer, embarked on the *Eveline* in January 1837 and reached London, to receive a hero's welcome, in June. His views, unlike those of so many others, had not changed. He became a Chartist and wrote a pamphlet, *The Victims of Whiggery*, in which he declared: 'I believe that nothing will ever be done to relieve the distress of the working classes unless they take it into their own hands; with these views I left England, and with these views I am returned.' He never returned to Tolpuddle (James Hammett was the only one of the six to do so); but with his brother James, the two Standfields, and James Brine, he first settled on a farm near Chipping Ongar in Essex and later migrated to Canada. George Loveless died there, in 'Methodist' country, on a farm at London, Ontario, in March 1874 at the age of 77. His tomb, in the Siloam cemetery a mile out of London, bears a simple inscription, redolent of filial piety but discreetly omitting all reference to the part he had played as a champion of human rights.[16]

The next small group of protesters to come to Tasmania were the three Kentish labourers who had hitched their fortunes to the spurious Sir William Courtenay and fought in 'the battle of Bossenden Wood'. They arrived together on the *Pyramus* in March 1839, were taken to Launceston and from there were assigned for service

[15] Tas. Arch., CON 31/2–43.
[16] *ADB*, ii, 132–3; G. Loveless, *The Victims of Whiggery* (London, 1837); Tas. Arch., CON 31/28, 18/22.

in different parts of the island: William Wills at Longford in the
north; William Price at Brighton in the south; and Thomas Mears,
described by the local parson at home as being the most intelligent
of the three, to work as a gardener on the Governor's domain at
Hobart. Price, who was serving a ten-year term, did little to besmirch
his reputation and received a ticket of leave in 1844 and a conditional
pardon two years later. Mears had a more turbulent career, being
repeatedly convicted of drunkenness and disorderly conduct, earning him a flogging on one occasion and terms of hard labour on the
roads on two others, and only receiving his conditional pardon in
1851, four years after it was first requested. Wills, who had no such
tarnished record, continued to live in the north—first at Longford,
later at Deloraine—and received his conditional pardon in October
1850. A couple of years later, having saved up a few hundred pounds,
he made a bid—he was the only one of the three to do so—to return
to England. He engaged a neighbour, Thomas Shackel of Deloraine,
to write on his behalf to the Revd. C. R. Handley, vicar of Herne Hill,
to explore the possibilities. The reply was far from reassuring: the
minister rightly pointed out that to return to England without a free
pardon would be to court disaster. So Wills let the matter drop; and
it must be presumed that, like his companions, he spent the rest of
his days in Australia.[17]

By now, the first of the Chartists to come to Tasmania—John
Frost and his fellows—had arrived on the *Mandarin* in June 1840.
The probation system was now in operation; and, on 3 July, a few
days after the ship's arrival in Hobart, Sir John Franklin, Arthur's
successor, reported to Lord John Russell that the prisoners would
be placed in a probationary gang on the roads—'with the exception
of John Frost, Zephaniah Williams and William Jones, whom
I have thought it right to *forward direct from the vessel to Tasman
Peninsula*'. And he added primly: 'Before their departure, however,
according to my usual custom, I inspect them.'[18] So, in accordance
with the Governor's instructions, Frost, Williams, and William
Jones went to spend their two-to-three years' term of probation at
Port Arthur and Impression Bay; while their fellow rebels from Newport, Jeremiah Howell, John Jones, and Francis Roberts were sent
to work on the roads at Bridgewater and Brown River and on the
docks at the New Wharf at Hobart. During the year that followed,
Howell was sentenced to two years in chains at Port Arthur for

[17] Tas. Arch., CON 31/32, 36, 47; P. G. Rogers, *Battle in Bossenden Wood*,
pp. 194–7.
[18] Tas. Arch., GO *Despatches (Outward)*, xxx, 593–7 (italics in original).

'gross insubordination', John Jones had his probation extended by fifteen months for 'making fals statements', Francis Roberts followed Howell to Port Arthur for attempting to abscond; and Zephaniah Williams, for the same offence, was put in chains for two years and became superintendent of mines at Port Arthur.

Frost himself escaped such dire penalties and became a clerk in the commandant's office at Port Arthur and completed his probation as a schoolmaster at Impression Bay. His probation completed, he went to Hobart New Town and Bothwell and held teaching posts in various parts of the island. In 1854 he received a conditional pardon and, though forbidden entry to the British Isles, was allowed to sail for New York. Here he received news of his freedom (February 1857) and returned to England where he lectured on convict life in Australia. Unlike Loveless, however, he gradually abandoned his old political beliefs. As age crept on, he took to spiritualism and, after many years of retirement from public affairs, he died at Stapleton, near Bristol, at the ripe old age of 90 (or maybe 93) in 1877.[19]

Zephaniah Williams and William Jones stayed on in Australia. Jones, after a blameless record, received his conditional pardon several years before the others, in 1847; but, like them, he had to wait for his full freedom until February 1857. He had already been living in Launceston for the past twelve years; and he died there in poverty in December 1873, his funeral expenses being paid for by the Oddfellows to whose Order he had belonged for many years.[20] Williams, his probation ended in November 1843, went to New Norfolk as a constable at 12s. a week and remained there for three years. He next became a barman at a Launceston hotel and, having made another attempt to escape, was sent back to the Tasman Peninsula for a further twelve months in chains. He was released in November 1848 and found service at Hobart and at Providence Valley near by. Like Frost, he was given a conditional pardon in 1854 and a free pardon in February 1857. He took no further part in public life but returned to his old occupation as a mineral surveyor and prospector of mines. There were opportunities to hand; and he discovered a long-neglected coalfield in New Town and started his own mining company at the Mersey River, where he acquired 2,000 acres, formed a miners' camp, and opened the Denison colliery at Tarleton, near Launceston, in 1853. He went on to extend his opera-

[19] *ADB*, i, 419–20; Tas. Arch., CON 31/1; *DNB*, vii (1922–3), 729.
[20] Tas. Arch., CON 33/1; D. Williams, *John Frost. A Study of Chartism, passim*; *ADB*, i, 419–20.

tions, bringing miners from England, entering into new and profitable partnerships, and was managing three groups of mines when business failed around 1859. He then reverted to his other earlier occupation by becoming a publican at Ballahoo and built a large house at Tarleton. Meanwhile, his family had come out from Wales to join him. His wife, Johan, died in 1863 and Zephaniah himself at Launceston in May 1874 in his eightieth year. He lies buried, together with his wife and daughter, at East Devonport, on the island's north coast.[21]

Richard Boothman, who was convicted of killing a policeman in a Chartist riot at Colne in August 1840, arrived on the *Barossa* in January 1842. He completed his two years' probation at Impression Bay without any untoward incidents and went to work in the northern part of the island, first at Westbury and later at Quamby and Launceston. From Launceston he wrote to his father on 17 April 1845 (his first letter since arrival) to tell him of his experiences during and after probation, stressing that his conduct had been beyond reproach and that he hoped for something to be done at home to secure his early release; and as evidence of his good behaviour he enclosed a signed statement from his present employer, Silas Pearce. His father died soon after, and his next letter, addressed to his brother and dated 14 December 1846, expressed his satisfaction, 'as it is the will of Divine Providence to take him out of this troubled world'; and he urged his brothers and sisters to 'be true and just in all [your] dealings' and to 'act humbly with God' and (more practically) to persuade the 'Rev. Mr Henderson' and other gentlemen to sign a petition to have him set free. The movement to do so, if ever it began, must have failed as the next we hear is that Richard Boothman died at Launceston, thirty years later, in 1877, leaving an estate of £559. 3s. 10d., or (after deduction for funeral and legal expenses) £455. 3s. 5d., to be shared among his heirs.[22]

In April 1843 the *John Renwick* arrived with seventy-two of the Chartists sentenced by Special assizes at Lancaster, Chester, and Stafford for their part in the northern riots of 1842; a handful of others followed on the *Equator* and *Lord Auckland* twelve to fifteen months later. There were no notables among them to be given any kind of special treatment and all but those who had already served a part of their probation at home (as was the case with the later arrivals) were sent to probation stations for two, two and a half, three, or four years according to the length of their sentence. Tickets

---

[21] Tas. Arch., CON 33/1; Williams, op. cit.; *ADB*, ii, 601–2.
[22] Tas. Arch., CON 33/16, 14/12; Lancs. RO, DDX 537/14–17.

of leave followed two or three or four years later and certificates of freedom (except in the case of a small number of 'lifers') when the original sentence expired. In this respect, William Ellis, whom we noted earlier as 'one of the most dangerous men in the Potteries', was as typical as any other. He arrived with a twenty-one-year sentence and was sent to serve a three-and-a-half-year term at the Cascades on the Tasman Peninsula. Emerging with a pass in October 1846, he worked for six months at Swansea, along the east coast, and, after a brief spell as a constable at Hobart, went up north to work for a Mr. King at Launceston. Here he tried to abscond and, in November 1847, was sentenced to six months of 'unpleasant and hard labour' and, in consequence, did not have his ticket of leave approved until January 1850, followed by a conditional pardon in December 1852. Less fortunate were two of the older prisoners, Jervis Phillips (aged 42 at the time of his conviction) and Thomas Owen (43). Phillips, who was serving a fifteen-year sentence, following a three-year probation at Southport, became a constable at Hobart; but he was dismissed the service for being drunk and disorderly and did not receive his ticket of leave until May 1849. He did not enjoy it for long: he died at the hospital at Hobart on 20 April 1850. Thomas Owen, a 'lifer', spent his probationary term of four years at the Cascades and emerged with an excellent record. But he spoilt it a year later, when working at Bothwell, by being sentenced to two consecutive terms of three months with hard labour for perjury and indecent conduct. So his ticket of leave was refused in October 1850. It was his last chance, as he died from an accident at Glenorchy, near Hobart, a month later.[23]

The most fortunate of all these prisoners was Richard Wright, who, as we saw in an earlier chapter, was an 18-year-old collier from Orton convicted of the same crime as William Ellis and, like him, given a twenty-one-year sentence. He served his three and a half years' probation in the Government coalmines on the Tasman Peninsula; and, his probation completed, worked for a number of private employers at Fenton Forest, Black Marsh, Hamilton, and Sandy Bay. But unlike Ellis, and Phillips and Owen, he had an almost unblemished record, being merely reprimanded for a couple of minor misdemeanours over a period of seven years. So he was given an early free pardon in April 1854 and, in February of the next year, he was discharged from the police barracks at Hobart and sailed on the *Derwentwater* back to England.[24] Another man that

[23] Tas. Arch., CON 33/38.
[24] Tas. Arch., CON 33/38, 14/21.

returned was George Colclough, miner of Hanley, who sailed back
to his home in the Potteries when his sentence expired in 1863.[25]
They appear to have been the only Chartists of 1842 to do so.

The third main group of Chartists—those of 1848—came on half
a dozen ships between November 1849 and May 1851. The last to
come were the seven Scots who had been transported for rioting
at Glasgow and Stonehaven, south of Aberdeen. As was common at
this time, most of them had served their term of probation in prison
before they came and were therefore free to work for wages on
arrival. The exception was John Lafferty, a Glasgow man, who,
although he had already stopped at Millbank, Portland, and Parkhurst before he sailed, had still fifteen months to serve. Apart from
this all seven went through the usual penal routine, finishing up with
a certificate of freedom when their seven or ten-year term came to
an end.[26]

The nine Englishmen arrived together on the *Adelaide* in November 1849.[27] Although 'lifers' convicted of sedition, they were allowed
favours denied to the Scots: receiving tickets of leave on arrival and
a free pardon seven years later (December 1856). Two men, however,
did not live long enough to attain their freedom. One was William
Lacey, who, having spent some years 'in respectable circumstances'
as a bootmaker, died at Launceston in February 1854, aged 44.[28]
The other was Joseph Ritchie, the bricklayer from Newcastle upon
Tyne, who died in poverty in Launceston Hospital in August of the
same year. Another who died, but after gaining his freedom, was
William Dowling, the painter, who died in 1857 at 128 Collins
Street, where, the local Directory tells us, he had been painting
portraits for several years.[29]

The most renowned of the transportees of 1848, William Cuffay,
lived on until July 1870, when, at the age of 82, he died at the Brickfields Invalid Depot where he had been living since October 1869.
His wife, Mary Ann, had come out on the packet *Panama* to join
him in April 1853; and they went to live at 177 Elizabeth Street, in
Hobart Town, where he worked for various shops as a tailor. After
he received his free pardon in 1856, Cuffay returned to political

[25] I am indebted to Dr. Robert Fyson of Newcastle-under-Lyme for this information.

[26] Tas. Arch., CON 33/97–9, 102.

[27] Tas. Arch., CON 37/5, 14/38, 18/50.

[28] *Launceston Examiner*, 14 Feb. 1854. On 29 May 1852, the *Star of Freedom*,
a Chartist paper in England, had published a letter from Dowling, giving a brief
account of the 'Tasmanian Chartists'.

[29] *Hobart Town Directory and Book Almanac* (Hobart, 1857).

activities; he was the only one of the numerous Chartist exiles to do so. He played a leading part in the campaign against the oppressive Master and Servant Act and, after he had addressed a crowded meeting in the Albert Theatre in March 1857, the *Tasmanian Daily News*, in reporting it, described him as having 'a big reputation as a Chartist'.[30] More specifically, the Hobart *Mercury*, in an obituary notice written a few weeks after his death, recorded that 'he particularly distinguished himself in the agitation for the amendment of the masters' and servants' law in the colony, and being a fluent and an effective speaker, he was always popular with the working classes'; and, the report continued, 'the exertion of Cuffey and other prominent advocates for the popular classes, contributed in a great degree to the settlement of the masters' and servants' question on a satisfactory basis'. Moreover, the report went on, 'he took a prominent part in election matters, and went in strongly for the individual rights of working men'. In the Brickfields establishment, it concluded, Cuffay was an occupant of the sick ward, where he was described as a quiet man and an inveterate reader. He was buried at Hobart in the Trinity burial ground and, 'by special desire his grave has been marked, in case friendly sympathisers should hereafter desire to place a memorial stone on the spot'.[31]

There remain to be considered the ninety-five American-Canadians of 1838, the five 'Daughters of Rebecca' of 1843, and some 350 Irishmen who had been sentenced for their part in the land-war of the 1840s and the events of 1848. The Canadians came on three ships—eight on the *Marquis of Hastings* (with twenty-three Canadian military deserters) in July 1839; five on the *Canton* (with half a dozen deserters) in January, and eighty-three on the *Buffalo* in February 1840.[32] Like the French-Canadians, the prisoners had been well conducted on board; and an officer on the *Buffalo* recorded on arrival that 'the [American] prisoners on the whole behaved remarkably well owing, in all probability, to the very strict guard kept upon them; for [he added] they came on board with a most infamous character, as a most daring and villainous set'.[33] The eight that came on the *Marquis of Hastings* had a high rate of mortality: Alexander

[30] *Tasmanian Daily News*, 24 Mar. 1851.

[31] *Mercury* (Hobart), 11 Aug. 1870. I am indebted to Dr. F. B. Smith, of Canberra, for giving me copies of these newspaper reports.

[32] For description and appropriation lists, see Tas. Arch., CON 18/5 (*Canton*), 18/16 (*Marquis of Hastings*); and Arch. NSW, Tas. Papers 27, A1054, pp. 233–51 (*Buffalo*).

[33] Cit. F. Landon, *An Exile from Canada to Van Diemen's Land* (Toronto, 1961), p. 180.

McLeod, a Canadian farmer, died of consumption two days after landing; and Garret van Camp, a Canadian labourer (described by Wait as 'a poor innocent, simple, quiet Dutchman'), died from an accident three weeks later. Of the survivors, Samuel Chandler, a wagon-maker of St. John's in Upper Canada, and Benjamin Wait were assigned to work for the Assistant Commissary-General, Roberts, on his property at Ashgrove, where they were employed on teaching and clerical duties. In December 1841 they were permitted to go to Hobart for Christmas, hired a small boat to go fishing and were picked up by an American whaler out at sea.[34]

The five *Canton* men (with Linus Miller as their chronicler) were first sent to work at the Brown's River road station, felling and carrying trees; they attempted to escape and were soon after moved to Sandy Bay, nearer Hobart. The main body of prisoners—those from the *Buffalo*—landed soon after; and William Gates records that a large crowd gathered to see them; for 'to a great many people of that country we were almost as great an object of wonderment as were the followers of Cortez to the simple-minded Aztecs'.[35] They were sent to Sandy Bay, where Sir John Franklin came to address them and expressed concern that they should not be treated like common felons. Yet his suggestion, made to London, that they should be offered tickets of leave at his discretion was as coldly received as Arthur's earlier representations on behalf of the Yorkshire weavers. But some concessions were made, such as being allowed Saturday afternoon free from stone-cutting and carting; though this bonus was offset for some (for Gates, in particular) by compulsory Sunday attendance at St. George's Anglican church. After some months at Sandy Bay the Americans were divided up: some (including Gates and Miller) were moved to Lovely Banks where they completed the construction of the probation station. Others went to Green Ponds, and later to Bridgewater where they worked on the causeway. Further attempts to escape were made and Linus Miller and Joseph Stewart, a tailor from Pennsylvania, were sent to Port Arthur for two years' hard labour. After Bridgewater, there were further divisions, some going on to complete their probation at Jericho and Jerusalem, others to Jerusalem and Campbelltown. Tickets of leave began to be given out in February 1842, but residence was restricted to half a dozen inland centres (such as Oatlands, chosen by Gates, and Campbelltown, where Daniel Heustis took to

---

[34] Mary M. McRae, 'Yankees from King Arthur's Court', *Tas. Res. Assoc. Papers & Proceedings*, xix (1972), 155.
[35] W. Gates, *Recollections*, p. 52; cit. McRae, p. 154.

cradling wheat); and, during the next months, Aaron Dresser, Elon Fellowes, Emanuel Garrison, and Stephen Wright (all *Buffalo* men) had the good fortune to be involved in catching two notorious bush-rangers and, as a reward, were offered early pardons: Dresser and Wright already in June 1843, while Fellowes was promised consideration 'whenever he may apply for indulgence'. A year later, pardons arrived for forty of the prisoners (including Fellowes); and there is a record of thirty-five of them coming to Hobart to sign for them (some with crosses) between 31 July 1844 and 9 January 1845.[36] Other pardons followed, but (as in the case of the French-Canadians at Sydney) pardons did not include tickets for the journey home; and when Linus Miller sailed for home in September 1845, he noted that thirty-three Canadian State prisoners still remained on the island, of whom twenty were still holding tickets of leave and twelve, though pardoned, had not yet been able to raise the money for the homeward voyage.[37]

Meanwhile, most of the prisoners were on their way home. The first to return were the three Short Hills prisoners (Wait, Chandler, and Gemmel) who had absconded in 1841. Next came Stephen Wright and Aaron Dresser, pardoned in 1843; on their arrival in America, they wrote an account of their experiences which was published by the New York *Tribune* in February 1844. Later that year, over thirty men worked their passage, as far as Honolulu at least, on the whaler *Steiglitz*; among them was John Tyrrell, a Canadian dairy farmer, who went back to his farm at Malahide, in Upper Canada; he died there in May 1874. Others left in smaller parties, like Gates (whose passage cost him $200) and Elijah Woodman, the Presbyterian merchant, who sailed in separate ships in early 1847. Gates arrived home at Cape Vincent in 1848; but Woodman died on the voyage off the Juan Fernandez Islands and was buried at sea. One of the last to leave was John Berry, a Canadian ploughman captured at Prescott, who had been working as a shepherd in the hinterland and only heard news of his freedom in 1857. He worked his passage on a South Sea whaler and disembarked in New York in June 1860. Apart from twelve men who died in captivity, a small number still stayed behind: among them Moses Dutcher, a carpenter from Montgomery county, who had married Sarah Burchell, a young convict woman, in 1841 and is

---

[36] Tas. Arch., CON 60/1.
[37] L. W. Miller, *Notes of an Exile to Van Diemen's Land*, pp. 90-1, 376-7. See also McRae, pp. 156-7. For the fullest, but highly tendentious, account, see Edwin C. Guillet, *The Lives and Times of the Patriots*, pp. 209-32.

believed to have settled on the island;[38] Edward (or Edwin) Merrett, a Worcestershire man, who died at Port Arthur in 1867; and James Aitcheson, a Scot, who (rumour had it) had crossed the Straits to New Holland (Victoria); so he, too, probably stayed on in Australia.[39] Today all the Canadian rebels—whether 'English' or French—are remembered and their hardships recalled in a commemorative monument that was unveiled at Sandy Bay, Hobart, in September 1970.

So, after an interlude of over twenty years, we return to the Irish. They fall into two highly disparate groups: the 340 or so Whiteboys, Ribbonmen, and other land-warriors who arrived on a score of ships between 1840 and 1853; and the dozen Young Irelanders of 1848. The first group, like the English north-country rioters of 1842, were more or less insignificant men whose stay in Australia was only rarely touched by drama and has left no mark in the history books. Again, all but a handful served their term of probation in the colony: most of the seven-year men for twelve months (with a few exceptions, like John Rice, of Co. Armagh, who served eighteen months, and Denis Reilly, of Co. Cavan, who served twenty-four), the fourteen-year men for two years, and the 'lifers' for two and a half or three. A great many were sent to the Tasman Peninsula; others to Maria Island, Swanport, or Bridgewater in the south; others again to Jericho or Jerusalem in the midlands, or to Fingal or Deloraine in the north; while a small number, among those arriving in 1844, stopped at Norfolk Island, to serve their probation, on the way.

Nearly all of the seven-year and fourteen-year men received their certificate of freedom according to plan, that is, seven or fourteen years after conviction; while the most a 'lifer' could hope for (for here there were few favours given) was a conditional pardon some fifteen years after conviction or three years after receiving his first taste of relative freedom with a ticket of leave. This almost clock-work precision only failed to apply where *serious* misdemeanours had been committed on the voyage or after arrival on the island. Thus the brothers Michael and Thomas Madigan, both seven-year men, who arrived together on the *Egyptian* in December 1840, served their twelve-months probation at Jerusalem and Saltwater Creek and became passholders at the same time in December 1841. But, once they went on to work for private employers, Thomas committed a number of misdemeanours, one of which earned him a term of six months' hard labour in chains for insolence and

---

[38] Tas. Arch., CON 52/2 (marriages); also CON 40/2 (for *Navarino*).
[39] Guillet, pp. 221–30. For Woodman, see also Landon, *passim*.

disobedience of orders; while Michael had an unblemished record. So it is hardly surprising that while Michael was given his ticket of leave in June 1844 and his conditional pardon in November 1846, Thomas received his in both cases a year later. Yet Thomas's crimes (in spite of his six months in chains) were not considered sufficiently serious to prolong his servitude and, like Michael's, his certificate of freedom arrived seven years after conviction almost to a day.[40]

There was also the case of two of the suspected mutineers of the *Isabella Watson* in 1842: Francis Gafney and Richard Jones, both seven-year men but the first sentenced at Cavan in February 1842 and the second at Dublin in June 1840. They both had unusually long periods of probation on the island: Gafney served two years at Bridgewater and Deloraine, and Jones (in spite of a preliminary long stay in prison in Ireland) served two and a half years at Port Arthur and Brown's River; so the first man's probation ended in August 1844 and the second's in February 1845. At this point Jones, though acquitted by the Supreme Court at Hobart of the charge of conspiracy to seize the *Isabella Watson*, incurred a number of relatively minor penalties (four days' solitary or thirty-six lashes) for 'positively refusing to attend the place of Divine Worship on the Sabbath': this happened four times in a couple of months. Meanwhile, Gafney (like Michael Madison) had a blameless record and received a ticket of leave in March 1846 and a conditional pardon in August 1848, followed by a certificate of freedom, roughly according to schedule, in March 1849. Jones received neither ticket of leave nor conditional pardon (a sure sign of disapproval), but his 'free' certificate turned up just seven years and one day after his conviction at Dublin.[41]

Some, on the other hand, won rewards and remissions for good conduct. Patrick McDonald, for example, another Ribbonman (*Richard Webb*, March 1842), although he was eventually dismissed from the police and fined £1 for neglect of duty, was earlier, when a constable at Brighton, 'commended for zealous conduct in extinguishing a fire at the station on 3 March 1843'; and, in consequence, was rewarded with an early ticket of leave in September 1845 and a conditional pardon two years later. Philip O'Reilly (*Blenheim*, February 1849), who had been given a seven-year sentence for 'writing a seditious letter relative to bad landlords', had an outstandingly good record: not only did he commit no offence in the colony, but the surgeon-superintendent of the *Blenheim* had asked that 'his very excellent and deserving conduct on the voyage be recorded . . . with a view to some remission of his sentence'. This

[40] Tas. Arch., CON 33/3.   [41] Tas. Arch., CON 33/26.

'remission' took shape in an early conditional pardon, received in February 1853. But the authorities, while benevolent in this respect, had proved churlish when, in August 1850, he petitioned for a free passage for his wife and six children and was told he would have to find the passage money himself and noted later: 'to pay expense of passage before receiving a C.P.'[42]

In some cases other factors intervened to disturb the neat time-table from conviction to freedom 'by servitude'. Thomas Shiels, a seven-year man from Co. Cavan (*Pestonjee Bomanjee*, January 1849), absconded on 18 September 1852, after being in the colony for three years and eight months; and, from the *Tory* (March 1847), there were two absconders: Michael Egan, a fifteen-year man from Co. Clare, in June 1852 after five years in the colony (a ticket of leave had been refused him ten months before); and Reynolds Kelly, a 'lifer' from Co. Leitrim, who had been in the colony six and a half years when he escaped, three months after receiving his ticket of leave, in October 1853. And among those who died before completing their term were John Cahill (*Waverley*, September 1841), a 'lifer', who died in hospital at Hobart on 22 May 1847; and two seven-year men, both from the *Tory*, who died while serving a two-year probation at Darlington, Maria Island, in 1847: John Trimble ('accidentally killed') on 24 July and Michael Crene on 3 December. John Deegan, on the other hand (*Hyderabad*, August 1849), long survived his certificate of freedom and was accidentally drowned in the Derwent on 3 July 1884.[43]

Some died a violent death—or appear to have done so. Matthew Mahide, a seven-year man from Tipperary (*Waverley*, 1841), was sentenced by the Launceston Supreme Court on 4 April 1848 to be hanged for armed robbery. (There is some irony in the fact that his certificate of freedom had come through four days before!) In another case we know that the execution was not only decided but carried out. On 3 December 1851 two brothers, Michael (24) and Denis Conlan (22), who had both arrived on the *Pestonjee Bomanjee* with tickets of leave in January 1849, were sentenced to be hanged— 'and dissected'—by the Supreme Court at Hobart 'for the wilful murder of Francis Burt'; and, three weeks later, Michael, the elder of the two, was executed at Hobart. Denis had his sentence commuted to one of transportation for life and was sent to Norfolk Island for ten years instead. Actually, he was given a remission of five and a half years—partly as a reward for 'service at a fire at N. I^sd', and was back at Port Arthur to serve two years' probation

---

[42] Tas. Arch., CON 33/93.   [43] Tas. Arch., 33/85, 92, 94.

in May 1855. But, of course, his free pardon had become considerably delayed: though it was due in February 1853, he only received it in October 1867.[44]

We have seen that the seven most noted of the Young Ireland prisoners arrived in Tasmania on the *Swift*, the *Mount Stewart Elphinstone*, and the *Neptune* between October 1849 and April 1850; and that their five lesser-known comrades-in-arms came later on the *Hyderabad*, the *Blenheim*, and *Lord Dalhousie* in December 1850 to August 1852.[45] On arrival in Hobart, six of the seven leaders were given tickets of leave and directed to reside, on parole, in a number of appointed districts: Meagher went to Campbelltown, McManus to New Norfolk, O'Dogherty to Oatlands, O'Donaghoe to Hobart, and Martin and Mitchel shared a cottage at Bothwell. Smith O'Brien, the most illustrious of the prisoners, was denied the privilege as he flatly refused to give any undertaking not to attempt to escape. So he was sent to the penal station at Darlington on Maria Island and when he tried to abscond to America was transferred to Port Arthur; but here he was given the privilege of having a cottage of his own (now a youth hostel). In November 1850 he was persuaded to give his parole, was granted a ticket of leave and, after living at New Norfolk and Avoca (north of Campbelltown), was allowed to sail to Europe with a conditional pardon in 1854. Two years later, he was granted a free pardon and returned home to Ireland. In 1859 he went on a short visit to New York and in 1863 (another year of 'revolutions') to Poland. Returning home, he stopped in Wales and died at Bangor in June 1864, aged 61.[46]

Of the other leaders, Mitchel escaped from the island in June 1853, having first surrendered his parole and ticket of leave in person to the police at Bothwell. He sailed to Sydney, and from there to Batavia, San Francisco, and New York, where he arrived, to be acclaimed by Irish 'patriots', in November. In the United States, he successively edited the *Citizen* and the *Southern Citizen* and, in 1862, declared himself a champion of the South in the Civil War, three of his sons enlisting on the Confederate side. In 1868, he published *My Jail Journey, or Five Years in British Prisons*. In 1872 and 1874, he visited Ireland, where he died on 20 March 1875, leaving a widow, a son and two daughters.[47]

Thomas Meagher also escaped from the island after surrendering his ticket of leave and withdrawing his parole, but unlike Mitchel (who criticized him for doing so) he returned them by letter to the

[44] Tas. Arch., CON 33/2, 92.   [45] Tas. Arch., CON 33/100, 104, 109.
[46] *ADB*, ii, 294.   [47] *ADB*, ii, 235.

police magistrate at Campbelltown.[48] He sailed to Pernambuco and on to New York where he arrived in May 1852. At New York, he was admitted to the Bar, became a United States citizen and edited the *Irish News*, which, unlike Mitchel's *Southern Citizen*, supported the Northern cause. When war started, he raised and commanded an Irish brigade which fought for the North. Later, he served for a year as acting governor of Montana Territory, where his equestrian statue still stands. He died by drowning in the Missouri River in July 1867. He left behind him in Australia one tangible memory of his Tasmanian exile: his infant son, Henry Emmet Fitzgerald, who died at Richmond, aged 4 months, in June 1852, and lies buried there in the Catholic churchyard.[49]

The remaining leaders, although their histories are not told in the *Australian Dictionary of Biography*, have not been forgotten in Ireland. Among them, John Martin, on receiving his conditional pardon in June 1854, returned to Europe with Smith O'Brien and went to live with him in Paris. Like others, he went back to Ireland after his free pardon was granted and died there in March 1875.[50] Terence McManus, after being in trouble with the Tasmanian police on two or three occasions, absconded in March 1851. He reached San Francisco in June and, as he was refused entry into Ireland, stayed on in the United States and died there in 1860.[51] Patrick O'Donaghoe went on from Hobart (his first assigned district) to Richmond, Oatlands, and Launceston, where he withdrew his parole and attempted to escape. His plan failed and for this and other misdemeanours he spent some time at the Cascades and in jail and had his ticket of leave revoked on three occasions. In December 1852 he successfully absconded to Victoria and sailed on from there to San Francisco. Like other absconders, he was refused a free pardon and died in New York, aged 62, in January 1854. Kevin O'Dogherty, the one-time medical student, was also (like O'Donaghoe) in trouble with the police for leaving his assigned district to attend an unlawful meeting at New Norfolk and spent some time at the penal station of Impression Bay. On returning to Hobart, he worked as a junior surgeon at St. Mary's Hospital in Davey Street, and went to Port Cygnet, along the 'ocean road', and set up in private practice. When

---

[48] For Mitchel's disapproval of Meagher's manner of escape, see his letter from Bothwell of 4 Oct. 1852 to 'Miss Thompson', a family friend, in Ireland: 'It is painful to say this, but in leaving V.D. Land so as to let even a question be raised about his good faith, was a grievous wrong to us and to our cause.' PRO N. Ireland, T 413/2.

[49] *ADB*, ii, 217–18; D. R. Gwynn, *Thomas Francis Meagher*, pp. 34–61.

[50] *DNB* (1893), xxxvi, 170–2.

[51] Ibid., xxxv, 673.

his conditional pardon came through in June 1854, he went to Victoria and on to England, where he married Mary Eva Kelly in August 1855. When pardoned the next year, he returned with his wife to Ireland. But, in 1860, he went back to Australia—he was the only one of the Irish prisoners to do so—and settled in Queensland, where he became a member of the Legislative Assembly and Legislative Council in turn. Returning to Ireland in 1885, he represented North Meath for three years in the British House of Commons. After that, he went back to Queensland and resumed his medical practice. He died there, aged 82 and the last of the Young Irelanders, in 1905.[52]

As might be expected, we know far less of the five rank-and-file prisoners of 1848; here we have only the prison records to instruct us. All but one of them—Cornelius Keeffe, who had already spent three years in jail at Waterford—served a probationary term at the Old Wharf, Hobart, on arrival: Edmund Sheafy for fifteen months, Thomas Donovan and John Walsh for two years; and Thomas Wall, the only fourteen-year man, for three years and six months (without taking account of deductions). The three seven-year men received tickets of leave in November 1853 and conditional pardons in August and September 1854, while Edmund Sheafy, who was serving a ten-year term, received his in 1854 and 1855; and free pardons followed, according to plan, between 1856 and 1859. None of the five had had previous convictions and only one—Edmund Sheafy—had any conviction recorded against him in the colony; and that was for a trivial offence. But Thomas Wall, who had been given a fourteen-year sentence for attacking the police barracks at Waterford, appears to have been the most exemplary prisoner of all. During his probation at Hobart, he was allowed a remission of '2 days per month [to quote from his conduct record] for zealous attendance at school' (he could only read 'a little' on arrival) and a further remission of 461 days gained by task work'. He subsequently went on to Hobart Town and Snug (near Kingston) and received further commendation for 'meritorious service' in fighting fires at Huon. As a result, he was given an early ticket of leave in February 1854, and his conditional pardon a year later, a bare five years after his conviction.[53]

Finally, to look back to July 1844, when four of the five 'Rebecca's Daughters' arrived in Hobart on the *London*; the fifth man, John Jones—alias 'Shoni Sgubor Fawr'—went to Norfolk Island on the

[52] I am indebted to Dr. Peter Howell (now of Flinders University) for reconstructing most of this case history for me.
[53] Tas. Arch., CON 33/100 (Donovan, Wall, Walsh), 104 (Sheafy), 107 (Keefe).

Blundell and from there came on the *Pestonjee Bomanjee* to Hobart three years later.[54] At this point, let us allow Rebecca's historian, the late David Williams, to take up their story:

It was Shoni who was the first to be transported. He was separated from the others. Possibly this was done because he had received a life sentence whereas they had terms of years, but the separation may have been deliberate as he was a far more violent character than they were. He embarked on the *Blundell* on 8 March 1844 and reached his destination on 6 July, after a seventeen weeks' journey around the Cape. To begin with he was placed on Norfolk Island ... Three years later he was transferred to Van Diemen's Land, crossing the thousand miles of ocean in the ship *Pestongee Bomanjee*. While on Norfolk Island he had already served sentences of two months' hard labour and ten days' solitary confinement for stealing potatoes and for fishing without permission. In Van Diemen's Land his life should have been easier for he was indentured to various employers, but their rapid succession (he served about twenty before his conditional pardon) and the frequency with which they 'returned him to service' show that they could do little with Shoni. He was imprisoned with hard labour for three months for refusing to work unless he got extra rations, given two days' solitary confinement for being absent without leave, two months' hard labour (with the tread-wheel) for disobeying orders, seven days' solitary confinement for being drunk and resisting a constable and one month's hard labour for not proceeding to Launceston as he had been directed to do. At last, on 19 September 1854, he was given his ticket of leave, but within a month it was revoked for he had committed an assault for which he was given eighteen months' hard labour. He seems to have been released before the end of this sentence, but, in December 1855, he was given a month's hard labour for drunkenness, and, in the following March, another three months for the same reason. He got his ticket of leave on 2 December 1856. Yet within two days he was reprimanded for misconduct, and this was repeated on two later occasions, and in March 1857 he was given a month's hard labour. He was conditionally pardoned on 20 April 1858, and with that his sad, if far from simple, annals terminate.[55]

The other convicts embarked on the *London* four days after Shoni had left, and arrived in the antipodes also four days after he did. They were placed on probation on Maria Island ... and there, only a week later, on 17 July 1844, David Jones died. He was just twenty-one years of age. Is it fanciful to imagine that he died of grief, twelve thousand miles from his native Carmarthenshire?[56] John Hugh, who had been seriously wounded at Pontarddulais, fared better.

---

[54] Tas. Arch., CON 14/28; 33/56, 78.

[55] Shoni's record was certainly a bad one, but even among protesters it was not unique. For the case of Patrick Kearney, a Bristol rioter, see pp. 211-12 above; and for others see pp. 246-7 below.

[56] Arthur would not have thought it 'fanciful'. Writing to Lord Goodrich in March 1834 concerning the early deaths of a number of the machine-breakers of 1830, he reported that several of the *Eliza* men 'died almost immediately from disease, induced apparently by despair'. Arthur to Goodrich, March 1834; cit. Hammonds, *The Village Labourer*, ii, 291.

He was soon given his probation pass (6 March 1846) and his ticket of leave (11 January 1848). In December 1850 he had served his seven years' sentence and was free. A solitary fine of five shillings for being drunk is the only penalty recorded against him. He was married and had a child in Carmarthenshire, but presumably his wife had died, for in August 1852 he applied for permission to marry Mary Maher, a convict transported on the *Duke of Cornwall*. With that he, also, passes from sight. John Hughes was admonished once or twice for misconduct during his probation, but he won the commendation of the authorities for capturing a fellow-convict who had absconded, and was given his pass on 18 July 1846. During his period of indenture he was given fourteen days' solitary confinement for feigning illness. He obtained his ticket of leave on 22 February 1853. Three years later this was revoked, but it was soon restored and, on 19 May 1857, he was given a conditional pardon, six and a half years before his sentence was completed. A letter which he wrote to his father on 18 April 1864 is still extant. He was then a timber cutter and apparently hired men to work for him at times. He had forgotten most of his Welsh and wrote in English. Although he knew of some who had gone home and then returned to Tasmania because of the climate, he still hoped to be buried among his relations and friends. In October 1867 he was prosecuted in the Supreme Court of Tasmania for having stolen a bill of exchange valued £26. 10s., but the jury exonerated him. He married and settled down in Tasmania and never came home, but he corresponded with his relatives at Tŷ-isha until his death about 1900. Both his son and daughter were living and were in good circumstances in 1921.

Finally, the Cantwr [David Davies]. He had a rougher passage. He emerged from probation within a year, but then ran into heavy weather. He was indentured to about a dozen masters and was fined for drunkenness several times and given twenty-one days' hard labour for this offence on one occasion. He served a period of three months' imprisonment with hard labour for gross insolence, and a similar sentence for using indecent language and assaulting a constable. It is clear that his weakness was drink. He obtained a ticket of leave in March 1852, but it was revoked, as also was the conditional pardon given him in October 1854. This was restored to him in August 1855, eight years before his sentence of twenty years had expired. . . . In his freedom he tried to earn a living as a farm overseer, a lime burner, a small road-contractor and a general labourer. He was then known as Taff Davis. He died on 10 August 1874, in his sixty-first year. For several nights previously he had been sleeping in an outhouse of the hotel at Ross. He retired to sleep in an intoxicated state on the night of 10 August, and it is presumed that he set the grass on which he slept on fire by lighting his pipe, for he was found next morning suffocated and partly burnt . . .[57]

[57] David Williams, *The Rebecca Riots*, pp. 286-9. Sources cited by Williams are police and marriage records at Hobart and the Tasmanian press.

5. Western Australia

WESTERN AUSTRALIA was first settled as a British colony on the Swan River, along the south-west corner of the earlier 'New Holland', in 1829. Its location made it admirably suited to become an outpost for trade with the Indies; settlers were to be lured by the prospect of cheap land; labour was to be free and, at this stage, convicts were deliberately excluded from the colony. However, when the British Government, yielding to pressures from other quarters, raised the price of land in all the Australian settlements, the sale of land in the West almost ceased and an economic crisis and a severe shortage of labour followed. Prompted by such consideration, in 1846, the Western Australians petitioned the Government to solve their economic problems by declaring the colony a penal settlement. The Government, pulled in opposing directions by competing interests, at first refused but eventually agreed; and, in May 1849, an order-in-council made the colony a place to which convicts (or 'exiles') might be sent; and the first convict ship, carrying seventy-five English 'exiles', docked in Fremantle harbour on 1 June 1850. A steady influx followed; and even when Hobart followed Sydney in closing its port to further convict transports after 1852, Fremantle continued to receive them at a fairly steady rate of two shiploads a year until January 1868. By that time, 9,635 prisoners had arrived in thirty-seven ships. There were no women among them and virtually no Irish; in fact, only one Irish ship—the *Phoebe Dunbar* (arriving in August 1853)—sailed from an Irish port.[1]

The first ship—the *Scindian*—brought among its seventy-five prisoners three arsonists, all fifteen-year men who had spent nine to fifteen months in prison in England before they sailed and were given tickets of leave twelve or thirteen months after arrival. The second ship—the *Hashemy*—brought five arsonists and a poacher. One of the arsonists was Joseph Clayton, who had been sentenced to the usual term of fifteen years. He was a Birkenhead labourer, aged 36, with a wife and three children, who had been convicted, at the Chester assizes in March 1848 of setting fire to a dwelling-house.

[1] See Shaw, pp. 353-5. Even the *Hougomont*, with its large contingent of Irish political prisoners, sailed from London.

The architect of the Bull's Head at Birkenhead described him as a man 'of sound intellect but [who] sometimes indulges a little'. Clayton spent twenty-eight months in prison before sailing on the *Hashemy* in July 1850 and received his ticket of leave in September 1851. We know little about his later career; but it appears that one of his children married in the colony (probably at Toodyay) in December 1864 and that Clayton himself died in April 1889 at the age of 73.[2]

Of the ships that followed two in every three brought further groups or contingents of arsonists of every kind. There were 361, or an average of twenty a year, all (with the exception of a solitary Irishman) from Britain. In some years, as might be expected, there was a significantly greater influx of such prisoners than in others: peak years were 1855 (with 29), 1862 (38), 1863 (37), 1864 (41), 1865 (59), and 1866 (52); in fact, more arsonists arrived in the four years 1863-6 than in all the other years combined. But, though the rhythm of arrivals changed abruptly, corresponding broadly (allowing for a twelve-to-eighteen months delay) to the rhythm of incendiarism in England, the pattern of sentence and operation remained comparatively constant. The punishment for burning down a house or a barn or setting fire to a stack of hay or corn continued, most typically, to be a fifteen-year term; and the prisoner continued to expect his ticket of leave a year to eighteen months after arrival and his freedom as soon as his nominal sentence expired.

Among the few exceptions, we may cite the case of two young Maidstone labourers, both convicted of maliciously firing a stack of corn and sentenced to the customary fifteen-year term, and both arriving, with nineteen other arsonists, on the *Stag* in May 1855. The younger of the two, Felix Morgan, had three months of his sentence remitted for saving a fellow prisoner from drowning and, in consequence, received his ticket of leave on 10 April 1857 instead of on 7 September as planned. The elder, George Jackson, had the opposite experience: he was punished eight times—five times for absconding, twice for robbery (in one case involving a three-year spell in prison with hard labour)—and had his certificate of freedom, due in March 1868, delayed until 15 April 1874.[3] But, in nearly all cases, punishment had lost the severity it had possessed even in the last dozen years in Tasmania, let alone in the earlier days in New South Wales; and now it was boredom rather than barbarity that

[2] Arch. WA, R.17, 21. I am indebted to Professor G. C. Bolton, of Murdoch University, Western Australia, for certain of these details.

[3] Arch. WA, R.12, 18.

must have been the constant bane of the convict's life. One relief was that once probation was over a man could work for wages and have some say in choosing his place of work. From the registers we learn something of the wages paid to convicts at this time. From these it appears that a man, doing a common labourer's job in the 1860s and early 1870s, might be paid 20s., 25s., or 30s. a month according to his age or the skill of the work performed. A general servant's wages were inclined to be lower, again starting at 20s. but rarely going above 25s. A butcher or a carpenter was paid 30s., or the equivalent of the labourer's top rate; but a sawyer earned £2 or £3 a month and some craftsmen considerably more. Daily rates were proportionately higher than the monthly, a labourer or general servant being paid 2s. 6d. or 3s. a day, a sawyer 7s. 6d. and a plasterer 8s. Piece-work might push earnings appreciably higher still; as in the case of James Collins, a young Hertfordshire labourer (not reputed to possess any particular skill), who, working as a reaper at York (seventy miles east of Perth), earned £8. 8s. on piece-work in December 1867.[4]

But how many of these arsonists—amounting to more than half of all British arsonists transported to Australia—may be considered to have been protesters? In their case, from the scanty information provided, it is almost impossible to tell the sheep from the goats. So there is perhaps no particular point in pursuing our inquiry further along these lines; and, for the purposes of this book, at least, it is more fruitful to turn once more to the sixty-two Fenians who arrived from England on the *Hougomont* in January 1868. On arrival at Fremantle the prisoners (who had still their probation to serve) were assigned to work in road parties at Clarence, Guildford, or Mount Eliza. From these they went on to Bunbury, Newcastle, Northam, York, or the Swan district in the neighbourhood of Perth. Nominally, the period of probation was strictly tailored to the length of sentence, the shortest period (for a five-year man) being two years ten months and fifteen days and the longest (for a 'lifer') twelve years and as many months and days. But, as we saw before, in their case theory bore little relation to practice. As one example of this, there was Patrick Doran, a 'lifer', who fell sick a few months after arrival

---

⁴ Arch. WA, R.1, 2, 8, 12, 18, 28. It is noticeable that while convict-craftsmen's wages tended to increase over the period 1860–74, labourer's wages appear to have remained static. But these, it appears from information kindly given me by Mr. Tom Stannage, of the History Department, University of Western Australia, had fallen steeply—by 'at least 40%'—between the late 1840s and the mid 1850s as the result of the full-time employment of convict ticket of leave holders. (See, in particular, a report on wages in the York District in the Perth *Gazette* of 28 July 1854.)

and was given a conditional pardon—allowing him to move anywhere he pleased within Britain's colonial dominions—on 9 July
1868.[5] Next, John Boyle O'Reilly made his escape to America on
the U.S. whaler *Gazelle* on 18 February 1869. O'Reilly had been
working as a clerk and librarian to the Roman Catholic chaplain
at Fremantle and, shortly after, when sent down the coast to Bunbury
to work in a road party, had been allowed to assist the parish priest,
Father Patrick McCabe, who helped him to plan his escape.[6] Then,
three months later (on 15 May 1869), the Government granted free
pardons to thirty-four prisoners who were serving various terms
for 'treason felony', while making no concessions as yet to the
'mutineers', who, in most cases, had been sentenced to shorter terms.
On 21 July a Perth newspaper, the *Inquirer*, reported that money
was being raised, through an Irish State Prisoners' Fund at Ballarat,
to enable the freed prisoners to return to Ireland.[7] A large part of
the money appears to have been raised in the next two months; for,
on 21 September, the paddle-steamer *Rangativa* (460 tons) sailed
from Albany for Sydney with twenty-five Fenians (travelling
steerage) and twenty-nine cabin passengers aboard.[8] The *Rangativa*
reached Port Adelaide, in South Australia, on the morning of
26 September, dropped two cabin passengers, picked up half a
dozen more and a cargo of twenty tons of flour and fifty cases of
jam and, after three days in port, sailed on to Melbourne and
Sydney, where the Fenians who, up to now, had not been allowed
to go ashore, finally disembarked; and from there fourteen of them
sailed on to San Francisco four months later.[9]

Of the nine freed prisoners that remained behind, two brothers,
Lawrence and Luke Fulham, were by now reported dead (Lawrence
had been receiving medical treatment for the past year); James Flood
followed the *Rangativa* prisoners on the *Geelong*, which sailed from
Albany to Melbourne, on 16 December; and John Goulding left on
the *Queen of the South* for New Zealand on 11 May 1871 with four

[5] Arch. WA, V.10.
[6] Ibid.; *ADB*, v, 371; J. S. Moynihan, 'Fenian Prisoners in Western Australia',
Éire-Ireland, iii, no. 3 (1968-9), 8-9.   [7] *Inquirer* (Perth), 21 July 1869.
[8] The twenty-five Fenians were Thomas Bowler (alias Cullinane), John Casey,
Denis Cashman, David Cummins, Thomas Daly, Patrick Doran, Simon Downey,
Patrick Dunne, Maurice Fitzgibbon, Thomas Fogarty, Eugene Geary, Dennis
Hennessy, David Joyce, John Kenneally, Patrick Lahey, Eugene Lombard, Morgan
McSwiney, Robert May, Michael Moore, Michael Noonan, Jeremiah O'Donovan,
Patrick Reardon, John Sheehan, Patrick Wall, and John Walsh. Arch. WA, A/138.
[9] Ibid.; see also South Australian Archives, Port Adelaide Shipping Registers
1858-75; *S. Australian Register*, 27 Sept. 1869; *Advertiser* (Adelaide), 27, 29 Sept.
1869.

other men (Baines, Fennell, John Flood, and Kelly) who had been conditionally pardoned a couple of months before.[10] Three others sailed at various times to Melbourne—intended as a stopping-place for Ireland: Hugh Brophy in May 1872, James Reilly on the *Nubia* in May 1874, and Cornelius O'Mahoney on the *Bungalore* as late as 1877. The remaining two appear from all accounts to have stayed on in the colony.[11]

Meanwhile, plans were being made in America for the rescue of some of the prisoners still left behind. The vessel selected, the *Catalpa* (with George S. Anthony in command), sailed from New Bedford on 29 April 1875 equipped for a whaling expedition; and, in consequence, it was not until nearly a year later that she cast anchor off the coast at Bunbury, south of Perth. And it was here that Robert Cranston and his five companions,[12] who had come from Fremantle by a smaller craft, were picked up on 17 April 1876; they were landed in New York harbour four months and two days later.[13]

Several prisoners still remained in custody, most of them men serving additional terms in prison for crimes and misdemeanours committed in the colony. Among them was Thomas Delaney, a former private in the 5th Dragoons. After receiving his ticket of leave in July 1871, he accumulated a list of nineteen offences— mainly for drunkenness and disorderly conduct, but culminating in a sentence of three months' hard labour in Fremantle jail for absence from home. He was given a conditional pardon in March 1878 and sailed for Melbourne on the *Rob Roy* in July 1882. Another hardened offender and former 'mutineer' was John Shine (briefly mentioned in an earlier chapter), who was less remarkable for the number of his offences than for the frequency with which he changed his job: no less than twenty-three times between September 1871 and December 1875, taking him to places as far afield as the Arthur River, Bunbury, York, Tipperary, Geraldton, the Mines, and Champion Bay. He also received his conditional pardon in March 1878; as did James Kiely, a one-time private in the 53rd Foot, and James McCoy, a drummer of the 61st Foot, whose turbulent career

[10] Arch. WA, R.16, V.10. The Perth *Herald* reported on 27 July 1871 that four of these men were taken into custody on arrival in Auckland but later released on condition they left New Zealand within 14 days (*Herald*, 27 July 1871, p. 3).

[11] Moynihan, p. 13; Martin G. Carroll, 'Behind the Lighthouse', p. 524.

[12] They were Thomas Darragh, Michael Harrington, Thomas Hassett, Martin Hogan, and James Wilson. Hassett had made an earlier bid for freedom, having been found on board the *Southern Bell* in April 1871 after spending ten months at large; he was jailed for three months with hard labour for the attempt. Arch. WA, V.10.

[13] Ibid.; Moynihan, p. 11. For a fuller account, see Z. W. Pease, *The Catalpa Expedition* (New Bedford, Mass., 1897).

in the colony landed him in a variety of prisons and was at one time marked by a stern injunction that 'he be restricted to engagements within 2 miles of the City'.[14]

With the exception of Delaney, these men were added to half a dozen others who chose to stay on in the colony after receiving their free or conditional pardon. One of them, Patrick Keating, a former labourer and private in the 5th Dragoons, died at Perth, aged 48, in January 1874. Others lived on to a great old age; and William Redmond, the Irish nationalist leader, describes how, when he visited the Celtic Club at Perth after the turn of the century, he met 'three feeble old men, who were apparently regarded by all the members of the club with much respect. They were Duggan, Kileen, and Kiely, three survivors of the band of Fenians who suffered in Western Australia.'[15]

We know little or nothing, except in the case of O'Reilly, of what happened to those who sailed from Albany to Melbourne, Sydney, and the United States; but we must assume that most eventually returned to Ireland. One who did not was Cornelius O'Mahoney, who died in Melbourne in 1878.[16] Another who may not have done was Denis Cashman, one of the fourteen *Rangativa* prisoners who sailed on to San Francisco; from there he went to Boston and became assistant editor of O'Reilly's paper, the *Pilot*.[17] O'Reilly himself, the most renowned of the Fenian exiles, had sailed to America by way of St. Helena and Liverpool, arriving at Philadelphia on 23 November 1869. He became a United States citizen and settled in Boston, working first as a journalist, then editor, and eventually part-owner of the *Pilot*. In it he advocated Home Rule for Ireland, but by constitutional means, and condemned the Fenian invasion of Canada in 1870. He also played a prominent part in the plan to send the *Catalpa* to Western Australia and rescue Cranston and his fellow Fenian prisoners. O'Reilly won a reputation in America as a poet and lecturer; his verse lacked distinction (as it always had), but his novel *Moondyne* (published in 1879) made a useful addition to the literature of transportation. In 1885, he was awarded an honorary doctorate of laws by the University of Notre Dame. He had married a few years after his arrival in America and left four children when he died at Hull in August 1890. There is a bust of him in the Catholic University of Washington.[18]

[14] Arch. WA, V.10.

[15] W. Redmond, *Through the New Commonwealth* (Dublin, 1906), pp. 133–5; cit. Moynihan, p. 13.

[16] Arch. WA, A/138.   [17] Carroll, p. 509.   [18] *ADB*, v, 371–2.

PART FIVE

ARTFUL DODGERS AND VILLAGE
HAMPDENS

1. Who were the Convicts?

THE debate on what sort of men the convicts were has gone on almost since Governor Phillip disembarked with his First Fleet at Botany Bay in January 1788. In the early days, little good could be seen in men so utterly depraved. First there were the off-scourings of London, soon to be followed by those of Birmingham, Liverpool, and Glasgow. With the 1790s came the Irish whom the colonial authorities at first considered utterly beyond redemption: not only for the nature of their crimes, but for their religion which made them suspect from the start. When the Defenders, the first of the Irish protesters, came out on the *Cornwallis* and the *Britannia* in 1796 and 1797, Governor Hunter described them as 'turbulent', 'worthless', and 'horrid'; and the rebels that followed were written off as men 'of a very bad description' and, moreover, of such 'credulous ignorance that an artful priest may lead them to every action that is either good or bad'.[1] And although Hunter displayed some concern for those prisoners on the *Minerva* and *Friendship II* who 'have been either bred up in genteel life or to professions unaccustom'd to hard labour',[2] they were generally considered lawless and criminal types whose very presence in the infant colony filled the authorities with fearful foreboding and alarm.

Later, as the first generation of convicts gave way to the next, the subject of debate shifted from the new arrivals to the emancipists, or those who had already served their term (or had been pardoned in the course of it) and were attempting to live down their crimes of the past by finding an accepted position in the society of the day. They found a champion in Governor Macquarie (1810–21) who fervently believed that 'tried good conduct should lead a man back to that rank in society which he had forfeited';[3] and we have seen before how he applied this principle to the case of William Redfern, the naval mutineer, and James Meehan, a rebel of 1798. Others, however, demurred, including many of the legal profession and officer corps, Commissioner John Bigge—and, not least, the Revd. Samuel Marsden, who believed that man was born in sin and that convicted

[1] Cit. T. J. Kiernan, *Irish Exiles in Australia* (Dublin/London, 1954), pp. 13, 29, 37.
[2] Ibid., p. 17.
[3] C. M. H. Clark, *A History of Australia*, i (Melbourne, 1962), 75.

felons, being more sinful than others, were utterly beyond redemption whatever their previous station in life.[4]

But, sooner or later, as Australia began to shed its penal and colonial past, the history of the founding-fathers began to be seen in a new light. No nation likes to see its origins painted in such uniformly sombre and unflattering colours; and, as Sir Keith Hancock wrote a generation ago, 'the tendency of a folk to idealize its origins is universal among mankind and may be observed even in Australia'.[5] So Australian historians, like the Hammonds in England, began early in this century to picture the convicts as more sinned against than sinning and as victims of a harsh and vindictive criminal code which made little distinction between a murderer and a man convicted of resisting enclosure, stealing a loaf of bread, or taking elementary precautions to protect himself against the grosser evils of an industrial revolution.[6] The best-known of the academic proponents of such a view was George Arnold Wood, whose paper on 'convicts' appeared in the *Journal of the Royal Historical Society* in 1922. Echoing the Hammonds' thesis of the 'village Hampdens', Wood asks the rhetorical question:

Does anyone now consider that the labourers who sailed to Australia with the convict brand upon them surpassed in moral wickedness the politicians, lawyers, and bishops who put that brand upon them? Is it not clearly a fact that the atrocious criminals remained in England, while their victims, innocent and manly, founded the Australian democracy?[7]

Such opinions found eager readers; and it was somewhat in the same tradition that T. J. Kiernan, a distinguished Irishman and one well familiar with the story of the early Irish rebels and others sent to Australia in the first decades of the nineteenth century, wrote his two moving, and richly documented, studies of the 'Irish Exiles', one published in Dublin and the other in Canberra, in 1954.[8] Such works and the intentions of their authors are certainly not to be despised; but it was inevitable that once historians began to subject the history of transportation to rigorous scholarly inquiry, based on the extensive records at Sydney and Hobart, their findings would

---

[4] Clark, *A History of Australia*, i, pp. 271–2, 275, 282, 369–70. See also *ADB*, i, 99–100 (Bigge); ii, 370 (Redfern).

[5] W. K. Hancock, *Australia* (London, 1930), p. 33; cit. Shaw, *Convicts and the Colonies*, p. 146.

[6] Ibid.

[7] G. A. Wood, 'Convicts', in *JRAHS*, viii, 177 ff.; cit. L. Robson, 'Male Convicts Transported to Van Diemen's Land, 1841–53', *Tas. Hist. Assoc.* ix (June 1961), 40.

[8] Kiernan, *Irish Exiles in Australia*; *Transportation from Ireland to Sydney 1791–1816* (Canberra), also of 1954.

be challenged and a new critical, and more discriminating, assessment of the nature of the convicts would take their place. The first historian to begin to undermine this rosy 'Whiggish' interpretation of Australia's earliest European settlers was A. G. L. Shaw, who, in an article in the *Sydney Morning Herald* in June 1953, argued that most convicts, far from being the innocent victims of an unjust system, were urban thieves, pickpockets, and shoplifters, the product of urban overcrowding and unemployment of whom a large proportion (varying from a quarter to a third) came from London and Lancashire and had already, far from being first offenders, been in and out of jail before. In short, in reply to the question, who were the convicts?, Shaw answered quite simply that 'the great majority were ne'er-do-wells from the city slums'.[9] Writing three years later in two consecutive issues of Australia's *Historical Studies*, Manning Clark, having made a sample of various shiploads of convicts between 1813 and 1840, came to broadly similar conclusions: that theft was by far the most common offence for which both English and Irish convicts were sent to Australia; that most offenders of both sexes were young; and that, by 1837, when the death penalty was rarely imposed, transportation to the Australian colonies had become reserved for hardened and dangerous criminals, most of whom came from the working classes in the cities and towns.[10]

And there the matter stood, apart from relatively minor amendments made by Shaw and Clark in their longer studies of the 1960s,[11] until L. L. Robson, in 1965, devoted a whole volume to 'an enquiry into the origin and character of the convicts transported to the two eastern colonies' (Western Australia was omitted from his study, as it was largely from all other general studies of the kind).[12] Robson's views are not startlingly different in any major respect from those already expressed by Clark and Shaw: he, too, concludes that the majority of the convicts from England and Ireland—though more positively from England—were young urban thieves. But though limited to a sample of one in twenty of all convicts arriving in Sydney and Hobart, his study is far more detailed and specific than those that came before him and his conclusions are based on a far wider range of questions, such as: where did the convicts come from? what crimes had they committed, including the one that led to transportation? how many were men and how many were women? how

[9] Shaw, in *Sydney Morning Herald*, 29 June 1953; cit. Robson, op. cit., pp. 40–1.
[10] Cit. Robson, pp. 41–2.
[11] Clark, *A History of Australia*, i (1962); Shaw, *Convicts and the Colonies* (1966).
[12] Robson, *The Convict Settlers of Australia* (1965).

many were English and how many Scots or Irish? to which colonies were they sent? what happened to them when they got there? what further offences were committed in the colony? how old were they? what were their occupations, their marital status, the length of their sentence, their religion and place of birth? and why did they commit the crime that brought them to Australia?

Robson's answers (most of which are outlined in his introduction) are, briefly, as follows:

Numbers and destination. Approximately 123,000 men and 25,000 women were sent to the two eastern colonies, the great majority (about 130,000) after 1815.

Place of trial. Two convicts in every three were tried in England, rather less than one in three in Ireland, and a few hundred more in Scotland and abroad. Of the English, one-third of the males and one-half of the females, came from London and Lancashire combined.

Age and marital status. The average age was 26 and about three in every four were single.

Social class and occupation. The great majority were from the labouring classes (agricultural workers, common labourers, and craftsmen), with a higher proportion of craftsmen among the English and Scots.[13]

Religion. Two-thirds were Protestant and one-third Roman Catholic (nearly all of these from the south of Ireland and Lower Canada).

Literacy. The English are shown (from partial evidence) to have been considerably more literate than the Irish and the men than the women.

Nature and causes of crime for which sent out. Eight out of every ten were transported for larceny of one kind or another. Causes were many, but poverty and the environment it bred were the most common.

Previous convictions. Certainly one-half, and maybe two-thirds (the records from New South Wales are deficient on this point), had been sentenced before, usually for some form of theft.

Offences in the colony. Male convicts transported to Tasmania committed an average of six offences per head in the colony up to 1840 and four between 1841 and 1853 (New South Wales records, once more, are inadequate for purposes of comparison).

English and Irish. Yet there were important differences between the Irish and the rest. The Irish were older (average age at time of trial nearly 28), more were married, more came from the countryside (in spite of a heavy leavening from Cork and Dublin); they were less likely to have committed previous crimes and these (except in the case of the Dubliners) were less likely to have been concerned with theft. So there was an Irish 'model' that, in several

---

[13] From the point of view of practical social analysis, however, Robson's categories and presentation are unsatisfactory: (1) because there is no breakdown into shorter (e.g. five-year) periods: thus the picture appears (falsely) to remain unchanged; and (2) because occupations are strictly based on those provided by the United Kingdom census of 1951, which bears little relation to the realities of the pre-industrial, or early industrial, society with which we are here concerned.

respects, was different from the English 'model' or that of the young urban thief.[14]

As for the moral character of the convicts—over which a fair amount of ink has been spilt—Robson is convinced (and here he moved back again to the English) that the women as a whole were considerably more depraved than the men. The men, he believes (and this is a minor concession to the traditionalist-Whiggish view), 'were neither simply "village Hampdens" nor merely "ne'er-do-wells" from the city slums'. Yet, he concludes, 'if the Hampdens are placed on one side of the scale and ne'er-do-wells on the other, the scale must tip toward the ne'er-do-wells'.[15]

Yet one important question has tended to drop out of the whole debate. It is the degree to which the 'complexion' of the convict settlers changed with the changes brought about in Britain (and parts of Ireland) by the twin forces of industrialization and city growth. In fact, in addition to all the other questions, a further one should have been asked: not only *who* were the convicts but how did they change from one generation to the next?

[14] *Convict Settlers*, pp. 9, 101, 119, 130, 143-58; also article from *Tas. Hist. Assoc.* (see p. 238 n. 7 above), pp. 66-7. For a critique of the author's methods and conclusions in handling the Irish data, see James Waldersee, *Catholic Society in New South Wales 1788-1860*, pp. 42-70.

[15] *Convict Settlers*, pp. 157-8.

2. Who were the Protesters?

IF the last chapter has broadly answered the question, what sort of men (and women) were the convicts?, in this one it is proposed to ask the same question about that relatively small part of them, the three or four thousand, whom we have termed protesters and who are the subject of this book. What sort of people were they? In brief, is there anything to distinguish them from the rest other than the crime that sent them to Australia? Were they older than other convicts? were they more, or less, married? more, or less, literate? more, or less, likely to have had a criminal record before they sailed and more, or less, likely to have added to it in the colony? Other writers—Shaw and Robson, in particular—have touched upon such questions and given some answers to them. But they have never spelled them out—either the questions or the answers—and that is the purpose of this final chapter.

But, first, we have a more general question that concerns the protesters less as individuals than as a group. Were they of the same social composition as that which Robson (without tying ourselves too closely to his method of classification) found among the convicts as a whole? Up to a point, this is so. Broadly, for Ireland, we find the same prevalence of labourers, smallholders, and tenants as was found before. Equally, in the English (or Scottish) countryside, it is the same mixture of farm labourers and rural craftsmen (though not in the same proportions)[1] who were sent out after conviction as machine-breakers or poachers or incendiaries as for any other rural crime. Again from the northern manufacturing towns of the 1840s (say from Lancashire or Scotland in 1842), we find men of the same occupations—colliers, potters, weavers, shoemakers, brick-makers—whether they have been transported for riot or for larceny or murder or common assault. So far, apart from the distinguishing features of the leaders, the two sets of prisoners look much the same. But if we left it at that we should leave out an important element in Robson's picture: the almost ubiquitous urban thief, as represented by the wide spectrum of crafts and occupations from all the cities of the British Isles, whether manufacturing towns or not. This is

---

[1] The proportion of craftsmen among English rural rioters appears to have been appreciably higher, but I have not attempted an exact calculation.

the element that is virtually missing from our protest chart; for, as we have argued already, protest (unlike common crime) was not a significant feature of either British or Irish cities at this time. Of course, there were exceptions: we have noted that of English and Scottish manufacturing towns after 1840; and there was, apart from the peculiar conditions of the Potteries (the last scene of the old-style urban riot in England), the typically urban explosion at Bristol in November 1831, among whose transported protesters we find the same sort of social complexion—the sailors and servants and butchers and drapers—that is common among Robson's London or Dublin thieves.[2]

To come to the more *personal* features—such matters as age, literacy, marital status, and criminal record. In order to attempt some comparison with Robson's findings (summarized at the end of the last chapter), some of these 'vital statistics' are set out in columns within the Tables of different types or generations of protesters in the Appendix at the end of the book (see p. 249). By following the 'ages' column through each of the Tables, we see that the average age of protesters very rarely corresponds to that in Robson's model of the urban thief: only, in fact, in cases of urban riot as at Bristol in 1831 and the manufacturing districts in 1842, when the average is shown to have been as low as 24 and 26½. Otherwise, with one further exception (the female arsonists), the average is appreciably higher, particularly in the case of the early rebels, whether Irish or British, arriving in either of the two eastern colonies up to 1830: this is as true of the Irish of 1798 and the 1820s as it is of the Luddites, the Yorkshire Radicals, the Pentrich rebels, and the Scots of Bonnymuir.

Marital status (not recorded before 1825) appears, as is hardly surprising, to bear a fairly close relationship to age; there appears, for instance, to be a tendency for a marriage rate of one in three to rise to one little short of one in two around the age of 29. The most striking case is that of the two groups of Canadians of 1839 (Table 6), with its sharp contrast between the relatively youthful and under-married Anglo-Americans and the mature and much-married 'French'. In their case, too, there is a similar sharp contrast in literacy—in this case limited to an ability to read and write—between

---

[2] Over all, an approximate calculation reveals that 410 (or 11·5 per cent) of the 3,600 protesters were from cities or towns: two in nine of the Britons, one in seventeen of the Irish and one in thirty of the Canadians. The typical convict-protester, in fact, was not a townsman but a country dweller and, in this respect at least, was almost as far removed from Robson's picture of the typical (English) convict as chalk is from cheese.

the highly literate (79 per cent) Americans and the comparatively un-literate (44·9 per cent) French-Canadians. It is probably significant, too, that the small urban groups among the English appear to be more literate than the larger rural groups; but the only surprise perhaps is that the rural Irish of the mid 1820s to the late 1840s are shown to be so decisively more able to read and write than the English machine-breakers of the 1830s. But, inevitably, such tests, carried out by the surgeon-superintendents on the ships without any possibility of enforcing a common standard, cannot claim to be accurate and can, therefore, serve only a limited purpose—in this case hardly any purpose at all as Robson (probably wisely) decided to abandon literacy as a common denominator and has therefore left us no figures with which to compare our own.

So far, then, in terms of age and marriage (though probably not in terms of literacy) the protesters approximated more closely to Robson's Irish than to his English or general model. But the decisive question still remains. Can they be seen to be distinguishable from other convicts in terms of their conduct or moral character? Is the protester, in fact, as shown by these records, a different sort of human being or is the record so confused and indecisive as to make it an almost irrelevant question? To settle the issue, we must look at two types of evidence—the literary and the statistical. We have seen quite a lot of the literary evidence already, as in the highly significant tribute paid to 'political convicts' in general by Captain Irvine of Elderslee, in New South Wales, who, when soliciting for skilled labour from this source in 1822, wrote of 'political convicts' as being 'men of industrious habits and fair moral character'.[3] We also saw the unusual step taken by Lieutenant-Governor Arthur, in a dispatch to the Colonial Office, to press the claims for special consideration of the treasonable weavers and shoemakers of York who were petitioning for reconsideration of their sentence in 1826— a step that earned him a rebuke from Sir Robert Peel.[4] Arthur, in fact, like Governor Macquarie in New South Wales, was inclined to distinguish between convicts 'of different characters and classes'; and it was certainly protesters (whom he was willing to respect as men of moral worth) that he had in mind rather than common-or-garden offenders. We have already referred to the high regard he had for the moral qualities of the machine-breakers of 1830. First, he wrote to London, a few days after the arrival of the *Eliza* at Hobart, that the men's conduct had been 'exemplary' (and later sent

[3] Arch. NSW, 4/1760, p. 135 (see p. 196 above).
[4] Tas. Arch., GO *Despatches (Outward)*, i, 1154–64; iv, 30–5, 37.

statistical evidence to support his view); and he followed this up six years later when, giving evidence before the Select Committee on Transportation, he picked them out for special mention as convicts of 'the better sort'. His views were shared—or, rather, anticipated— by the Directors of the Van Diemen's Land Company who, it may be remembered, attempted to get as many of them as possible to work for them on their estates; and, on the eve of their departure, John Capper, the Superintendent of Convicts at London Docks, said of them that 'he never saw a finer set of men'.[5] And to these we may add—though they are never quite as impressive—the innumerable tributes paid by magistrates, farmers, parsons, and priests to the sterling qualities of the many hundreds of Irish 'patriots' awaiting transportation after the '98, not to mention the far more numerous hulk and gaol and superintendents' reports from the convict ships that tell a similar story of the excellent qualities of the large majority of the political and social protesters that came as convicts to Australia.

Inevitably, however, it is the statistical evidence—largely provided by the conduct registers at Hobart—that carries the greater conviction; and certainly it is the only source that makes it possible to compare the behaviour of one set of convicts with another. If we turn again to the Appendix at the end of the book, we shall see that there is one group that is sadly out of tune with the rest. This is the notorious case of the eighteen Bristol rioters sent to Hobart who, as we saw before, had an average toll of colonial offences nearly twice that of Robson's urban thief. This is the only group to exceed Robson's average other than the small group of Rebecca's Daughters (1843), whose high score is largely due to the unusually turbulent record of one of its members, 'Shoni' (alias John Jones). Otherwise, only the first and smallest of the Chartist groups (1839), with an average of 4·5 colonial offences, comes near to Robson's average of five for the 1840s as a whole.[6] Apart from these, there is a clear tendency shown in these Tables for the protester's toll of crime in the colony to fall well below that recorded by Robson—most certainly below his English model and most often below his Irish model as well. In the case of previous convictions, a somewhat different picture emerges: it shows that even in the case of protesters,

[5] Hobsbawm and Rudé, *Captain Swing*, p. 248.

[6] There are also the arsonists: the men sent to Tasmania in 1818–39 (with an average of 5·5; not recorded here); and the women of 1840–53 (average of 3·25). But it is not practical to attempt any comparison between the protesting and the non-protesting 'marginals'. (It is even doubtful if, after laborious research, any sort of intelligible pattern would emerge!)

two in seven or three in seven Englishmen had been convicted before, whereas the proportion of previously convicted Irishmen was appreciably less.

Of course, behind these averages there lurks many an exception, suggesting that many of the protesters, like most of the Bristol rioters of 1831, can hardly be ranked among the 'village Hampdens'. This was true of every group. 'Shoni', of the Rebecca rioters, as we saw, had over twenty offences to his name. Others had even higher scores. For example, among the Irish land-warriors of the 1840s, there was Daniel Burke (alias Rourke), who committed 35 offences (mainly of a minor character) in all; in 1846, there was James Ryan, with 26; in 1843 and 1845, there were Thomas Moran and John Costello with 22 offences apiece; Thady Kelly, in the same year, committed 21; and, in 1842, Abraham Dekeliah, one-time teacher and clerk, recorded 21 offences ranging over a varied repertoire that included absence without leave, leaving work, destroying government property, insolence and disobedience of orders, stealing food and clothing, refusing to work, forging passes, absence from muster, and ill-using a fellow prisoner.[7] There were at least a dozen protesters, scattered over the years, who were hanged at Sydney, Launceston, or Hobart for committing crimes of violence, like armed robbery or murder, in the colonies. And even the machine-breakers, whose sterling qualities marked them out for special commendation, had their full quota of black sheep. The two women among them, for example: Elizabeth Studham and Elizabeth Parker. Studham, though 'well behaved and orderly' on board, was described as being a young woman 'of loose habits' and was sentenced for ten offences in the colony, mainly for bad language and disorderly behaviour but also (on two occasions) for theft. Parker's record was worse. She was convicted on eighteen separate occasions on charges ranging from drunkenness and assault to 'indecent exposure' and 'being found in bed in a disorderly house after hours'.[8] Of the men, some dozen had served sentences in England of six, nine, or twelve months or more for relatively serious offences: John Ingram, an Essex ploughman, for example, had spent three years and four months of a seven-year sentence in prison for stealing a watch. In New South Wales, Alfred Darling, one of the Kintbury (Berks.) leaders, served a twelve months' sentence for an attempted rape and Joseph Arney, a Hampshire wheelwright, was sent to Norfolk Island for eight years for stealing cattle. The Tasmanians'

---

[7] Tas. Arch., CON 33/18, 34, 69, 75, 94.
[8] Tas. Arch., CON 40/9, p. 105; 40/7, p. 48.

record was probably worse (and it was certainly more fully recorded):
forty-eight men were found guilty of serious misdemeanours; and
of these a dozen had substantial criminal records, involving sentences
of two, seven, or fourteen years' hard labour; one even served a life
sentence for 'breaking and entering'.[9] One of the worst was John
Ingram, the Essex ploughman, whose master wrote to the Lieutenant-
Governor that he had 'given [him] more trouble than anyone [he
had] ever had'.[10]

So there was many a protester who could quite easily, without
injustice, be counted in the company of Robson's 'ne'er-do-wells'
rather than in the select minority of 'village Hampdens'. But, in
relation to the three to four thousand I have termed 'protesters', they
are not so many, though it is not possible to draw an exact dividing-
line between the sheep and the goats. But, by and large, it does appear
from these records (supplemented by those of a more impressionistic
nature) that it is among these protesters that we must look for the
'village Hampdens', men whose sentence of transportation should
not be allowed to blot out otherwise exemplary records and deny
them the respect that their descendants owe them.

The names of two dozen of such men, at most, appear in the
Australian Dictionary of Biography and a few more in the *DNB*;
so these will not be forgotten. But there are many others, no less
worthy to be remembered, among the several hundred recorded in
this book; and of these the great majority (as we have seen) stayed
on in the country to which they had been exiled. They, too, no longer
deserve to be hidden in the shadows with all the other unsung heroes.
Let them be allowed to emerge and bask a little in the approval that
posterity has too long refused them.

[9] Hobsbawm and Rudé, p. 249.
[10] John Archer, farmer, to Sir John Franklin, 27 Sept. 1837, CSO, 5/87/1906.

APPENDIX

(see Pt. V, chap. 2)

Protesters classified according to age, marriage, literacy, and criminal record

TABLE 1   *Irish sent to NSW, 1800–40*

	No.	Av. age	% Married	% Literate (= R and W)	Criminal Record	
					Prev. convicted	Colonial crimes per head
Rebellion 1798/1803	241	31	*	*	*	*
Land-and-Tithe War 1815–40**						
1815–20	178	29·0	*	*	*	*
1821–5	379	29·0	*	*	*	*
1826–30	85	28·5	48	43·5	*	*
1831–5	427	26·2	30·5	38·5	*	*
1836–40	109	27·0	32	48·6	*	*

TABLE 2   *Irish sent to VDL, 1818, 1840–52*

	No.	Av. age	% Married	% Literate (= R and W)	Criminal Record	
					Prev. convicted	Colonial crimes per head
1818	10	33·3	*	*	*	3·7
Land-and-Tithe War**						
1840–4	180	27·25	28·3	46	1 in 4	2
1845–9	110	27·25	30	46·3	1 in 7	2·2
1850–3	34	26·5	19	53	1 in 8	0·9
Young Ireland, 1848	12	35	41·5	75	0	0·9

* Inadequate data.   ** Date of ships' arrival.

TABLE 3   *Irish sent to WA, 1868*

	No.	Av. age	% Married	% Literate (= R and W)	Criminal Record	
					Prev. convicted	Colonial crimes per head
Fenians	62	27	16	98	1 in 20	2·8

TABLE 4   *Britons sent to NSW, 1793–1840*

	No.	Av. age	% Married	% Literate (= R and W)	Criminal Record	
					Prev. convicted	Colonial crimes per head
Scots Jacobins, 1793–5	6	37	83	(100)	*	*
Naval mutineers, 1797	15	32	*	*	*	*
Luddites, 1812–17	42	30·7	*	*	*	*
Isle of Ely, 1816	7	31	*	*	*	*
Pentrich rebels, 1817	14	37·5	*	*	*	*
Cato Street, 1820	5	29·4	*	*	*	*
Scottish rebels, 1820	19	28	36	*	*	*
'Swing' rioters, 1830	144	27	54	33·3***	*	*
Bristol rioters, 1831	8	24	25	50	*	*
Tolpuddle, 1834	6 (1 to VDL)	28·5	66·6	83	1 in 6	*

TABLE 5 *Britons sent to VDL, 1821, 1840-53*

	No.	Av. age	% Married	% Literate (= R and W)	Criminal Record	
					Prev. convicted	Colonial crimes per head
Yorkshire Radicals, 1821	12	35	90	*	*	3
'Swing' rioters, 1830	332	29	55	33·7***	2 in 7	1·7
Bristol rioters, 1831	18	25	55·5	*	2 in 7	10
Welsh rioters, 1831–5	7	32·5	60	14	0	*
Bossenden Wood, 1838	3	37	66·6	33	0	4
Rebecca, 1843	5	27	20	60	0	7
Chartists:						
1839	7	34	57	71	2 in 7	4·5
1842	75	26·5	42·6	43	3 in 4	2·6
1848	16	31	33	68·75	0	2·5

* Inadequate data.   ** Date of ships' arrival.   *** 1 ship only.

TABLE 6 *Canadian Rebels, 1838-9*

	No.	Av. age	% Married	% Literate (= R and W)	Criminal Record	
					Prev. convicted	Colonial crimes per head
Lower Canadians to NSW	58	38	79·3	44·9	0	*
Upper Canadians to VDL	95	28·5	36·5	79	*	1·5

TABLE 7   *Irish Arsonists sent to VDL, 1841–53*

	No.	Av. age	% Married	% Literate (= R and W)	Criminal Record	
					Prev. convicted	Colonial crimes per head
Men	50	28	38	64·3	3 in 10	2·7
Women	232	23	8	10·7	6 in 10	2·1

TABLE 8   *British Arsonists sent to VDL and WA 1840–68*

	No.	Av. age	% Married	% Literate (= R and W)	Criminal Record	
					Prev. convicted	Colonial crimes per head
Women to VDL, 1840–53	46	24·5	8	41	1 in 2	3·25
Men to VDL, 1840–53	150	28	25	64	1 in 3	2·7
Men to WA, 1850–68	361 (290 cases)	27·4	17 (192)	77 (175)	*	*

* Inadequate data.

BIBLIOGRAPHY

I. *Manuscript Sources*

A. GREAT BRITAIN, IRELAND, CANADA

(1) Public Record Office, London:
   HO 11/1-123: Transportation Registers 1788–1868.
   HO 26, 27: Criminal Registers for (*a*) Middlesex, 1791–1849; and (*b*) England
      and Wales (inc. Middlesex 1850–68), 1805–68.
   HO 40-2, 52: Disturbances: correspondence.

(2) County Record Offices, England:
   Kent RO, Maidstone: Papers relating to Bossenden Wood, U 951. C 37.
   Lancs. RO, Preston: T. Holden correspondence, DDX 140; Boothman
      correspondence, DDX 537; Depositions relating to events of 1842,
      QJD 1/89.

(3) Bodleian Library, Oxford:
   Clarendon Papers: Irish 'Outrages', 1826–38.

(4) Scottish Records Office, Edinburgh:
   Trials before Courts of Judiciary, JC 4, 11–13.

(5) PRO, Northern Ireland, Belfast:
   Papers relating to Rebellion of 1798, D 272.
   John Mitchel correspondence, 1852–3, T 413.

(6) State Paper Office, Dublin:
   Rebellion Papers, 620.
   State of the Country Papers, vol. i (1780–1821).
   Prisoners' Petitions and Cases, 1778–1836.
   Prisoners' Petitions (O'Farrell), 1836–41.

(7) Public Archives of Canada, Ottawa:
   Confiscations in Lower Canada, 1837–8: RG4, B37.
   Courts Martial at Kingston and London, 1838–9: RG5, B36, B41.
   Commission on Rebellion Losses, 1849–53: RG4, B37.

B. AUSTRALIA

(1) Mitchell Library, Sydney:
   Census, 1828. Mutch Index of Births, Deaths and Marriages (1815–1915).
   Convict records on microfilm, e.g. HO 11 and HO 26-7.
   Convicts Landed in the Colony of New South Wales, 1830–1842 (11 vols.,
      Sydney, 1831–43).

(2) State Archives of NSW, Sydney:
  Convict records:
    Indents: bound, 1788–1835: 4/3996–4022; printed, 1835–42: 4/4023–58;
      Irish, 1822–40: 4/7076–8.
    Musters of convicts, 2/8240–82.
    Assignment and distribution lists, 1814–26: 4/3493–518.
    Ticket of leave butts, 1827–75: 4/4063–234.
    Conditional pardons, 1826–70: 4/4432–77.
    Certificates of freedom, 1810–33: 4/4423–7; 1827–67: 4/4289–418.
    Free pardons of 'machine-breakers', 1835–9: 4/1123.1.
    Applications to marry, 1825–51: 4/4508–14.
    House of Correction (Carters Barracks) register, 1837–41: 4/4569.
    Death register, 1828–79: 4/4549.
  Tasmanian papers held in NSW.
(3) Tasmanian State Archives, Hobart:
  Lt.-Gov.'s Despatches: GO.
  Col. Sec.'s Correspondence: CSO.
  Letter Books of Van Diemen's Land Co.
  Convict records: indents; conduct registers; assignment and description
    registers; record books, 1803–53; CON 13–53; esp. 13–53, 31–3, 40–2, 52.
  Census returns, 1842–51; marriage registers, 1834–50; index of publicans.
(4) State Archives of Western Australia:
  Convict Registers: A.128; R.1–31; V.10.
(5) State Archives of South Australia:
  Shipping Registers, 1858–75.
(6) Public Record Office, Victoria, Melbourne:
  Victoria. Shipping Lists of Immigrants, vols. 2–3 (Feb. 1842–July 1848).

II. *Parliamentary Papers*

(1) England and Wales:
  Convictions under Game Laws, 1827–30, PP 1830–1, xii.
  Criminal offenders committed for trial or bailed, 1834–53: PP 1835, xlv;
    1836, xli; 1837–8, xliii; 1839, xxxviii; 1840, xxxviii; 1841, xviii; 1842,
    xxxii; 1843, xlii; 1844, xxxix; 1845, xxxvii; 1846, xxxiv; 1847, xlvii;
    1847–8, lii; 1849, xliv; 1850, xlv; 1851, xlvi; 1852, xli; 1852–3, xxxi;
    1854, liv.
(2) Scotland:
  Criminal offenders committed for trial, 1839–58: PP 1841, xviii; 1842,
    xxxii; 1843, xlii; 1844, xxxix; 1845, xxxvii; 1846, xxxiv; 1847, xlvii;
    1847–8, lii; 1849, xliv; 1850, xlv; 1851, xlvi; 1852, xli; 1853, lxxi; 1854,
    liv; 1854–5, xliii; 1856, xlix; 1857, xlii; 1857–8, xlvii; 1859, xix.
(3) Ireland:
  Conviction under Insurrection Act, 1822–4: PP 1823, xvi; 1824, xxii.
  Outrages reported to the Constabulary Office in 1836–8, 1844: PP 1837–8,
    xlvi; 1845, xxi.

Criminal offenders committed for trial, 1845–60: PP 1846, xxx; 1847, xlii; 1847–8, lii; 1849, xliv; 1850, xlv; 1851, xlvi; 1852–3, lxxxi; 1854, liv; 1854–5, xliii; 1856, xlix; 1857, xlii; 1857–8, xlvii; 1859, xix; 1860, lvii; 1861, lii.

Riot Commission's Report on Belfast riots, 1857: PP 1857–8, xxvi.

(4) Canada:

Papers relating to Canadian rebellions of 1837–8: PP 1840, xxxi, xxxii.

III. Periodicals

England: *Annual Register*; *Gentleman's Magazine*; *Leeds Mercury*; *Reynolds' Political Instructor*.

Ireland: George Faulkner's *Dublin Journal*.

Australia: *Adelaide Advertiser*; *Hobart Town Advertiser*; *Hobart Town Gazette*; *Hobart Mercury*; *Launceston Examiner*; *Perth Inquirer*; *Perth Herald*; *Perth Gazette*; *Sydney Gazette*.

IV. Contemporary Accounts, Journals, etc.

Barrington, George. The History of New South Wales (London, 1810).

Ducharme, L. *Journal d'un exilé politique aux terres australes* (Montreal, 1845). English edn. *Journal of an Exile in Australia* (Sydney, 1944).

The Exile's Lamentations; or Biographical Sketch of Thomas Cook (Sydney, 1841).

Gates, William. *Recollections of Life in Van Diemen's Land* (New York, 1850).

Loveless, G. *A Narrative of the Sufferings of James Loveless, James Brine, Thomas and John Standfield* . . . *displaying the Horrors of Transportation* (London, 1881).

—— *The Victims of Whiggery* (London, 1837).

Madden, Dr. —. *Antrim and Down in '98* (Glasgow, n.d.).

Memoirs of Joseph Holt, General of the Irish Rebels in 1798, ed. T. C. Croker (2 vols., London, 1838).

Miller, Linus W. *Notes of an Exile to Van Diemen's Land* (New York, 1846).

Mitchel, John. *Jail Journey* (Dublin, n.d.).

O'Reilly, John Boyle, *Moondyne* (Melbourne, 1880).

Prieur, François-Xavier. *Notes d'un condamné politique de 1838* (Montreal, 1884). English edn. *Notes of a Convict of 1838* (Sydney, 1949).

Tench, Watkin. *Sydney's First Four Years*, ed. L. F. Fitzhardinge (Sydney, 1961).

Wait, Benjamin. *Van Diemen's Land, written during Four Years' Imprisonment* (Buffalo, 1843).

V. Printed Collections, Guides, Dictionaries, Reports, etc.

Australian Dictionary of Biography, vols. 1–6 (Melbourne, 1966–76).

Commons Journals of Ireland (vols. xxvii–xxix, 1798–1800).

Contemporary Sources and Opinions in Modern British History, ed. Lloyd Evans and P. J. Pledger (2 vols., Melbourne, 1966-7).

Dictionary of National Biography (London).

Eldershaw, Peter. *Guide to the Public Records of Tasmania* (3 vols., Hobart, 1957-65).

Evidence before the Select Committee on Transportation (London, 1837). [For full report, see PP 1837-8, xix, xxii.]

Guide to the Convict Records in the Archives Office of NSW (Sydney, 1970).

Historical Records of Australia, 1st series, vol. i.

Old Bailey Sessions Papers.

Proceedings of the York Special Commission, Jan. 1813 (London, n.d. [1814?]).

Report of the State Trials before a General Court Martial held at Montreal in 1838-9 (2 vols., Montreal, 1839).

Wood, H., *Guide to the Records deposited in the Public Record Office of Ireland* (Dublin, 1919).

VI. Books and Articles

Baillargeon, G. 'A propos de l'abolition du régime féodal', *Revue d'histoire de l'Amérique française* (1972), pp. 365-91.

Bateson, Charles. *The Convict Ships 1788-1868* (Edinburgh, 1959).

Blainey, G. *The Tyranny of Distance* (Melbourne, 1966).

Briggs, A. (ed.). *Chartist Studies* (London, 1959).

Broeker, Galen. *Rural Disorder and Police Reform in Ireland 1812-36* (London, 1970).

Brown, P. A. *The French Revolution in English History* (London, 1918).

Carroll, M. C. 'Behind the Lighthouse: the Australian Sojourn of John Boyle O'Reilly 1844-1890' (Ph.D., State Univ. of Iowa, 1955).

Clark, C. M. H. *A History of Australia*, vol. 1 (Melbourne, 1962).

Clarke, Marcus. *For the Term of his Natural Life* (2 vols., Sydney, 1929).

Cole, G. D. H. *Chartist Portraits* (London, 1965).

Crawford, W. H. 'Landlord-Tenant Relations in Ulster 1609-1820', *Irish Econ. and Soc. History*, ii (1975), 5-21.

Crotty, R. D. *The Land Question. Its Structure and Volume* (Cork, 1966).

Cullen, C. H. *Young Ireland in Exile* (Dublin, 1928).

Darvall, F. O. *Popular Disturbances and Public Order in Regency England* (London, 1969).

Disraeli, Benjamin. *Sybil, or the Two Nations* (London, 1845).

Dunbabin, J. P. D. *Rural Discontent in Nineteenth-Century Britain* (London, 1974).

Dunham, Aileen. *Political Unrest in Upper Canada 1815-1836* (Toronto, 1927).

Ellis, Peter B., and Mac A'Ghobbain, Seumas. *The Scottish Insurrection of 1820* (London, 1970).

Engels, Frederick, *The Condition of the Working Class in England in 1844* (London, 1952).

Fauteux, A. *Patriotes de 1837-1838* (Montreal, 1950).

Gatrell, V. A. C., and Hadden, T. B. 'Criminal Statistics and their Interpretation', in ed. E. A. Wrigley, *Nineteenth-Century Society* (Cambridge, 1972), pp. 336–96.

Gertzel, Cherry. 'The Convict System in Western Australia 1850–70' (B.A. Hons. Thesis, Univ. of Western Australia, 1949).

Guillet, Edwin C. *The Lives and Times of the Patriots* (Toronto, 1938).

Gwynn, D. *Thomas Francis Meagher* (Dublin, 1961).

Hammond, J. L. and B. *The Skilled Labourer 1760–1832* (London, 1919, etc.).

—— *The Village Labourer* (London, 1911, etc.).

Hancock, W. K. *Australia* (London, 1930).

Hanham, H. J. 'The Problem of Highland Discontent, 1880–1885', *Royal Hist. Soc. Transactions*, 5th series, xix (1969), 21–65.

Harper, F. *Joseph Capper* (London, 1962).

Hasluck, Alexandra. *Unwilling Emigrants. A Study of the Convict Period in Western Australia* (Melbourne, 1959).

Hobsbawm, E. J., and Rudé, G. *Captain Swing* (London, 1969).

Hoyle, William. *Crime in England and Wales. An Historical and Critical Retrospect* (London, n.d. [1876]).

Jones, David. *Before Rebecca. Popular Protests in Wales 1793–1835* (London, 1973).

—— 'Thomas Campbell Foster and the Rural Labourer. Incendiarism in East Anglia in the 1840s', *Social History*, Jan. 1976, pp. 5–43.

Kiernan, T. J. *Irish Exiles in Australia* (Dublin/London, 1954).

—— *Transportation from Ireland to Sydney 1791–1816* (Canberra, 1954).

Kitson Clark, G. 'Hunger and Politics in 1842', *Journal of Modern History*, xxv (1953), 355–74.

Landon, Fred. *Western Ontario and the American Frontier* (Toronto, 1967).

Lee, Joseph. *The Modernisation of Irish Society 1848–1918* (Dublin, 1973).

—— 'The Ribbonmen', in *Secret Societies in Ireland*, ed. T. Desmond Williams (Dublin, 1973), pp. 26–35.

McRae, Mary M. 'Yankees from King Arthur's Court: a Brief Study of North American Political Prisoners Transported from Canada to Van Diemen's Land, 1839–40', *Tas. Hist. Assoc.* xix (1972), 147–62.

Malcomson, A. P. W. 'Absenteeism in Eighteenth Century Ireland', *Irish Econ. and Soc. History*, i (1974), 15–35.

Mansergh, Nicolas. *The Irish Question 1840–1921* (London, 1968).

Mather, F. C. *Public Order in the Age of the Chartists* (Manchester, 1959).

Mayhew, H. *London Labour and the London Poor* (London, 1864, repr. 1961–2).

Moynihan, J. S. 'Fenian Prisoners in Western Australia', *Eire-Ireland*, iii, no. 3 (1968–9), 6–13.

Neal, John. *The Pentrich Revolution* (n.d. Reprint, Derby, 1966).

Nowlan, Kevin B. 'Agrarian Unrest in Ireland 1800–1845', *University Review* (Dublin), iv (1967).

O'Farrell, Patrick. *Ireland's English Question* (London, 1975).

O'Tuathaigh, G. *Ireland before the Famine 1798–1848* (Dublin, 1972).

Ouellet, F. *Histoire économique et sociale du Québec 1760–1850, structures et conjonctures* (Montreal, 1966).

Ouellet, F. 'Les Insurrections de 1837-38: un phénomène social', *Histoire sociale*, no. 1 (1973), pp. 54-82.

Pakenham, Thomas. *The Year of Liberty* (London, 1972).

Palmer, Stanley. 'Police in England and Ireland, 1780-1840: a Study in Contrasts'; paper read to American Historical Association, New York (December 1971).

Parsons, George. 'The Cato Street Conspirators in New South Wales', *Labour History* (Canberra), May 1965, pp. 3-9.

Payne, H. S. 'A Statistical Study of Female Convicts in Tasmania, 1843-53', *Tas. Hist. Assoc.* ix (1961), 56-69.

Pease, Z. W. *The Catalpa Expedition* (New Bedford, Mass., 1897).

Perry, T. M. *Australia's First Frontier. The Spread of Settlement in New South Wales 1788-1829* (Melbourne, 1963).

Petrovitch, P. 'Recherches sur la criminalité à Paris dans la seconde moitié du XVIIIᵉ siècle', in *Crimes et criminalités en France sous l'Ancien Régime, 17ᵉ-18ᵉ siècle*, in *Cahiers des Annales 33* (Paris, 1971), pp. 187-261.

Philips, D. 'Riots in the Black Country, 1835-1860', in *Popular Protest and Public Order*, eds. J. Stevenson and R. Quinault (London, 1974).

Prest, J. *The Industrial Revolution in Coventry* (London, 1960).

Quinault, R. 'The Warwickshire County Magistrates and Public Order, c. 1830-1870', in *Popular Protest and Public Order* (see Philips, D., above).

Radzinowicz, L. *A History of English Criminal Law and its Administration from 1750* (4 vols., London, 1948-68).

Richards, Eric. 'Patterns of Highland Discontent 1790-1860', in *Popular Protest and Public Order* (see Philips, D., above).

Robson, L. L. *The Convict Settlers of Australia* (Melbourne, 1965).

—— 'Male Convicts Transported to Van Diemen's Land, 1841-53', *Tas. Hist. Assoc.* ix (1961), 39-55.

Rogers, P. G. *Battle in Bossenden Wood. The Strange Story of Sir William Courtenay* (London, 1961).

Ronan, M. V. (ed.). *Insurgent Wicklow* (Dublin, 1948).

Rosenblatt, F. *The Chartist Movement* (rev. edn., London, 1967).

Rudé, G. 'The Archivist and the Historian', *Tas. Hist. Assoc.* xvii (1970), 111-28.

—— '"Captain Swing" and Van Diemen's Land', ibid., xii (1964), 6-24.

—— '"Captain Swing" in New South Wales', *Hist. Stud.* (Melbourne), vii (1965), 467-80.

—— *The Crowd in History* (New York, 1964).

—— 'Early Irish Rebels in Australia', *Hist. Stud.* xvi (1974), 17-35.

—— 'English Rural and Urban Disturbances on the Eve of the First Reform Bill', *Past and Present*, no. 37, July 1967, pp. 87-102.

—— 'Protest and Punishment in Nineteenth-Century Britain', *Albion*, v (1973), 1-23.

Ryerson, Stanley R. *Unequal Union* (Toronto, 1968).

Schoyen, A. R. *The Chartist Challenge* (London, 1958).

Shaw, A. G. L. *Convicts and the Colonies* (London, 1966).

Smith, F. B. 'The Plug Plot Prisoners and the Chartists', *ANU Historical Journal* (Canberra), Nov. 1970, pp. 3-15.

Stevenson, J. 'Food Riots in England, 1792-1818', in *Popular Protest and Public Order* (see Philips, D., above).

Storch, J. D. 'The Plague of the Blue Locusts. Police Reform and Popular Disturbance in Northern England 1840-57', *Internat. Review of Social History*, xx (1975), 61-90.

Thomis, M. *The Luddites. Machine-Breaking in Regency England* (Newton Abbot, 1970).

Thompson, Dorothy (ed.). *The Early Chartists* (London, 1971).

Thompson, E. P. *The Making of the English Working Class* (London, 1963).

—— *Whigs and Hunters. The Origin of the Black Act* (London, 1975).

Tobias, J. J. *Crime and Industrial Society in the 19th Century* (London, 1967).

Waldersee, J. *Catholic Society in New South Wales 1788-1860* (Sydney, 1974).

Wallot, J.-P. *Un Québec qui bougeait* (Montreal, 1973).

White, R. J. *Waterloo to Peterloo* (London, 1957).

Williams, David. *John Frost: a Study in Chartism* (Cardiff, 1939).

—— *The Rebecca Riots. A Study in Agrarian Discontent* (Cardiff, 1955).

Williams, John. 'Irish Convicts and Van Diemen's Land', *Tas. Hist. Assoc.* xix (1972), 100-20.

Williams, T. Desmond (ed.). *Secret Societies in Ireland* (Dublin, 1973).

Wood, G. A. 'Convicts', *JRAHS*, viii (1922), 177-208.

Woodham-Smith, C. *The Great Hunger* (London, 1974).

GENERAL INDEX

SELECT INDEX OF PROTESTERS